GUI Design Handbook

GUI
Design
Handbook

Susan Fowler

Illustrations by
Victor Stanwick

McGraw-Hill
New York • San Francisco • Washington, D.C. • Auckland • Bogotá
Caracas • Lisbon • London • Madrid • Mexico City • Milan
Montreal • New Delhi • San Juan • Singapore
Sydney • Tokyo • Toronto

Library of Congress Catalog Card Number 97-75529

McGraw-Hill

*A Division of The **McGraw·Hill** Companies*

1 2 3 4 5 6 7 8 9 0   DOC/DOC   9 0 2 1 0 9 8 7

ISBN 0-07-059274-8

*The sponsoring editor for this book was Scott Grillo and the production supervisor was
Pamela A. Pelton. It was set in Vendome by Multiscience Press, Inc.*

Printed and bound by R. R. Donnelley and Sons Company.

McGraw-Hill books are available at special quantity discounts to use as
premiums and sales promotions, or for use in corporate training programs. For
more information, please write to the Director of Special Sales, McGraw-Hill,
11 West 19th Street, New York, NY 10011. Or contact your local bookstore.

 This book is printed on recycled, acid-free paper containing a minimum
of 50% recycled de-inked fiber.

To the constantly curious Sally, Lucy, Mohammed,
Gilgamesh, and Enkidu

CONTENTS

LIST OF TABLES

PREFACE

This book is our answer to the friends and colleagues who read our first book, *The GUI Style Guide*, and said, "Wow! This is great! Lots of information! But do I have to read it all? Can't you just tell me how to do an icon? A check box? A message?"

Yes, as it turns out, we *can* write a book that you don't have to read. This book, *The GUI Design Handbook*, is a list of common graphical user interface (GUI) components in alphabetical order. It works like most programming guides: You look up the component that you're interested in, and we supply a definition, guidelines, usability tests, and pointers to similar components.

Each description of a component has these sections:

- *Good For.* This section explains what the component is and what it's used for (as well as what it's *not* used for, if that's pertinent).

- *Design Guidelines.* The guidelines attempt to cover all of the sore points and questions identified during our work with developers over the years. They have been culled from experience, e-mail conversations about usability, and printed sources.

- *Usability Tests.* This section describes the types of usability tests that tell you whether you've chosen the right component and whether you've avoided the pitfalls known to be associated with that component.

- *See Also.* Since many GUI components have overlapping functionality, you may have a choice of components. This section points you to other likely candidates.

Seeming Duplicates

Because we concentrate on functionality, we've broken certain components into parts that might strike you as odd at first. For example, you'll find three types of dialog boxes, three types of fields, two types of list boxes, and three types of online help. The reason is that each type is used differently. Therefore, each different type has its own section.

Synonyms and Similarities

If the component you are looking for does not appear in the main body of the book, check the index. We've tried to list all synonyms for various components there.

Also, if you're looking for a particular function but don't know which component might embody that function, check components' "Good For" and "See Also" sections as well as the index. We've tried to cross-reference functions and components wherever possible.

A Method for Designing GUIs

There are two exceptions to the dictionary approach: Appendix A, which describes a GUI design methodology that we've successfully taught to software development students and professionals, and Appendix B, which lists the usability tests and procedures we recommend in the main part of the book.

Our approach to both design and usability testing is quick and dirty. It is our experience that many software companies fly by the seats of their pants, and, although we don't think a business maturity level of 1 is the right place to be, we've tried to be realistic. When you're ready to design and test more thoroughly, you'll find the resources you need in the appendices and in the bibliography.

Thanks and Apologies

No book is written only by its authors, and this one is no exception. We would like to thank the readers of our earlier book, *The GUI Style Guide*, who offered so much useful criticism as well as encouragement. We are especially grateful to Stuart Burnfield, one of our Australian readers. Also important to the genesis of this and the earlier book were our colleagues at CFI ProServices, ComWare Systems, EJV Partners, J.P. Morgan, Reuters Analytic Group, Small Computer Company, and many other companies. They taught us most of what we know about software development and management.

We would also like to thank two reviewers, Steven Feldberg, New York, and Chauncey Wilson, Massachussetts. Their close readings have made what you hold in your hands much better than the draft that they saw. Any remaining mistakes are all ours. Thanks also to Jeff Rubin, The Usability Connection, and Donna Timpone, UserEdge, Inc., whose formal and informal lessons in usability made the appendices possible. (Any mistakes there are all ours too.)

Many thanks to Alan Rose, Multiscience Press, who put this book together for McGraw-Hill, Multiscience Press editors Carol Parikh and Ben Goffman, who saved us from some very silly errors, and Multiscience Press production editor Lauralee Reinke, who created this thing of beauty out of messy Word for Windows files. We are grateful to John Wyzalek, editor at McGraw-Hill, who waited so patiently for the book to be done, and to Mark Smith, Spinnaker Reach, N.J., who started us on this book.

Thanks also to Jack Putnam, writer, editor, and book-party master, who has always been a good advisor ("You're writing *another* book? Don't you ever learn?"), to Brian Lathrop, who was at least able to describe what sanity feels like, and to Henry Spira, animal-rights activist, for the pleasure of his company and the example of his extraordinary courage, humor, and intelligence.

GUI Design
from A to Z

Check Box

A button used to turn attributes or states on and off. Users can set any number of check boxes, including none.

Check boxes are square (radio buttons are round) and can have either text or iconic (picture) labels. The "on" setting is usually indicated by a check mark or an X inside the box. However, Motif and iconic check boxes (see Figure 3) simply look pushed-in.

Good For

■ Toggling a small number of independent attributes or states on and off (Figure 1).

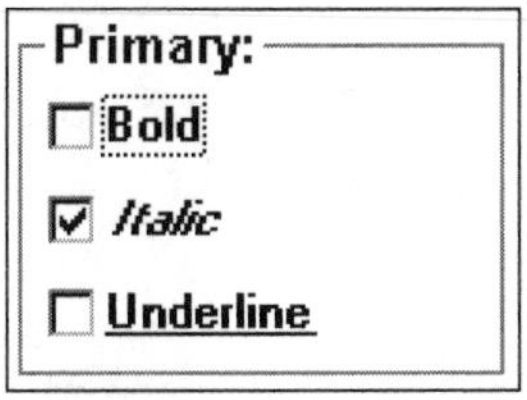

Figure 1

A set of check boxes.

```
┌─Primary:──────────┐
│  □ Bold           │
│  ☑ Italic         │
│  □ Underline      │
└───────────────────┘
```

■ Toggling *one* setting on and off. Use a single check box for a toggle (Figure 2). See "Two-state toggles" below.

Figure 2

A check box used as a toggle.

```
┌──────────────┐
│ ☑ Toggle on  │
└──────────────┘
```

Not Good For

■ Transition changes such as starting applications, opening dialog boxes, or navigating to another screen. Use pushbuttons instead.

■ Two-state toggles in which the two states are not opposites. Use radio buttons instead. See "Not opposites" below.

- Three-state toggles. Avoid this:

  ☐ Select redeemed bonds?   meaning "No"

  ☒ Select redeemed bonds?   meaning "Yes"

  ■ Select redeemed bonds?   meaning "Doesn't matter"

Use radio buttons or single-selection list boxes instead. However, see "Mixed-value states" below.

Design Guidelines

Although check boxes can be used on menus (for example, to toggle settings on and off) and in windows (for example, to toggle data points on and off on graphs), they are most common in dialog boxes, toolbars, and palettes simply because the reason that these components exist is to hold settings.

Text labels appear on the side of the button (in countries where the writing runs left to right, on the right side).

    ☐ Show text labels

Iconic labels appear on the check box itself (Figure 3). For more on iconic labels, see Iconic Labels.

Figure 3

A toolbar-based check box, with an iconic rather than text label.

TWO-STATE TOGGLES   Every check box is a toggle—the setting is either on or off. When you have a group of check boxes, you have a group of independent and mutually *inclusive* toggles.

When you have a single-button toggle, on the other hand, you are taking advantage of the fact that a check box's two states or settings are mutually *exclusive*—either yes or no, on or off—in a Boolean sort of way. For example:

    ☐ Capitalize first letter of sentence meaning "No" or "Off"

    ☒ Capitalize first letter of sentence meaning "Yes" or "On"

Problems occur, however, when either:

- The two states are not opposites.
- The check-button label contains negatives.

NOT OPPOSITES

☐ Full duplex

What is the opposite of full duplex? To the uninitiated, probably empty duplex (or a single-floor apartment, depending on the context). For modem connections, however, the right answer is half duplex.

One solution is to change the label depending on the setting, but that becomes confusing for two reasons (Microsoft 1995a, 138):

- Changing labels makes the interface seem inconsistent, which is a usability failure.
- Until the user clicks the button a few times, he or she may not realize that clicking sets the *other* state, not the state shown on the label:

  ☐ Half duplex   First state
  ☒ Full duplex   Second state

It's confusing to describe, and worse to specify and program. Here are some better ideas:

- Only when the setting's two states are opposites or can be easily inferred, use a single check box. For example, "Allow fast save" or "Button sounds enabled."
- When the two states are not opposites or are not easily inferred, use two radio buttons. For example, say that you have two types of color fill—spot and flood. Spot and flood are not natural opposites. To be clear, you'd use two radio buttons (Leavens 1994, 237–240):

  ⊙ Spot fill
  ○ Flood fill

NO NEGATIVES   The rule is, if the box is checked (true), then the answer to the question (actual or implied) is yes. Otherwise, the answer is no.

Therefore, to avoid double negatives when the boxes are empty, always label the buttons with positive statements. For example, "Disable sound card" means, if unchecked, "Don't disable sound card," which *really* means, "Do enable sound card." Eliminate the negative *dis-* and use "Enable sound card."

MIXED-VALUE STATES   As mentioned in "Do Not Use For" above, avoid three-state buttons (Yes, No, Doesn't Matter, for example). Since users have little or no experience with three-state buttons, they either won't notice the different states or won't know what to do with them if they do notice the differences. Radio buttons or list boxes are better choices.

However, the Microsoft guidelines allow a mixed-value toggle when it *reflects* rather than *sets* an actual user choice. For example, say that you've selected an entire paragraph, some of which is roman, some of which is *italic,* and some of which is **bold**. If you then open a font palette containing check boxes, the italic and bold check boxes show a gray "mixed value" state, as in Figure 4. If you click italic once, italic is turned on for the entire selection, which is indicated by an X or check mark in the box. If you click twice, italic is turned off for the entire selection and you see an empty check box. If you click three times, the value returns to the mixed state (Microsoft 1995a, 148–149).

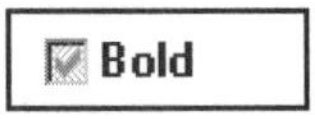

Figure 4

A mixed-value toggle in Microsoft Word for Windows.

☑ **Bold**

If a mixed-value toggle is important to your application, test it on users. They may not notice the change in values or, if they notice it, they may not understand it. If you do identify difficulties and you can't eliminate them, you might want to add a note right on the interface or in a tooltip. Also flag the issue in your "getting started" documentation and online help.

HOW MANY ARE TOO MANY?   *If the settings are related.* Unless you have a lot of spare room on the screen, switch to a multiple-selection list box when you get to about seven check boxes.

If the settings are visual (colors on a palette for example). Use as many check boxes as you need, but group them into categories or some natural order (the spectrum, for example). See List Box, Multiple Selection for more information on categorization styles.

If you have a long list of toggle check boxes. Try to break them into chunks of five or so buttons, or divide them in some natural way among tabbed dialog boxes.

INTERNATIONALIZATION If you have an international audience, watch out for terminology problems. Carl Zetie points out that "in British English, we 'tick' a box, we don't 'check it.'" If the documentation says "Check the Italic button," instead of clicking it, your international users may look to see if the button is there. He adds that, in many cultures, X means "wrong" and is used to cross something out, not to select it. Use checkmarks (✓) rather than Xs as the selection cue (Zetie 1996, 164).

Alternatives to "check" are "click on" and "click off," or "select" and "unselect."

Usability Tests

TOGGLES On single-button toggles, make sure that:

- The two settings are true opposites. A quick test: If the labels were questions, could you answer them with yes and no?
- There are no hidden double negatives in the unset version of the buttons. Look for *not* and *dis-, un-,* and *in-* prefixes. (In some contexts, you might look for *a-* as well: "Client atypical?")

SETS OF BUTTONS For groups of check boxes, test that the labels (text or icon) make sense to users. You can use a paper and pencil test in early iterations.

Also test that the groupings make sense. Ask your participants to categorize the buttons themselves, and use the groupings for which there is agreement. In complex systems, however, make sure that you use expert participants. Subject-matter experts and novices may have different conceptual models, and you need to match the expert model.

See Also

Combo Box; Dialog Box, Tabbed; List Box, Multiple- and Single-Selection; Pushbuttons; Radio Buttons.

Combo Box

A combination of a list box and a text-entry area. The list box allows only single selections. The text-entry area has two functions: searching and data-entry. Depending on the type of combo box, the text-entry area may simply show whatever item was selected from the drop-down list, let users type in search items, or let them add new entries to a database.

Good For

Presenting a list of suggested choices (Figure 5). Combo boxes let the user:

- Select from a list.
- Type in a new entry.
- Search for and jump to an item on the list by typing its first character or first few characters.

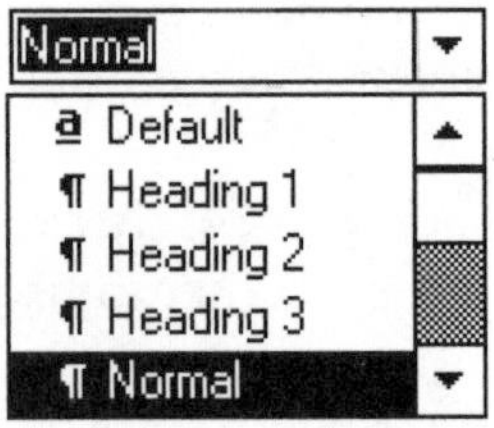

Figure 5

A drop-down list box, one of the three types of combo boxes.

Not Good For

■ Selecting more than one item at a time. Combo boxes allow only single selections.

■ Fewer than five items (unless you expect to add more items later). Use radio buttons instead.

■ Restricting users to predefined items (except for the drop-down list box—see Drop-Down List Box). Use a list box instead.

Design Guidelines

Visual Basic and other development packages offer three styles of combo boxes: Simple, drop-down combo, and drop-down list. Users can add new items to the simple or drop-down combo boxes, but not to a drop-down list. Users can search all three types by typing the search item in the entry area.

The simple combo box (Figure 6) is an entry area with a list below it. Use this style whenever you have enough space—being able to see the list items is always good.

Figure 6

The simple combo box.

The drop-down combo box (Figure 7) is an entry area with a down-arrow button to its right. Use this style when space is limited—for example, on a toolbar. Note that, in Windows 3.x (but not in Windows 95), the down arrow is separated from the entry area by a space to distinguish it from a drop-down list box, described below. This cue may be too subtle for all but the most detail-oriented users. On the other hand, it does no harm.

Figure 7

The drop-down combo box. Note the space between the entry area and the arrow button—it indicates that the control is a combo box rather than a drop-down list.

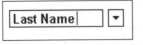

The drop-down list box (Figure 8) looks the same as a drop-down combo box except that there is no space between the entry area and the arrow button. It acts differently, however: Users cannot enter new items. They can only select from the items already on the list. See Drop-Down List Box for details.

Figure 8

The drop-down list box. There is no space between the entry area and the arrow button.

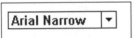

SEARCHING The text-entry area of a combo box has two functions: searching and data-entry. The search (or "jump-ahead") feature is useful when the list is very long and scrolling takes too much time. Users can search for items on the list by typing one character (Figure 9 and Figure 10), or more than one if the combo box is set up to do progressive searching (Figure 11 and Figure 12).

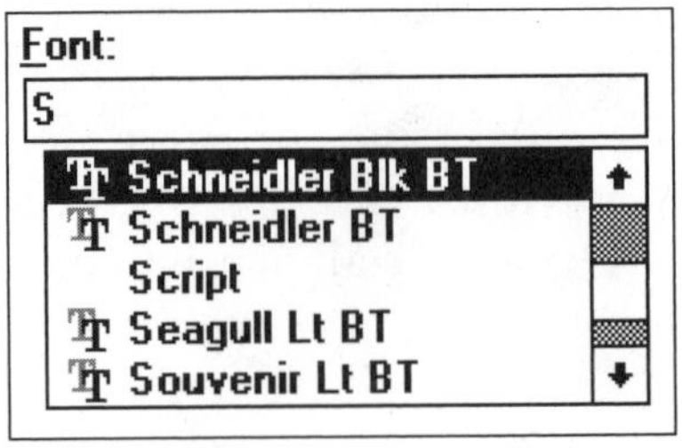

Figure 9

In one-character searches, pressing "S" goes to the first S item.

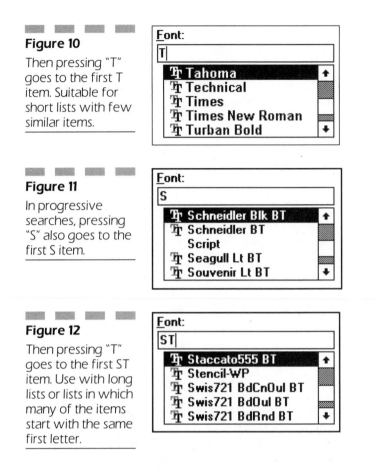

Figure 10

Then pressing "T" goes to the first T item. Suitable for short lists with few similar items.

Figure 11

In progressive searches, pressing "S" also goes to the first S item.

Figure 12

Then pressing "T" goes to the first ST item. Use with long lists or lists in which many of the items start with the same first letter.

Once the item is highlighted, the user can select it. The item is then displayed in the entry area.

DATA ENTRY   The data-entry feature is useful when:

- The list is unfinished (you haven't captured all alternatives yet).
- You can anticipate some but not all values that the user may want to enter.
- The list changes often (for example, stock changes daily and the stock database may not be up to date).

WHEN TO LET USERS ENTER NEW ITEMS   A general usability rule is: Don't force users to pick items from a fixed list if the list is incomplete. Aside from the frustration this creates, if your users don't have the information they need, they may pick *any* item and thereby invalidate your data-collection efforts.

For example, if your program insists that every client entry have an SIC code (standard industrial classification), but SIC codes are often missing from the source material, typists who are under pressure to enter hundreds of records a day are not going to look up the client company and find its SIC code. They are going to pick the first code on the list or pick codes at random, just to get through the record.

Instead of creating situations in which users are forced to pick incorrect items, let them enter new codes. However, keep in mind that if you let users enter new items, they may enter misspellings or synonyms for items that already exist elsewhere on the list. Whether you can let users enter wrong information depends on the results of your task analysis:

- If the combo box entries affect a corporate database, do the users have the authority to add new items to the database?

- Can you save the data locally while the user waits for an answer, then save it permanently on the server once the supervisor validates the entry?

- Can you accept any entry, then do a lookup and offer alternatives at the exit point?

As Carl Zetie says, "One of the major conflicts in any application is balancing freedom against constraint. Free taskflow allows the user to work as he finds best. Constrained taskflow guides the user to a successful conclusion" (1995, 91). For a detailed discussion of methods for handling constraints, see Zetie's chapter 3, "Taskflow."

SIZE OF THE LIST   The size of a combo-box list has two parameters: depth and width.

DEPTH OR LENGTH   First, make sure you can do what you want to do. Your development package (or other considerations) may restrict the number of items on the list. Check your specifications against your tools before committing yourself to a combo box (or any type of list box). For example, say you want to create a combo box for ZIP codes (a good idea because the U.S. Post Office does add ZIP codes occasionally). If your development kit only lets you create 100-item lists, you can't use a combo box for ZIP codes.

Second, figure out where you want to set the trade-off between ease of use and available real estate. Research and experience indicate that the more options you can display at once, the more quickly users will select the correct item. Having to click the drop-down arrow and scroll through the list slows users down. However, the combo box's search options can mitigate some of these delays.

In general, the part of the list that users see should be about seven items long. Go to 10 or even 20 items if the entire list is long—a longer list may prevent users from closing the list box by mistake, because they won't be scrolling as much and therefore won't make a slip of the mouse (Leavens 1994, 287).

WIDTH Make sure that all items can be viewed horizontally. If you can't make the entry area or the list as wide as the widest item on the list, make it at least as wide as the average item. Then include a horizontal scroll bar, make the width of the list dynamic, or show the entire list item when the user touches it with the mouse (like tool tips). Too many file-name list boxes (for example) are so narrow that they show only the first part of the path names and never the file names. These lists are, therefore, utterly useless.

If your application may ever be internationalized, keep in mind that items will expand. Design for automatic text expansion wherever you can. See Label for information on rates of expansion between languages.

Usability Tests

Make sure that users know that they can type in the box as well as select from the list of options. If you find that this feature is not apparent, highlight it in your "getting started" documentation and online help.

See Also

Drop-Down List Box; List Box, Multiple-Selection; List Box, Single-Selection; Spinner Button. For information on organizing lists, see List Box, Multiple-Selection.

Command Line

An entry area from which users can run commands and searches.

Good For

▦ Letting users define searches (Figure 13).

Figure 13

A command line used for searching in Alta Vista.

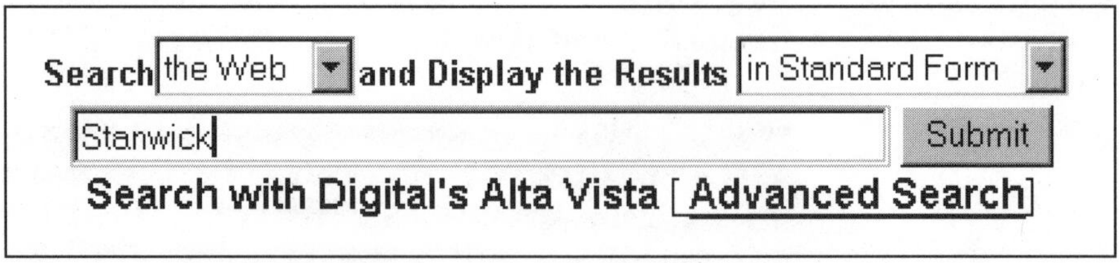

Search the Web ▼ and Display the Results in Standard Form ▼

Stanwick | Submit

Search with Digital's Alta Vista [Advanced Search]

▦ Providing shortcuts for expert or professional users, especially in programming, spreadsheets, and financial applications (Figure 14). Typing can be faster for experienced users.

Figure 14

The command line in Excel is the third area from the top, where the statement "A1 + A2 + A3" appears.

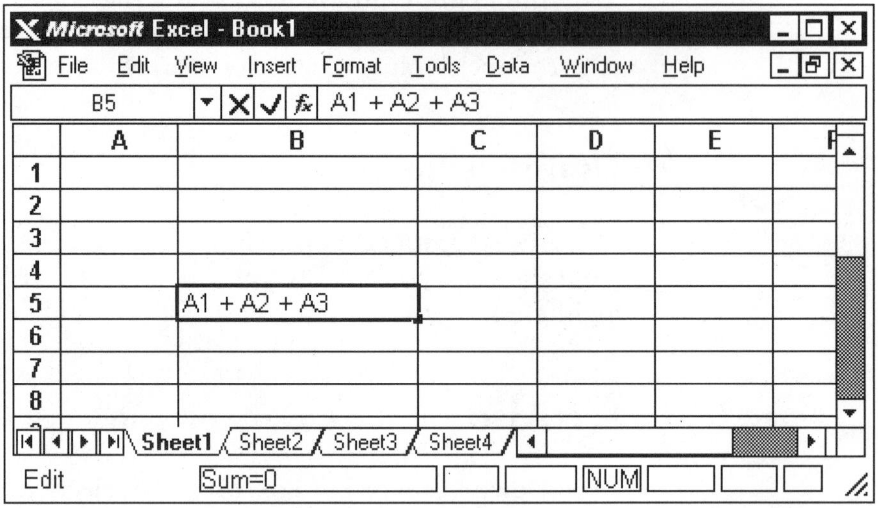

Microsoft Excel - Book1

File Edit View Insert Format Tools Data Window Help

B5   ▼ X ✓ fx A1 + A2 + A3

	A	B	C	D	E	F
1						
2						
3						
4						
5		A1 + A2 + A3				
6						
7						
8						

Sheet1 / Sheet2 / Sheet3 / Sheet4 /

Edit   Sum=0   NUM

▦ Supporting already defined DOS and UNIX batch files or scripts that perform repetitive or customized work. Customers are usually not willing to give up their script files (unless you are willing to rewrite them as GUI macros).

Not Good For

■ Inexperienced or occasional users because expert use depends on memorization, which generally requires long-term familiarity.

Design Guidelines

One of the benefits of GUIs is visibility: All available actions, for example, are made visible in the menus. In the same way that recognition is more effective than recall (memorization), GUIs, which show users all choices rather than make them try to remember a command, are more effective than command-line interfaces. If there is no way to access an operation other than recall, you cannot count on most users to remember all the options.

Menus also give new users an intellectual advantage. Test participants who are taught to use the menus first and commands second, "fared better in their overall knowledge of the functionality of the system. Participants in the command language condition learned only a limited number of task-specific functions" (Norman 1991, 317–318). In other words, although a command line is a good tool, use it in addition to—not as a replacement for—menu access.

WHEN TO KEEP OR ADD A COMMAND LINE   There are certain users for whom command-line interfaces are suitable. Consider including (or retaining) a command line when:

■ Many of your customers are familiar with the old command-line version of the program (Figure 15). Including a command line may help ease them into the new GUI version (OSF 1993, 6–14).

■ The GUI adds too much overhead or is too restrictive for expert users. For example, people who normally use SQL to access databases are not going to be happy with canned data views and queries that require lots of mouse and button activity.

■ The user has to type an entry anyway. Typing the entry on a command line is much faster than accessing the menu, opening a panel, typing the entry, and then pressing OK or some other button.

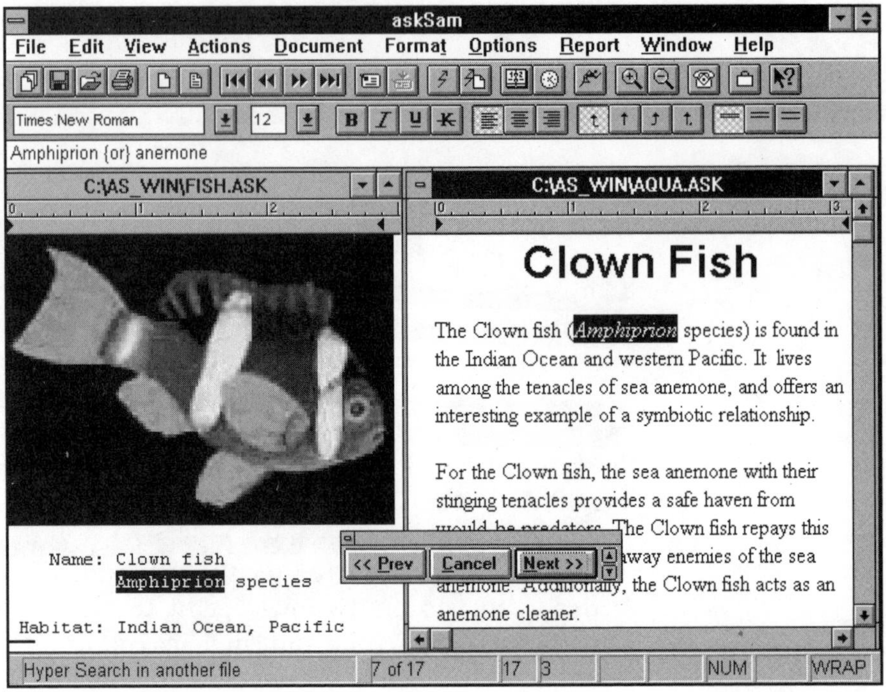

Figure 15

The askSam
command line
appears below the
formatting toolbar
(under "Times New
Roman").

When askSam Systems[1] ported askSam, a text database program, from DOS to Windows, the company retained the command line. According to Phil Schnyder, president of askSam Systems, "In askSam, you can search for any word by pressing one key to get into the command line, typing the word, and pressing Enter. I've tried other databases— you can put information in theirs just as quickly as ours, but to get it out, you had to go through too many dialog boxes." (We asked Schnyder if askSam's long-time DOS users still used the command line to start programs or access commands. "Not really," he said. "You get tired of typing in the commands. It's easier to use the menus than the command line for the programs.")

ANALYZE USERS CAREFULLY Good deployment of GUI command lines requires in-depth user analysis. It isn't enough to say, "Well,

---

1. askSam Systems, Inc., P.O. Box 1428, Perry, FL 32347; voice: 800/800-1997 or 904/584-6590; fax: 904/584-7481. askSam for Windows is available in English, German, Italian, and Spanish.

our audience is UNIX system administrators and they really *like* command lines. So we won't bother about adding menus." The problem is that, even if your audience is truly restricted to UNIX system administrators:

- Not all commands are used equally often—some are used once and then forgotten.
- Many useful commands may never be noticed.
- Some of your commands may work differently from what your users expect.
- There may be a terminology mismatch. You may use DEL as the delete command, but your users expect rm.

Also, in spite of your expectations, your audience may not be homogeneous. End-users start picking up shortcuts from the local gurus, and suddenly everyone is mucking around in the guts of the application and needing more support than you expected.

The solution is to find out which operations are most likely to be used often and define command-line shortcuts for those operations. Less popular operations should be added to a menu system, bundled together into macros or wizards, or described in detail in a readily accessible help system. (Make sure that the help system contains an index with lots of synonyms for the various operations.)

Note that some applications offer command-line functionality that is not available through the GUI, says Steven Feldberg. "Typically, however, these are systems that suffered the grafting of a GUI onto a prior, command-driven interface. [But other types of] examples abound, such as Access (or pretty much any database product) that allows you to put inline commands from the 'Application Development Language' into the command line. Another example is searching via command lines which often allows for complex Boolean expressions that cannot be constructed via the GUI" (Feldberg, 1997).

It is probably a mistake to have hidden functionality, but sometimes it can't be helped. For example, existing users may want to be able to use old commands, but since you don't want to support the old functionality for new users, you don't document it; a function is new and untested, but it's so cool you want the digerati to try it anyway, so you mention it at a user's group meeting; your application has both end-user functionality and a behind-the-scenes application programming interface (API). Sometimes these disjunctions are resolved by time—in other words, the old users die off, the hidden functionality becomes public, the technical writing department writes a separate API manual, thereby letting your company package the end-user and programmer versions separately. Nevertheless, for both usability and support reasons, it is best to push the process along as quickly as possible.

WHERE TO PUT A COMMAND LINE   The Motif guidelines suggest putting the command line at the bottom of the window or, if the window also has a message area, just above the message area (OSF 1993, 6-12–6-13).

Windows 3.x and Windows 95 systems have Run options on File (3.x) and the Startup (95) menus.

Spreadsheets put the command line below the toolbars, to the right or middle of the window, and above the cells.

Commercial financial applications seem to put command lines at the top left just below the menubar.

If there is any question about the right location, test the various possibilities on users.

Usability Tests

Make sure that users both notice and recognize the command line.

Find out which commands are actually used and rank them by usage levels.

If appropriate, test whether users refer to the commands the same way you do—for example, if you create a delete command, do the users lean toward RM, DEL, ERASE, or CUT? If there is no clear-cut winner, set up aliases for the top three or four.

Also check the use of punctuation. For example, how do your users indicate a Boolean AND on a search command line?

BLACK AND WHITE

BLACK, WHITE

(BLACK WHITE)

BLACK + WHITE

BLACK & WHITE

black and white

Rank the styles and make sure your program treats the most common ones as synonyms. (The simplest way to do this is to make copies of the commands and use all the synonyms as the names of the copies. For example, in a DOS batch system, you could copy DEL.BAT to RM.BAT, CUT.BAT, and so on.)

Note: BLACK + WHITE may seem really wrong to you, but if users use +, and + isn't used for anything else in the system, you should consider using it as a synonym. However, if it is used elsewhere and you can tell that the command-line entry is not mathematical, display an error message and teach the user something helpful about the system.

See Also

Keyboard Shortcuts; Menu, Drop-Down.

Cursor

A character that visually indicates the point at which the user's next action will occur. (Note that there are audio as well as visual cursors.)

Good For

- *Text cursor.*   In text windows or entry areas, marks the insertion point.

  abc|de

- *Selection cursor.*   For objects, indicates what has been selected (Figure 16).

Figure 16

The lasso is the selection cursor; the outline is the selected area. (Cursor from CorelDraw.)

Design Guidelines

Text cursors come with the operating system and in development kits; they do not have to be designed.

A selection cursor is more of a visual effect than a cursor. It indicates the location at which the next keyboard event will occur.

Since a cursor is a form of feedback, the only design issues are whether the user can spot the cursor and whether the cursor gets in the way of the user's action.

Usability Tests

If you have designed your own cursor or have modified the system's text cursor in some way, observe users carefully to make sure that:

- They can see the cursor. For text cursors, check the size and the default blinking rate.
- It doesn't get in their way when they try to do something. (It is more likely that a pointer will cover text or another item, however.)

Most platforms let users change standard cursor shapes and sizes at the operating-system level. You might want to add this functionality to your own cursors as well.

See Also

Pointer.

Dialog Box, Expanding

A dialog box or palette that becomes larger when the user clicks an "expand" button.

Good For

- Showing advanced or application-specific functionality without opening another dialog box (Figures 17 and18).

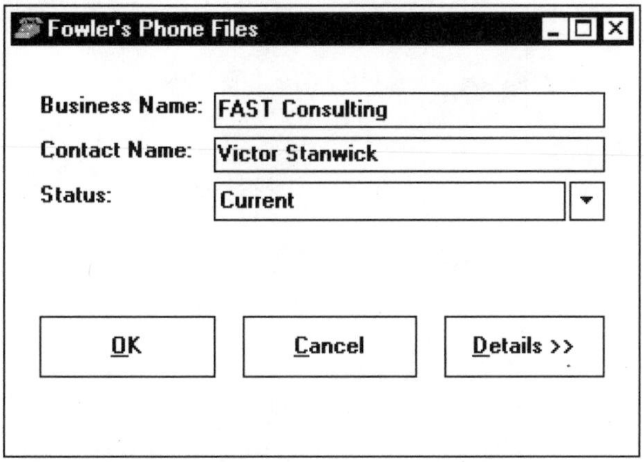

Figure 17

An expandable dialog box.

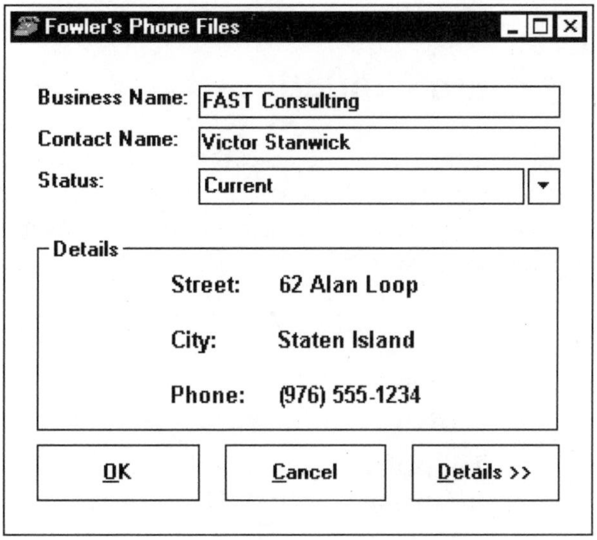

Figure 18

The expanded version.

- Showing details of system operations in error and progress messages (Figure 19).

Figure 19

Details of a communication, unexpanded and expanded.

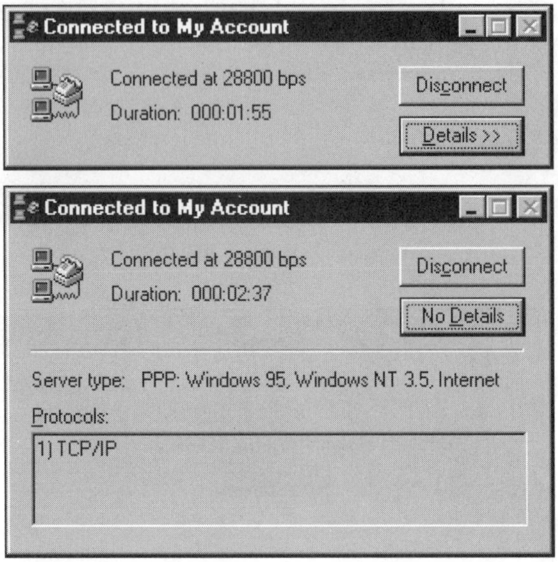

Not Good For

- Holding primary functions. Don't put important functions in the expandable part of the dialog box.

Design Guidelines

Expanding dialog boxes can make an application look less choppy than opening secondary dialog boxes can (Weinschenk and Yao 1995, 42). However, since expanding dialog boxes are rarely used for settings, their affordances can be poor for this purpose. Try tabbed dialog boxes instead.

If you must create an expanding dialog box for settings:

- To indicate that the dialog box expands, label the pushbutton with two right angle-brackets: Expand >>.
- The primary pane should contain all controls needed to complete the dialog box's task. Use the expansion area for advanced or infrequently used options.

- Expand the dialog box downward if the workflow moves from top to bottom. Expand the dialog box to the right if the workflow moves left to right. (See "Where to put the pushbuttons" in Dialog Box, Standard.)
- Position pushbuttons in the expanded dialog box wherever they were positioned in the unexpanded version. In other words, if the pushbuttons appear at the bottom of the unexpanded dialog box, put Close and any additional buttons on the bottom of the expanded pane.

Usability Tests

Check for affordances:

- Will users recognize the meaning of the >> button?
- If not, will they abandon the dialog box and look through the menus for the missing functionality?
- Will users be surprised by the expansion?
- Will they even notice the >> button?

Make sure that the users can contract the box, once expanded.

See Also

Dialog Box, Standard; Dialog Box, Tabbed; Palette.

Dialog Box, Standard

A window used to hold settings or secondary information and to gather information from the user. Whereas the main window contains the user's actual task (a what-if analysis, for example), dialog boxes let users change how the application itself works (the currency type used during the analysis).

Good For

Dialog boxes have three equally important functions:

■ *Transactional.* Gathering the details needed to complete a command—for example, which file to save or which file to open (Figure 20).

Figure 20

A transactional dialog box.

■ *Tools.* Holding tools such as spelling checkers, floating toolbars, and palettes (Figure 21). Tools usually float on top of main windows, are always visible, and are not confined to any secondary window or document in a multiple-document interface (MDI). A common subtype is the property window or property sheet (in Windows 95), which is used to set properties for GUI objects—for example, selecting the default font for a spreadsheet.

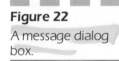

Figure 21

A tool dialog box.

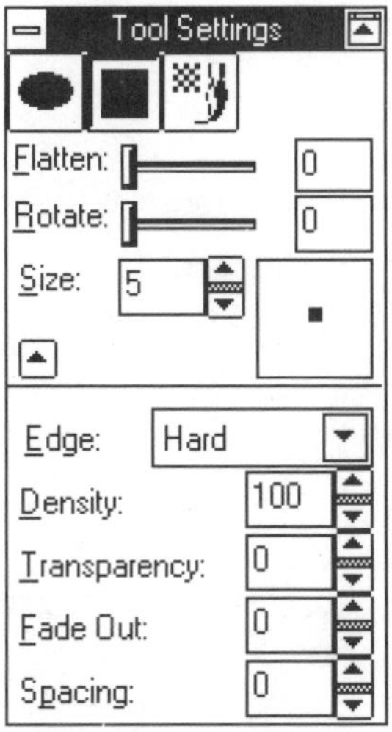

> *Messages.* Delivering messages and providing feedback (Figure 22). Message boxes are used to ask questions, confirm actions, and warn of problems. See Message Box for details.

Figure 22

A message dialog box.

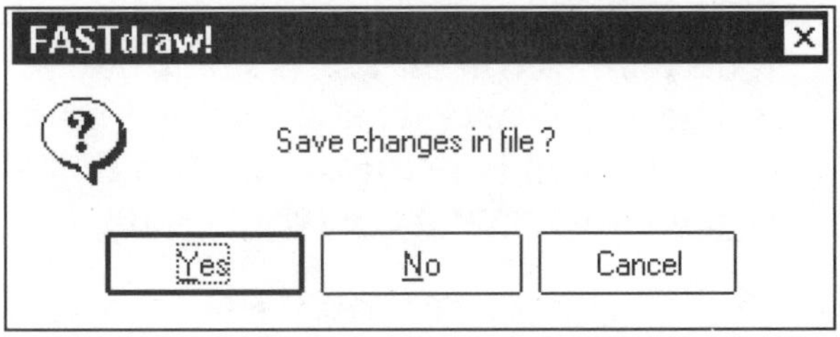

Not Good For

> Holding top-level business information. Dialog boxes are, by nature, hidden under pushbuttons or menu options. They can be used to modify primary tasks or add to primary information, but they are not the user's main view of the application or the data.

Design Guidelines

A dialog box:

- Is usually smaller than the main window or windows.
- Has no menu of its own (except for control menus and minimize/maximize buttons in the title bar).

The development platforms now supply common or standard dialog boxes—for example, File Open, File Save, Print, and a handful of others are available in the development kits. Microsoft suggests that you use the standard dialog boxes but, if you need to create your own for some reason, that you model yours on the standard dialog boxes rather than create new designs from scratch.

LAYING OUT DIALOG BOXES   As Leavens says (1994, 187), "Users will gain an understanding of what your dialog box does and why simply by the way the controls are laid out. Of course, if your controls are laid out badly, the user won't get this information."

MAKE GROUPS OF RELATED ITEMS   Related items should be visually grouped. (In fact, in the case of check boxes and radio buttons, most development packages require that you group related buttons inside a frame or group box.) Unrelated items should not be grouped (because grouping always implies a relationship).

FOLLOW THE WORKFLOW   Lay out your windows to match the user's workflow. Put the most common or critical information at the top left (for language systems in which text reads left to right, top to bottom; adjust for other systems). Then add entry areas and buttons from top to bottom and left to right.

PUT THE PUSHBUTTONS IN THE RIGHT PLACE   The rules for locating pushbuttons and other controls are:

1. Pushbuttons that affect only part of the dialog box should be located inside that part, at the bottom or right side (in countries where text is read from left to right).

2. Put pushbuttons that affect the entire dialog box (OK, Cancel) at the bottom or right side of the dialog box.

3. Whenever possible, place buttons in this order: affirmative buttons used to save any changes and leave the dialog box (OK); negative buttons to cancel changes and leave the window (Cancel); buttons unique to that window (Weinschenk and Yao 1995, 11).

4. Whether the pushbuttons appear at the bottom or the right depends on the flow of movement through the dialog box. For example, if users will move horizontally through entry areas, put the buttons to the right. If they will move vertically, but the buttons on the bottom. See Figure 23 and Figure 24.

Figure 23

When the general movement is horizontal, put the pushbuttons to the right.

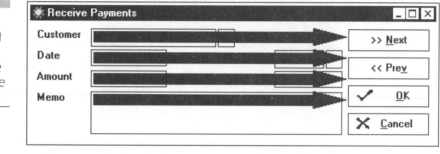

Figure 24

When the general movement is vertical, put the pushbuttons at the top or bottom.

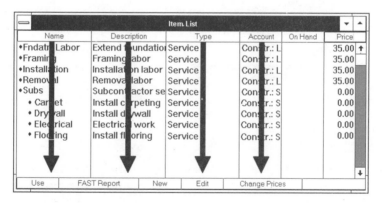

BEHAVIOR GUIDELINES   Dialog boxes must behave appropriately, not just look right. Following are guidelines on dialog box activities.

ALWAYS ON TOP   If a dialog box has Always on Top set, make sure that this behavior is restricted to your own application (Microsoft 1995a, 181). (Overbearing "Always on Top" settings are sometimes a problem with online help systems.)

TO MINIMIZE OR NOT?   In Windows 95 applications, do not put dialog boxes on the taskbar.

Dialog boxes are not officially minimizable on any platform, although some applications do allow users to minimize or compress palettes and toolbars (see the CorelDraw roll-up palette in Figure 25 and Figure 26).

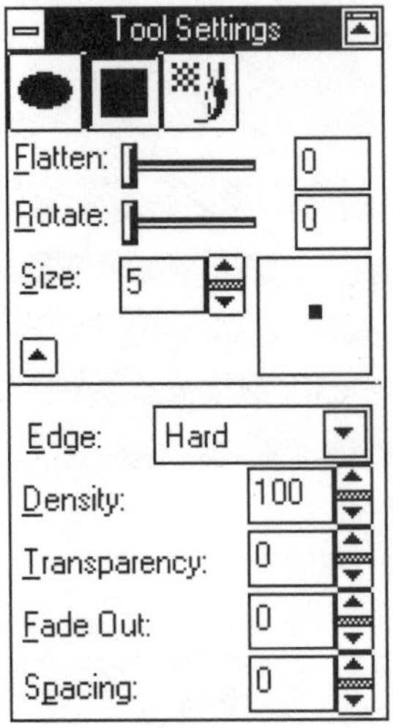

Figure 25
A CorelDraw palette, full-size.

Figure 26
The same palette, rolled up (minimized).

LEVELS   In Windows 95 (and other platforms as well), a dialog box can contain a pushbutton that opens another dialog box. The Microsoft guidelines say:

- If the second dialog box is independent of the first, close the first dialog box and show only the new window. (Do usability testing before implementing this approach, however. For reasons you would never think of, users may actually want to leave all of the dialog boxes open.)

- If the intent of the second dialog box is to get information for the original dialog box, put the new window on top, offset to the right and below the first.

Go no deeper than one level to avoid "creating a cluttered cascading chain of hierarchical windows" (Microsoft 1995a, 182).

SCROLLING Avoid horizontal scrolling of lists in dialog boxes (Weinschenk and Yao 1995, 40–41). Instead:

- Use a larger dialog box.
- Break the information up into more than one dialog box or view (see Dialog Box, Tabbed).
- Allow the dialog box to expand (see Dialog Box, Expanding).

CASCADE OR TILE? In general, use cascading dialog boxes unless users need to see all the information at the same time—for example, a real-time news or stock-market window (Weinschenk and Yao 1995, 40).

RESIZING DIALOG BOXES Resizing the dialog box in which a list box appears can affect the list box. If the dialog box gets bigger, the list should get longer or wider as well. (Why else would a user bother to make the dialog box larger?) If the dialog box gets smaller, the number of choices in the list box should drop to your default minimum but no further (see List Box, Multiple-Selection and List Box, Single-Selection). Remember to set also a reasonable minimum size.

TITLES OF DIALOG BOXES Whenever possible, the name in the title bar should match the name of the menu option or pushbutton used to display the dialog box. Table 1 contains specific guidelines for titles.

MODES IN DIALOG BOXES The paradox of dialog boxes (and windows) is this: Computer screens offer significantly less real estate than

TABLE 1

Guidelines for
Dialog Box Titles

Dialog Box Type	Title Contains	Example
Detail collection, transaction	*parent name — action name*	CLIENTDB – Find
Settings, property sheet	*action name or situation name. parameters*	Font
Spelling: English (US)		
Message	parent name	Stock Picker

the printed page. To do the same work on a computer that one would do on paper means working with many small pages rather than one large page. In short, as a developer you are forced to offer the job in chunks, sequentially, whenever you move a task to a computer. As Dave Collins puts it, "Information that cannot be presented all at once must be presented over time" (1994, 218).

When you have to present a task progressively, one strong temptation is to keep it on track with modes—in other words, until the user finishes one chunk, she cannot see or work on the next chunk. An equally strong temptation, however, is to find modes too restrictive and therefore philosophically abhorrent. As Carl Zetie says (1995, 105), there are two well-established and widely held principles about modes:

- Modes are fundamentally evil and should be avoided at all costs.
- Modes provide support and guidance and should be provided whenever possible.

With these two contradictory principles, how do you decide when to make a dialog box modal, partially modal, or modeless?[2]

Again, Zetie provides some help. First, he points out that a highly restrictive modal-dependent system may strike a self-directed, self-confident developer as unwarranted interference. However, it may strike an uncertain or busy user as a safe and comfortable route to his goal.

Secondly, Zetie says, you can use the distinction between tool-type dialog boxes and detail-gathering dialog boxes to pick modes.

Tool dialog boxes need to be modeless, moveable, and perhaps even minimizable (Figure 25 and Figure 26).

Picking modes for transactional dialog boxes is more difficult because transactional dialog boxes can affect a part or all of an application, and thereby interfere either with the activities of some local part of the application or the entire application. Mode failures occur when a dialog box's mode (its effect) is broader than (or, more rarely, narrower than) its sphere of influence.

For example, say that you develop an e-mail spellchecker that checks individual messages. If the e-mail application lets users edit more than one message at a time, then the users should be able to spellcheck more than one message at a time—they should be able to switch among messages modelessly, carrying the spellchecker with them. If they can't

---

2. There is another definition of mode that we are ignoring in this discussion—an operational state like "editing mode" or "drawing mode."

jump between messages without first closing the spellchecker, they will probably refuse to use it. The spellchecker, in other words, can't be modal at the individual message level, especially not while the more important message editor is modal at the application level.

You can analyze message-box modes in the same way—if the message is about a small part of the application, then it should be modal only for that part. If the message situation affects the entire application, then the message box should affect the entire application.

Since error messages tend to get lost under other windows, developers sometimes make them application-modal or even system-modal to keep them in front of the user until the error situation is cleared up. However, you don't have to make them modal to solve the visibility problem—just give them an "Always on Top" property.

Table 2 lists modes from a technological point of view. However, the true answer to whether a dialog box should be modal or not is the nature of the task or subtask. A single application may use different types of modes in different places. Sometimes the user may be strongly constrained; at other times he or she may have plenty of freedom. Some tasks may be inherently serial; others may be serial or parallel at the user's preference (Zetie 1995, 87).

For an excellent discussion of these issues, see chapter 3, "Taskflow," and chapter 4, "Dialog Design," in Zetie (1995).

GUIDELINES FOR USING MODES Following are guidelines for using modes in your application (adapted from Zetie 1995, 109–110):

1. Use modes consistently. If one tool, like a spellchecker, is modeless, another similar tool, like a thesaurus, should also be modeless.

2. Do not initiate modes unexpectedly. For example, don't suddenly trap a user in a required field.

3. Make it clear to the user that she has entered a mode. Offer feedback—for example, a pointer change or a status-bar message.

4. Make it clear how to escape from the mode. If the user starts a database query, for example, show him how to cancel the query with a Cancel Query button.

5. Always make it possible for the user to escape from a mode harmlessly—at the very least, make sure that every dialog box has a Cancel button.

	Type	Use and Behavior	Examples
TABLE 2 Dialog Box Modes	Modeless	Used for tools. Lets users make multiple changes easily by changing the settings or entries in the dialog box itself and by changing the selection in the main window. If the dialog box is used to change visual attributes, provide a preview area inside the dialog box that shows the effects of the user's changes.	• Toolbars and palettes • Find-and-replace panels • Spelling checkers • Online help
	Semi-modal (Windows 95), Primary modal (OSF/Motif)	Used for gathering details within an application. The user can access some windows outside the dialog box as a way of responding to the dialog. However, he or she cannot access any parent dialog box (any dialog box or window from which the current dialog box came).	In a spreadsheet, the user might have a font dialog box open but be able to change the range of cells. In a database, the user might be able to open a separate window or dialog box to find missing information.
	Movable (or Application) modal	Used to request input or complete a command—which file to save, how to format text. Lets the user switch to and work in another application but not the current application. The user can move the box so that it doesn't obscure the area in which he or she is working.	Dialog box used to change a password. Dialog box used to change application-wide settings—for example, in Internet applications, the list of local-access phone numbers.
	System modal Alert modal	Used for system-level messages and warnings. The user must respond to the dialog box before he or she can do anything in any application. Microsoft says to avoid using system modes unless your application operates as a system-level utility and then only for severe situations such as an impending fatal system error.	System warning message; alert box.

Usability Tests

If you notice that users are opening windows, dialog boxes, or other applications to get additional information, consider redesigning the application to pull in the information automatically with OLE (Object Linking and Embedding) functions.

If you notice that users are moving or canceling dialog boxes to get at "buried" information, consider redesigning the dialog-box sequences and modes.

If users seem to get hopelessly stuck—for example, they cancel the procedure without saving anything or they reboot the machine to start over—then look for feedback and mode failures:

- When feedback is poor, they may be unable to figure out what mode they are in and how to get out of it. Make sure that the mode change is blatantly obvious—for example, make the pointer change its shape.

- Overly restrictive taskflows may force users to exit from the dialog boxes prematurely because they cannot fill a required field or answer a question accurately.

With cognitive walkthroughs, you can test modes and taskflows even before you have access to users. When you do have users, try low-fidelity prototyping to test taskflow. See Appendix B, "Usability Tests," for details.

See Pushbutton for more on testing dialog-box pushbuttons.

See Also

Dialog Box, Expanding; Dialog Box, Tabbed; Field, Required; Palette; Toolbar; Window.

eil,

(Resetting.)

Dialog Box, Tabbed

A dialog box in which settings are grouped into sections. Each section has its own labeled "file" tab. Users switch among the groups by clicking on the tabs.

Good For

- Grouping related application features, attributes, or settings (Figure 27).

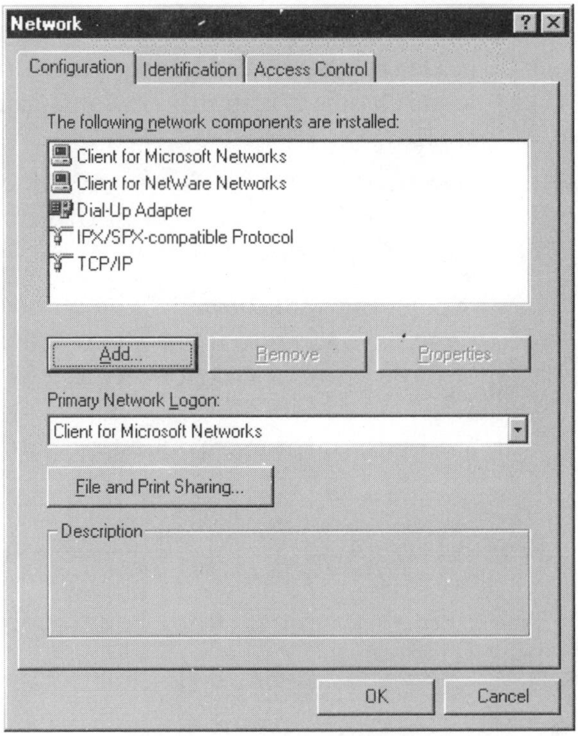

Figure 27

A tabbed dialog box.

Not Good For

- Presenting unrelated settings or too many settings. Don't have more than two rows of tabs. See "Single-level tabs" below.

- Presenting hierarchical information (tabs within tabs). Use methods other than tabs to select levels. See "Hierarchical tabs" below.

- Presenting sequential information. Use wizards instead.

Design Guidelines

The following guidelines are recommended by Chauncey Wilson, a human-computer interaction (HCI) expert who has been designing, reviewing, and testing standard dialog boxes for 12 years and tabbed controls for the last six years (Wilson 1997a).

Tabbed controls (dialog boxes and windows) are based on the metaphor of dividers in filing cabinets or ringed notebooks. The individual tabs, usually called "pages," have textual or graphic labels that indicate the general contents of each page. Microsoft has defined certain types of dialog boxes—property sheets, for example—as tabbed dialog boxes. See Figure 28 and Figure 29.

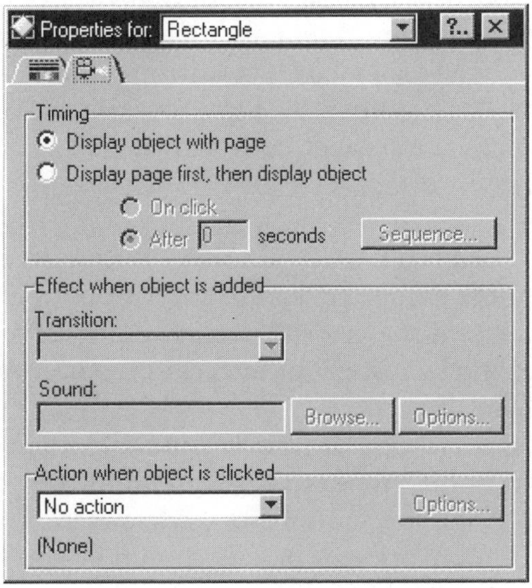

Figure 28

The standard tabbed dialog box style.

Figure 29

The notebook
tabbed window
style (see Window
for details).

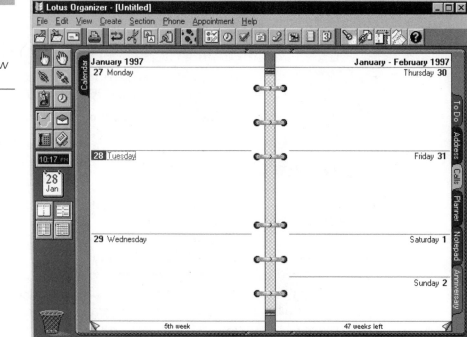

Tabbed dialog boxes are convenient for organizing product functions. Robinson (1996, 1) notes that developers like tabbed dialog boxs because they are a convenient method for grouping many functions.
However, tabbed dialog boxes can present a bewildering array of choices for users. For example, the Options tabbed dialog box in Word for
Windows 6 has 12 tab pages, each with at least 10 choices (and some with
many more).

GENERAL LAYOUT GUIDELINES   Wilson recommends using a consistent layout for tab pages because variations in margins, common button position, and the vertical starting point of components can result
in an annoying tachistoscopic effect as the user moves from tab to tab
(Wilson 1997a).

To facilitate transfer of training, use consistent GUI mechanisms for
similar tasks in different tab pages and in different tabbed dialog boxs.
For example, the mechanism for adding items (passwords, words in a
spellchecker, network equipment) should be consistent in general look
and feel across all tabbed dialog boxs and standard dialog boxes.

Make sure that components' vertical and horizontal starting points are consistent. A common design flaw in tabbed dialogs is to center data-entry areas, pushbuttons, and other components, especially when there are only a few of them. However, centering components means that they will seem to jump around as users flip between tabs. Left-justifying components and putting all pushbuttons on the bottom or at the right is visually more consistent.

DON'T HIDE INFORMATION   One of the advantages of tabs over menu access is visibility. Don't lose that advantage by hiding the information, says Wilson:

- Put the most frequently used controls or information on the first tab page that the user sees.

- If your users want to see or compare information on more than one tab, accommodate them either by using two or more modeless tabbed dialog boxes or by letting them tear the tab off (like a tear-off menu or palette). Making users remember information while they switch between tabs puts a serious burden on short-term memory.

- Avoid complex interactions among controls on different tabs. A user may not understand that a disabled control on tab 4 can only be enabled if the proper radio button is chosen on tab page 2.

- For the same reason, don't put required fields on more than one tab. Also, to reduce errors, provide feedback about which fields are required and which are optional. Consider grouping all required fields together or using visual cues to differentiate required and optional fields. See Field, Entry and Field, Required for more information.

HELP BUTTONS   Help buttons on tabbed dialog boxes should provide help on the current tab page, Wilson says, rather than on the dialog box as a whole. Tab-sensitive help buttons speeds up access to help.

ROWS OF TABS   Tabs can be arranged in rows on a single level (see Figure 28) or in hierarchical ranks (see Figure 32). The problems of the two styles differ.

SINGLE-LEVEL TABS   Once you move beyond two rows of tabs, you place a cognitive burden on the user, says Wilson. Put tabs on only one edge and use at most two levels of tabs, five to seven tabs per edge. If you think you need more than two levels, you probably have too much information going into each set. Try re-categorizing the tabs into smaller sets.

If you must have more than one row of tabs, don't compound the problem by moving them around when the user selects a tab. For example, the tabs in Figure 30 and Figure 31 are confusing to most users.

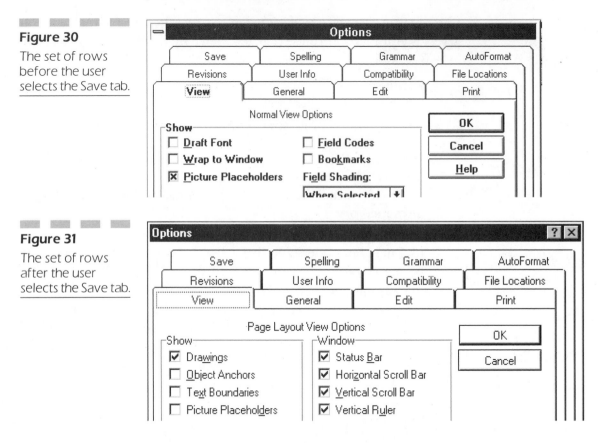

Figure 30

The set of rows before the user selects the Save tab.

Figure 31

The set of rows after the user selects the Save tab.

Expert users explore the interface to learn how to use the program, generally by starting at the top-left tab (in Western languages) and moving to the bottom-right tab. If the tabs move by themselves, however, the expert user will never get through all the tabs. She may decide, in fact, that the dialog box is unreliable and avoid it whenever possible.

HIERARCHICAL TABS   For property-type dialog boxes, avoid hierarchical sets of tabs—tabs in which one set of tabs is secondary to another

(Figure 32). Instead, try combining list boxes with tabs (Figure 33) when a set of properties can be applied to more than one object, as per Microsoft (1995a, 189). In this type of design, the user first chooses a type of control or data view from a drop-down list, then chooses the desired attributes tab from a group of related tabs. Although this approach is like having tabs within tabs, the use of the drop-down list reduces the visual complexity.

Figure 32

Hierarchical tabs.

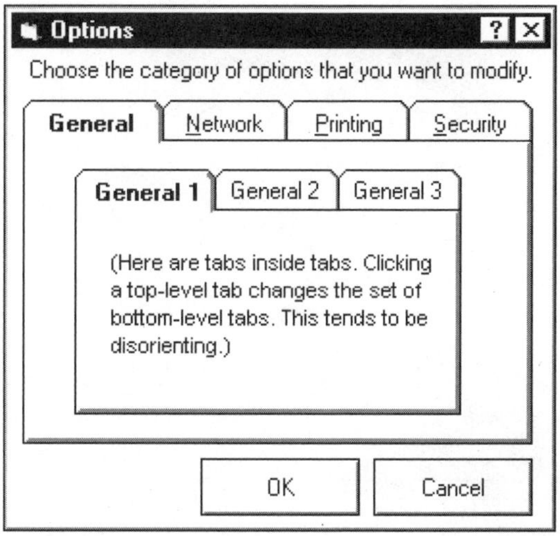

Figure 33

Combining list boxes with tabs.

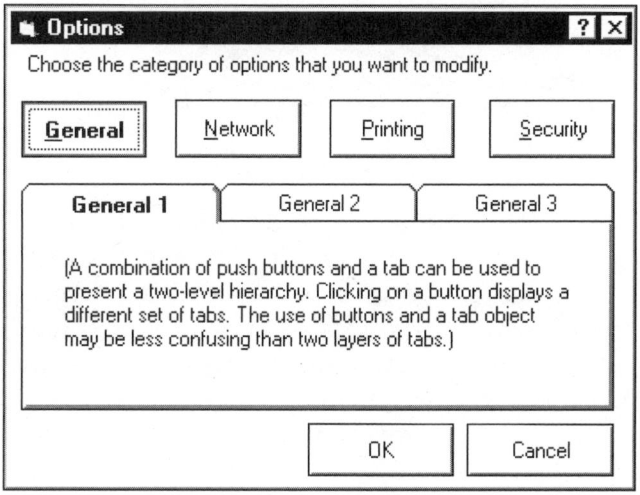

The same approach can be used in other circumstances as well, especially in tabbed windows. See Window for examples.

LABELS ON TABS   A set of tabs is functionally equivalent to a set of menu items. The important difference is layout: Unlike menus, the structure is always visible as a row of tab labels.

Make sure that the user can identify the current tab page—use good cues (Wilson 1997a). Common cues include changing the font of the label from normal to bold (Figure 34) and changing the background color of the tab. The use of multiple cues (bold text plus a white background) is also effective (Figure 35).

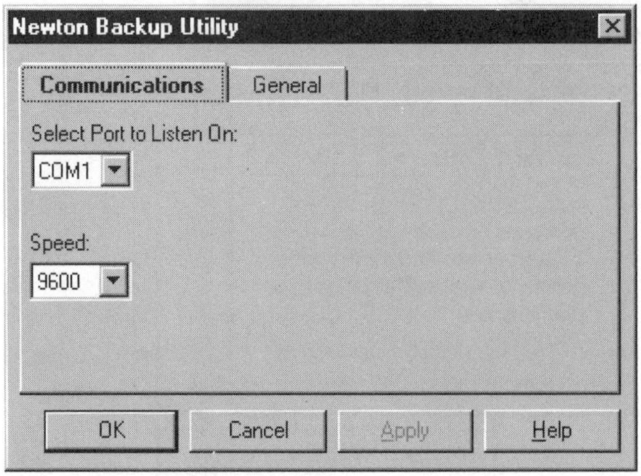

Figure 34

Show which tab is selected by changing the label from normal to bold.

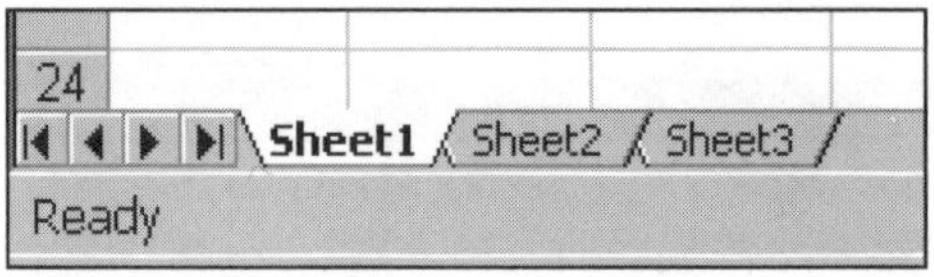

Figure 35

Excel tabs change the background and turn the text bold.

SCROLLING LABELS   Some development packages will automatically create scrolling tabs (Figure 36) if the labels become too long to fit in the dialog box (as they might when translated). Other packages will add new rows. If you plan to localize your product, translate a sample of your tab pages to determine the impact of text expansion. Text can expand from 30 to 200 percent and create major labeling and layout problems. (See Labels for more information on expanding text.)

KEYBOARD ACCESS   Provide a method for accessing tab pages through the keyboard. Access can be through accelerator keys like

Options
General
Network
Software
Hardware
Printing
OK
Cancel

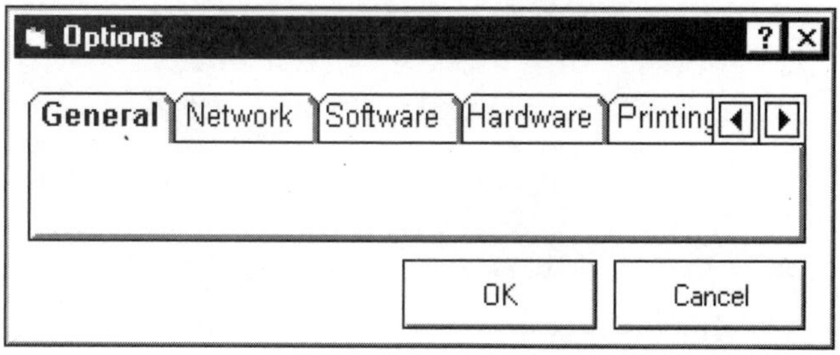

Figure 36
A scrolling set of tabs means that functionality is hidden.

Ctrl+Tab (common in Windows 95) or mnemonics for individual tab pages (for example, Alt+G might display the "Gridlines" tab page).

VERTICAL LABELS Avoid vertical or stacked text in labels. Vertical labels are difficult to read on a computer screen. Users can turn books on their sides if necessary, but most can't easily do the same with their monitors. If you need vertical labels, keep the text horizontal (Figure 38).

General
Print
Network

Figure 37
Don't stack the letters or turn them sideways.

General
Print
Network

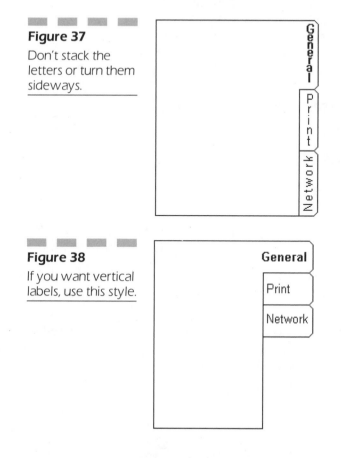

Figure 38
If you want vertical labels, use this style.

PUSHBUTTONS ON TABBED DIALOG BOXES   Usability experts have noticed that users are often unclear about when changes to settings in a tabbed dialog box take effect (Robinson 1996, 1). For example:

- Do the changes take effect when you move from tab to tab, when you click OK, the next time you start the program, when you click Apply, or when you close the tabbed dialog box?

- If you take some action on a particular page, such as adding a group of users to a network, are the new users saved when you click the Add button or are they saved when you click OK?

Use a consistent method for saving changes to the settings in all tabbed dialog boxs in a product. Avoid doing an auto-save in one tab dialog (changes in one tab are saved when you click on another tab) and manual save (clicking on the OK button) in others.

Also, researchers find that users are most satisfied with explicit information about effects. For example, adding an explicit Apply Settings button means that users no longer have to guess that clicking OK or switching tabs applies their changes. Although the Apply button might add an extra interaction, it eliminates unnecessary cognition. The idea, as ever, is to let users think about *their* tasks, not yours.

SAVING THE PAGE VERSUS THE DIALOG BOX   Another source of confusion is what OK, Cancel, or Apply actually affect—the entire dialog box or just the current page? Make effects obvious by positioning your pushbuttons inside or outside the page as needed:

- Place pushbuttons that affect all the pages outside the margins of the tab page (Figure 39).

- Place pushbuttons that affect only the page inside the page margins (Wilson 1997a).

RESTORE THE DEFAULTS   Tabbed dialog boxs are often used for complex system configuration tasks with many settings. Provide a mechanism for restoring the settings on the current tab page or on all tab pages, Wilson says. This could be a Restore Defaults button placed inside a tab page (which would affect only the settings on the page) or with the main pushbuttons (which would affect the settings on all tab pages). Just make sure that the user is clear about what the Restore Defaults button will do. See Pushbuttons for more information.

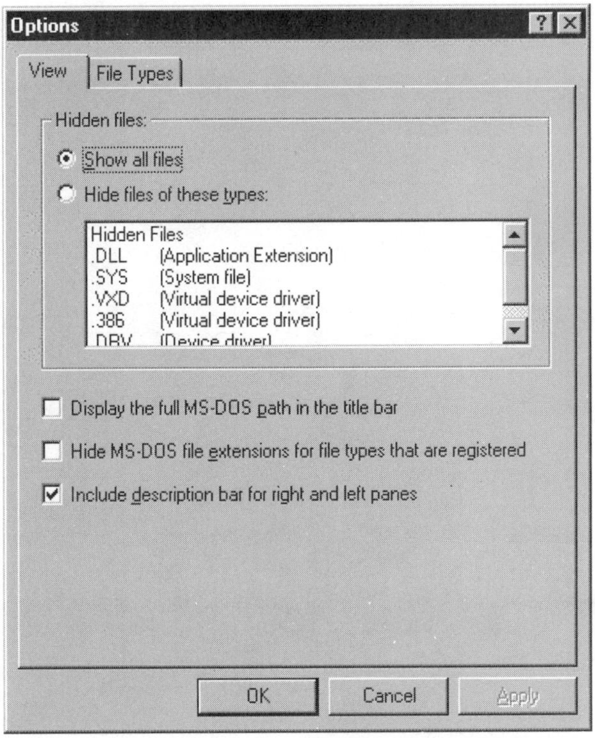

Figure 39

Figure 39

The pushbuttons
are placed outside
the tabs to indicate
that they affect the
entire dialog box.

WHAT THE TABBED DIALOG BOX REPLACED The tabbed dialog box has become a popular method for combining many individual "preferences" or "properties" dialog boxes into a compact package (Wilson 1997a). Before the tabbed dialog box was invented, a GUI designer would create a separate dialog box for each set of related features or attributes, or else use radio buttons, drop-down lists, list boxes, or pushbuttons to display dialog boxes within dialog boxes. Figure 40, Figure 41, Figure 42, and Figure 43 show some of the methods that tabbed dialog boxes replace.

Other methods include:

- Creating separate menu items for each dialog box, which increases menu complexity.

- Opening multiple levels of dialog boxes from the parent dialog box.

- Expanding dialog boxes to show second-level information.

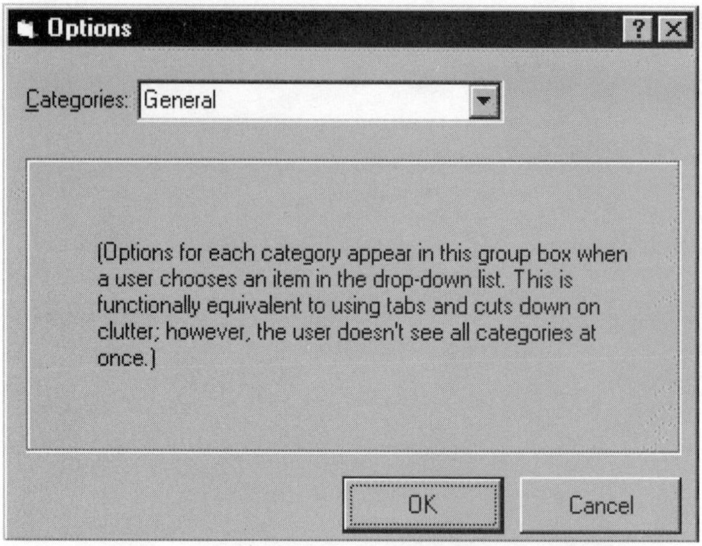

Figure 40

A drop-down list
instead of tabs.

Figure 40

A drop-down list
instead of tabs.

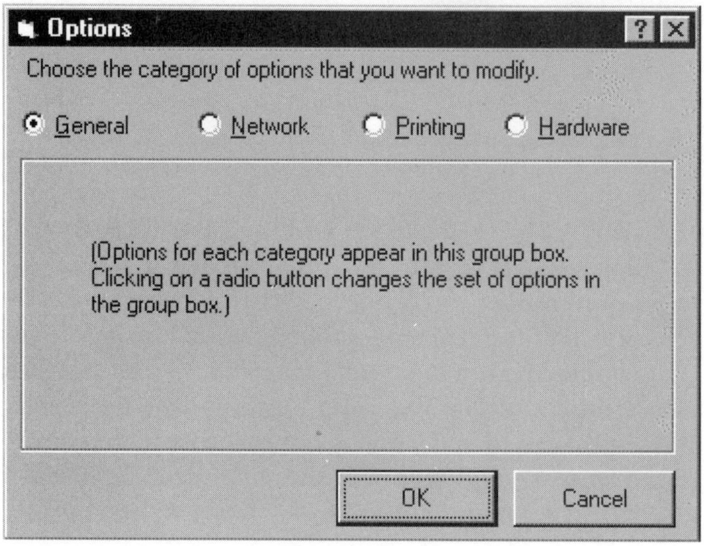

Figure 41

Radio buttons
instead of tabs.

Although expanding dialog boxes and opening multiple dialog boxes
from one dialog box still appear occasionally, most of them are also being replaced with tabbed dialog boxes.

Figure 42

Single-select list
box instead of tabs.

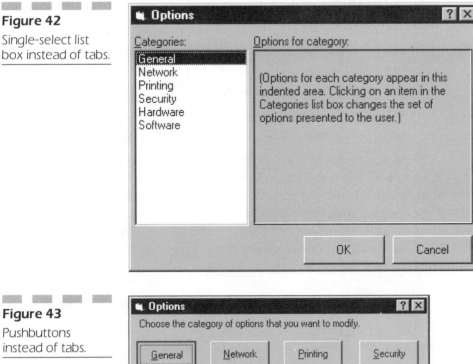

Figure 43

Pushbuttons
instead of tabs.

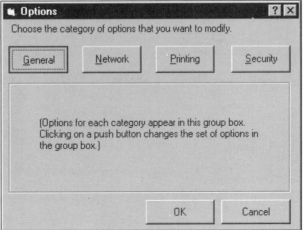

WHEN TO USE A TABBED DIALOG BOX   Tabbed dialog boxs are
most appropriate for random access to features, attributes, or task objects. Tabbed dialog boxes cue users that they can visit as many or as few
of the tab pages as they think are relevant, in any order.

However, the tab metaphor does not suggest that users *must* visit
each page in order. Thus, avoid tabbed dialog boxes for sequential tasks
(in which each tab represents a step in a process). Instead, consider using
a wizard to guide users through sequential tasks (Zetie 1995, 148).

If you must use tabbed dialog boxes for sequential tasks, provide clear feedback on:

- How the user can change things in previous steps.
- Whether steps can be skipped.
- What is required within each step.
- When the subtasks for each step are actually accomplished or saved—as each subtask ends or only at the end of all subtasks?

There is a recent trend to integrate tabbed dialogs into wizard designs (Figure 44). This approach, which lets users make many choices at each step, might be due to users complaining that the wizards are not flexible enough. However, adding multiple tabs to each wizard dialog box imposes an extra—and probably unexpected—cognitive load on the user. Wizards are supposed to take the simplest or default route through the task, not the most complicated one.

Figure 44

A wizard with tabs.

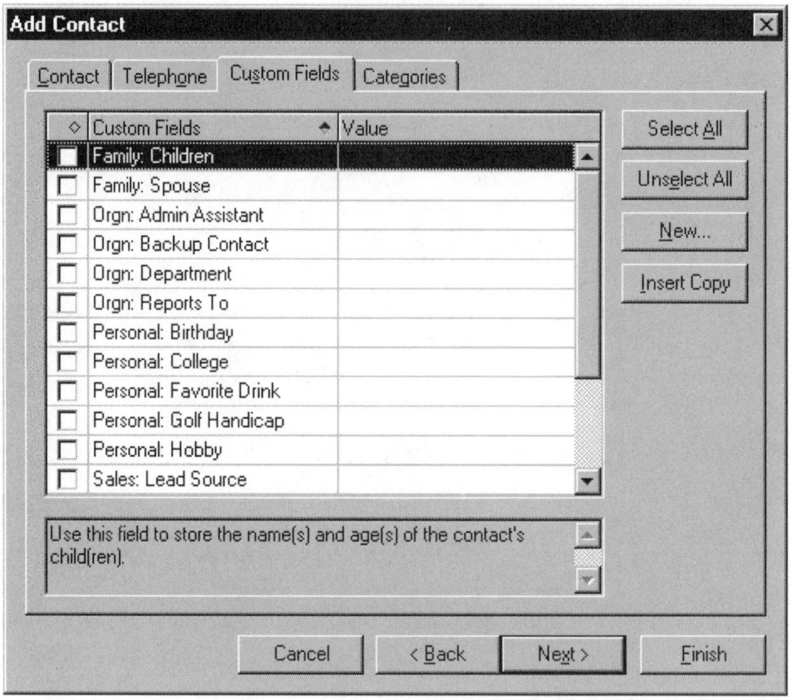

If you find yourself in this situation, check whether the "expert route" is missing. Your experienced users may be trying, unsuccessfully, to find out how to do the task more more quickly—i.e., without the wizard. Tell them somewhere in the wizard or in help how to make the change directly. Also see if you have a wider diversity in user needs than you expected. Multiple wizards might be an appropriate response. See Wizard for more information.

Usability Tests

Test whether users can locate functions inside tabbed dialog boxs. For example, with a paper and pencil test, ask participants to match functions to tab names. You can test this with a low-fidelity prototype as well.

Test the labels. Ask the participants to find an item and see whether they pick the right tab. For unsuccessful choices, ask them what label they would use. Change the labels between tests until most users pick the right tab.

Test for information overload—in other words, too many sets of tabs and too many unrelated dialog boxes in the same set. If participants have trouble matching functions and labels, try breaking the entire set of pages into smaller sets, then test again.

By direct questioning, see if participants know when their changes have taken effect.

See Also

Dialog Box, Standard; Window.

Drop-Down List Box

A data-entry tool that lets users pick items from a list rather than type entries.

Good For

- Limiting choices to the items on the list.
- When available space is limited (on a toolbar, for example) and when the mouse is the primary interaction device (as opposed to the combo box, which is more keyboard-oriented). See Figure 45.

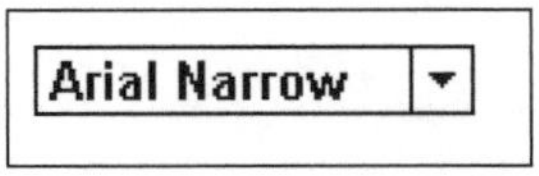

Figure 45

A closed drop-down list box.

> Arial Narrow ▼

Not Good For

- Letting users add new items. Use a drop-down combo box instead.
- Letting users select more than one item. Use a multiple-select list box instead.

Design Guidelines

In Visual Basic and some other development packages, a drop-down list box is a type of combo box. In other words, to create one, you select the combo box control, then change the Style property to "dropdown list."

Note that users cannot add new items to a drop-down list as they can with simple or drop-down combo boxes. They can, however, search the list by typing the first letter of the desired item when the list has focus. See "Searching" in Combo Box.

In Windows 3.x, the drop-down list box may be visually distinguished from the drop-down combo box by the *lack* of a space between the entry area and the down arrow (Figure 45).

Weinschenk and Yao (1995, 22) make these recommendations:

■ Since drop-down lists hide all but the first item, use a drop-down list if most users will select the first item.

■ Display a default value in the entry area if users will pick it more than half the time. For example, on a medical insurance form, "Self" is probably the most likely answer to "Relationship to Patient?" and would be a good default value. If there is no clear default, use alphabetical order or some other logical order (see Table 13. "Organization Styles for Lists" in List Box, Multiple-Selection).

■ Do not use a drop-down list if users need to see all options all the time. (To find out, check your specifications and do usability testing.)

■ Consider using filters when there are more than 40 items on the list. (Scrolling through long lists is difficult because there is a tendency for the mouse to slip off the scroll bar.) You can divide the list up alphabetically (for example, users click an M button to get the list of chart types starting with M) or by category (users click "Laser" to get the list of laser printers, "Bubble Jet" for bubble-jet printers, and so on).

Usability Tests

Make sure that users know they can search the list. If half or more users don't notice the search option, consider adding an instructional label or tooltip such as "Type item or click the down arrow." You can also flag the issue for your online help, documentation, and training teams.

See Also

Combo Box; List Box, Single-Selection.

Field, Entry

An area that lets users enter and edit data. Depending on the type of application, data-entry fields allow users to enter, edit, and save database and system information or to enter values for analyses. Some applications also use fields to run searches—for example, the user can enter a last name, Social Security number, or other key data, and then click Search to find a particular record. A subcategory of the data-entry field is the multiple-line field.

Good For

- For database operations, letting users create or change records (Figure 46). The entries are saved on permanent storage media.

Figure 46
Database field.

- For analysis operations, letting users run calculations and analyses (Figure 47). The entries are usually not saved.

Figure 47
Input area for part of an analysis.

- For system-level utilities, letting users save file names and other system information (Figure 48).

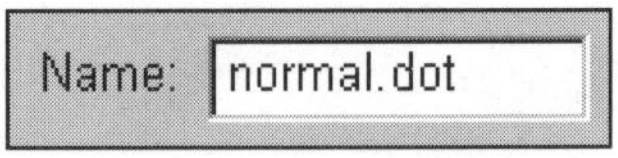

Figure 48
Entry area for a file name.

Not Good For

- Running commands. Use command lines instead.

■ Entering fixed kinds of information. Rather than making users type the same information repeatedly, use combo boxes, lists, check boxes, or radio buttons instead.

Design Guidelines

Note that data-entry, required, and protected fields overlap. Required fields are a type of data-entry field, and protected fields can change from protected to entry, depending on which business or data-integrity rules are in effect.

VISUAL DESIGN FOR DATA-ENTRY FIELDS   Entry fields should look like they accept data. Create this effect by:

■ Providing a frame or box for the entry area.

■ Using a beveled border that makes the field look inset (Marcus 1995, 141).

■ Using a different, lighter color for the entry area so that it contrasts with the background.

■ Except for passwords, always displaying the user's entries as he or she types them.

Other general design guidelines:

■ When a field appears, it should either be empty or contain an initial default value. (See Field, Required, for more information on default entries.) If the field contains a value, the value should become selected (and therefore editable or replaceable) when the cursor enters the field.

■ Provide a label. However, because the data are more important than the labels, make sure that the labels are smaller, lighter, or less visible than the data (Bellcore 1994, 5–46). See Label for details on label location and text case.

■ Group related fields. See Label for field layout guidelines.

DISABLED ENTRY FIELDS   Sometimes fields become unavailable or disabled temporarily (because of business or data-integrity rules). When fields are temporarily disabled, follow these guidelines:

- If users cannot change the contents of a field temporarily, turn the contents gray but do not change the color of the entry area.

- If the field itself is temporarily unavailable, gray out the label and background of the entry area (Marcus 1995, 141; Weinschenk and Yao 1995, 33).

Note that, in contrast, permanently protected fields use the window's background color for their data areas and have no beveled edges.

WIDTH OF ENTRY AREAS   It used to be that picking field widths was easy—in a monospaced-font interface, the entry area was the same width as the field. With the arrival of proportional fonts, however, the widths of fields and their entry areas parted company (Figure 49).

Figure 49

The difference between monospaced and proportionally spaced entry areas.

```
12345678901234567890123456789012345678901234 5
This is a proportional font against a 45-character ruler


12345678901234567890123456789012345678901234 5
This is a monospaced font against a 45-character ruler
```

To pick the appropriate entry-area width for a variable-length field:

1. Find the field size, if you haven't already done so, by averaging the lengths of typical sample data.

2. Create a text box, then type the average number of characters (a series of lowercase n's will do) into it. Adjust the width of the box until you can see all of the characters at once. You can make the actual field longer provided that you let the user navigate left and right beyond the edges of the displayed area. Keep in mind, however, that users dislike horizontal scrolling in fields.

If you are going to internationalize your interface, make sure that you repeat the average-field length tests for entries in the target languages. These entries can be 30 to 200 percent longer than their English counterparts. See Table 12 on page 111 in Label for details.

To find the best width for fixed-length fields (which are usually codes), create a text box for the field, then type in as many uppercase Ms (the widest letter in the Latin alphabet) as the code requires. For example, for a two-digit state field, you'd type MM. If the last M isn't cut off, the entry area is the right size.

When the widths of a number of fields are similar, match the widths rather than defining customized widths for each one. However, keep in mind that the size of the entry area signifies the data length to users. Don't be tempted to make entry areas too short or too long only for aesthetic reasons (Weinschenk and Yao 1995, 33).

MULTIPLE-LINE FIELDS   Most data-entry fields do not let users change the text font or size or enter more than one line of data. The exception is the multiple-line field, which let users type, edit, and read passages of text. Typical uses include e-mail messages and text files (Galitz 1997, 340; Microsoft 1995a, 159).

Multiple-line fields, especially those defined as "rich-text fields," can be printed and have OLE functions—for example, you can let users show part of a spreadsheet in the field (Microsoft 1995a, 159).

JUSTIFICATION   Don't force users to right-justify or left-justify entries themselves.

- If the entry is alphabetical, left-justify it.
- If it's numeric, right-justify it.
- If it's decimal, justify the entry around the decimal point.

Also don't force users to enter leading zeros and don't force them to change the text's case themselves (Bellcore 1994, 5–47).

Note that different writing systems have different justification rules. For example, Hebrew and Arabic writing systems are bidirectional—text is entered and displayed from right to left, but numbers (and any Roman-alphabet words) are entered and displayed from left to right (Apple Computer 1992, 105–107). See Figure 50.

Figure 50

A sample, done in English, of bidirectional text. Note that the number is (within the context) reversed.

$1,000,000—amanaP ,lanac a ,nalp a ,nam A

For more information on internationalization issues, see Fowler and Stanwick, 1995, chapter 6, "International Software" (1995, 241–242).

KEYBOARD NAVIGATION AND USAGE Users must move between fields and inside fields. Guidelines for moving between fields are:

■ Provide mnemonics (see Keyboard Shortcuts for details). Put the access-key underline on the label, but when the user presses the access key, put the cursor in the live entry area (Microsoft 1995a, 157).

Figure 51

"L" is the mnemonic for the "Last Name" field.

Last Name: Stanwick

■ Use Tab, Shift+Tab, and the up and down arrow keys to move between fields (Microsoft 1995a, 157; Digital 1995, 253).

■ If the users are familiar (from character-based interfaces) with pressing Enter to move between fields, also allow Enter even though it might seem like un-GUI behavior. Carolyn Snyder, usability expert at User Interface Engineering, points out that it's "not true that Microsoft has 'invalidated' using the Enter key. In some Windows products (Microsoft Money being one), the user can set a preference to navigate with Enter rather than Tab." Having this option is important, she says. "I have seen users accustomed to a DOS-based system get all hung up over the Tab/Enter thing because hitting Enter has become such a reflex for them. This sounds like a trivial thing, but I've seen it cause new users significant difficulty" (Snyder 1997).

Guidelines for moving inside single-line fields are:

■ The left and right arrow keys move the cursor left and right by one character.

■ In fields containing multiple words, Ctrl+← moves the cursor to the beginning of the previous word. Ctrl+→ moves the cursor to the next word (Digital 1995, 252).

■ The Begin or Home key moves the cursor to the beginning of the line or field. The End key moves the cursor to the end of the line or field (Digital 1995, 252). An alternate is Ctrl + left or right arrow (Marcus 1995, 141).

Guidelines for moving inside multiple-line fields are:

- The up and down arrow keys move to the previous or next line (note that in single-line fields, the up and down arrows move to other components).
- The left and right arrow keys move the cursor left and right by one character.
- Ctrl+← moves the cursor to the beginning of the previous word. Ctrl+→ moves the cursor to the next word (Digital 1995, 252).
- The Begin or Home key moves the cursor to the beginning of the line or field. The End key moves the cursor to the end of the line or field (Digital 1995, 252). An alternate is Ctrl+← or Ctrl+→ (Marcus 1995, 141).
- Ctrl+Begin or Ctrl+Home moves the cursor to the beginning of the file. Ctrl+End moves the cursor to the end of the file.
- Use double-clicking to select individual words (Digital 1995, 253).
- Use Tab for indenting (Digital 1995, 253).
- Use Return to insert a carriage return. The Digital guidelines suggest using Enter or Ctrl+Enter to invoke the window or dialog box's default action. This requires a keyboard with both Enter and Return (Digital 1995, 253).

Note that, if the window or dialog box has a default pushbutton activated with Enter, you may need to disable default access as long as the cursor is in the multiple-line field.

CUT, PASTE, UNDO, REDO   Applications should, at a minimum, allow cut, copy, and paste operations using the standard accelerators (Ctrl+X for cut, Ctrl+C for copy, and Ctrl+V for paste). Toolbar cut, copy, and paste buttons are always helpful.

Provide a method for selecting data using the keyboard (not just the mouse). The Digital guidelines suggest Ctrl and spacebar (1995, 253). In Microsoft Windows 3.x and 95 programs, Shift plus the left and right arrows select text.

When using Delete or Backspace, Microsoft recommends that the application not put the cut text in the Clipboard. Instead, provide at least one level of undo (1995a, 63).

INSERT AND OVERTYPE If the field supports replace mode, use the Insert key to toggle between insert and overtype mode (Digital 1995, 253; Microsoft 1995a, 63). For insert mode, use the text insertion cursor. For overtype mode, use a block cursor on top of the current character and reverse-highlight the character (Microsoft 1995a, 62–63).

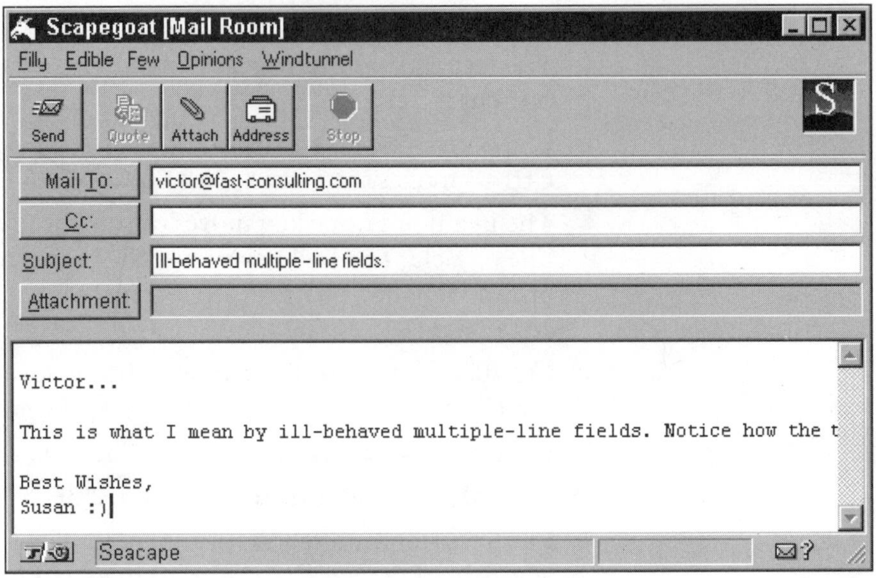

Figure 52

An ill-behaved
multiple-line field.

You can define multiple-line fields to accept paragraph breaks and font changes. Make sure that you support wraparound. Do not force users to enter their own line breaks or to type out of view—past the borders of the entry area—even if you supply scroll bars (Bellcore 1994, 5–47).

AUTO SKIP "Auto skip" or "automatic return" makes the cursor move automatically to the next field as soon as the last character in the previous field is completely filled. Theoretically, since auto skip eliminates pressing Tab or Return, it should be faster than manually tabbing between fields. However, it is not faster for data-entry personnel working on "heads-down" form-based data-entry windows. (See Windows for the three types of windows.)

Professional data-entry personnel have two characteristics that make auto skip problematic: They are usually touch typists and they rarely look at the screen while they work. Since not all fields are completely filled, the typists often have to stop, check the screen to find out where the cursor is, then either tab to the next field or just start typing again.

For example, Figure 53 shows auto skip under ideal circumstances. The typist fills in the street address, presses Tab, and types the two-character state abbreviation.

Street address: Main St.   State: CA   ZIP: 95555-1234

Figure 53

As long as the state is filled in completely, the cursor jumps automatically to the next field.

Figure 54 shows what actually happens much of the time. The street address is too long, but the typist isn't looking at the screen and doesn't notice. He continues typing, but now he's in the state field, which accepts the two letters (no editing) and moves the cursor into the ZIP code field. Since the ZIP code field doesn't accept letters, it beeps, finally breaking his concentration. At this point, he has three bad entries to fix.

Street address: Maria Hotchkis   State: SR   ZIP: DCT06700

Figure 54

An auto skip failure.

Like skiing or ice-skating, touch-typing is most satisfying when its practitioner can get into the flow. Auto skip, unfortunately, breaks that flow. Wilbert O. Galitz found in a 1972 study that "auto skip, while requiring fewer keystrokes, was found to result in longer keying times and more errors than manual tabbing because it disrupted the keying rhythm (1997, 151). It also requires learning and constant analysis, as he demonstrates in Figure 55.

Auto skip is also contraindicated when employee turnover is high and when users don't spend significant amounts of time doing data entry. New hires might have trouble learning the navigation style; infrequent users might have trouble remembering the rules and the codes.

However, auto skip can be helpful in either of two situations: if every field on the window is fixed-length or if the application uses a "heads-up" conversational-type window.

Figure 55

Decision trees for data entry with auto skip and without. From Galitz (1997, 152–153).

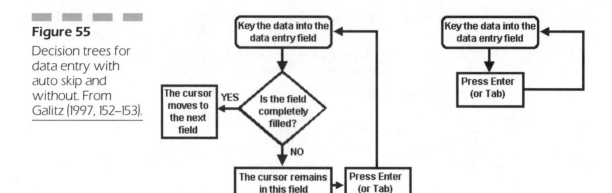

When every field contains a fixed-length code, the application need not make the experienced data-entry typist press Tab or Enter. Keep in mind, however, that the inexperienced user who has yet to memorize all the codes may have trouble keeping his or her place. If usability tests indicate a problem, let these users switch from manual skip to auto skip when they feel they've gotten up to speed.

A typical conversational application is a word processing program or a telephone reservations system. Since the data-entry personnel are looking at the screen while they input information, they see the auto skipping occur and therefore don't lose track of the cursor location.

Auto fill (auto-complete) is a good alternative to auto skip. See "Transformations and edits" below for details.

DATA-ENTRY AND TOUCH TYPISTS If your users complain about having to use the mouse too much, find out if they're touch typists. Touch typists like to keep their hands in the home position (on the middle row of keys, from A to F and J to the colon). They do not like to switch between mouse and keyboard. Accommodate touch typists by:

- Using the standard set of mnemonics (Ctrl+S for save, Ctrl+C for copy, and so on).
- Making sure that all lists use combo boxes (with combo boxes, you can either type or select an entry from the list).
- Making sure that all check boxes can be set by typing a letter or number (X, Y, or N, M or F).

DATA ERROR PREVENTION AND CORRECTION   Where there is data entry, there are errors. One of the reasons that your application uses field edits is to prevent and, if necessary, handle errors.

You can prevent misunderstandings by building your interface around the users' conceptual models (see Appendix A). You can make some errors unlikely by editing the data and by improving visibility, feedback, and mapping (matching computerized and actual items—for example, using an onscreen thermometer to set a temperature). You can prevent other errors by the judicious use of constraints. Once you've done as much prevention as you can think of, then you can offer graceful recovery methods.

TRANSFORMATIONS AND EDITS   To design fields most effectively, you must map the system model (in a database, columns, rows, data, flags) to the user's conceptual model (what stock is available, what needs to be reordered, what should be sent back to the manufacturer). In other words, your application must accept whatever seems sensible *to the user* as input (input transformation); display whatever makes sense *to the user* as output (output transformation); and constrain only when constraint is more efficient *for the user* (one-to-one transformation).

An *input transformation* is what many developers would call an edit. Carl Zetie (1995) uses dates as typical candidates for input transformation. For example, each of these dates are the same, if you accept that some are European versions of December 5, 2000:

- 12/5/00
- 12/5/2000
- 12-5-2000
- 05-12-2000
- December 5, 2000
- 5 December 2000

In a well-mannered application, the user would either know exactly which of these formats to use (because the label or the field says so) or the application would accept any of them. (For more on dates, see "Date formats" below.) The input is then transformed twice—once to its internal representation, which is usually the number of days since an arbitrary starting date; and secondly to its display or output state—for example, 12/05/00 (Zetie 1995, 79).

An *output transformation* extracts meaning from a mass of data. An output transformation generally starts with a totality of information from a database or analysis, but ends with a display of only the most significant points.

For example, an inventory system might know that the level of a particular item is so low that it is triggering a reorder and that crates of an out-of-stock item are waiting to be unloaded into the warehouse. However, no matter how much information it may have, the system will show only that some items are deliverable and some aren't. A sales clerk sees the available items in blue (not shades of blue corresponding to how available they are) and unavailable items in red (not shades of red). The output transformation pulls just the necessary information from the entire universe of information. "Choosing a good output transformation is always a question of reducing the information presented to the user to everything that she needs to know, but no more" (Zetie 1995, 79).

A *one-to-one transformation* means that there is a one-to-one correspondence between the user model and the system model—in Solitaire, for example, the cards in the user's mind match the cards on the screen. In a user interface, replacing a yes/no question with a checkbox would be a one-to-one transformation. In a printout, displaying the stock items' names rather than their catalog numbers (the sales clerk's input) would be another type of one-to-one transformation.

One-to-one transformations are more appropriate than standard input transformations whenever "it is useful to force the user to a single way of expressing an input. For example, replacing a yes/no question with a check box eliminates the user's doubt over whether the question can be answered with a simple 'Y,' or requires 'Yes' in full, or is case-sensitive" (Zetie 1995, 81).

Following are ways to handle errors and some of the most typical data-entry problems. However, keep in mind that any good solution requires a deep understanding of your users' goals and conceptual models. For detailed advice, see chapter 2, "Conceptual Models," in Zetie (1995); chapter 4, "Applying Object-Orientation to User Interfaces," and chapter 5, "Three Domains of OO Design for the User Interface," in Collins (1995); and chapter 3, "The Three Models," in Cooper (1995).

VISIBILITY, FEEDBACK, MAPPING To improve visibility, show users exactly what you expect from them. For example, if you want users to enter dates in DD-MON-YYYY format, put "DD-MON-YYYY" inside the field as a mask that the user overtypes (Figure 56), or put "DD-MON-YYYY" in the label.

Figure 56

Date-format masks and labels.

To improve feedback, let users know, when they make errors, both that there is a problem and what the solution is. For example, what if the user types a date in MM-DD-YY format—"12/05/00," say, but the required format is DD-MM-YY? In this case, the error message should include the right date format (see Figure 57).

Figure 57

Error message with the right level of feedback.

To improve mapping, more closely match software components to items in the user's universe. For example, you can let users enter dates in any format that makes sense to them, and then change them internally to the format your application requires. For even better mapping, you can let users select dates from an onscreen calendar (Zetie 1995, 210).

Make sure that the mapping is efficient as well as effective, however. For setting up appointments in a week or so, a scrollable calendar is fine; for setting a maturity date 30 years out, a scrollable calendar would be an abominable waste of time. (You need to be able to type in a date in that case.) However, in the financial application, having a calendar as a *backup* would be useful: If the chosen maturity date fell on a weekend, a pop-up calendar set to the appropriate week and year would make it easy to pick a weekday.

You also can prevent range errors with good mapping. A range error occurs if the user is asked to enter a range of dates, numbers, or other items, and he or she types an entry for the small end that is larger than the entry for the large end. Of course you can test for the error and put up a message, but why not use a scale instead and thereby prevent the issue from even coming up? For example, if the only valid temperatures range between 0° and 100°, let users pick a temperature by dragging a selector on a 0°–100° thermometer widget (Figure 58). Just make sure that you add an entry area for fine adjustments and for touch typists.

Figure 58

Effective temperature mapping. Users can drag the mercury up and down the thermometer.

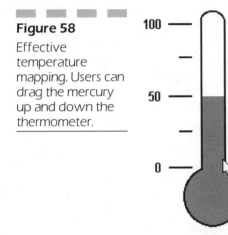

100 —

50 —

0 —

CONSTRAINT   By constraining users with lists, you can prevent "set" errors—in other words, you can restrict users to a set of entries known to be valid. For example, you can let users select one item from a small set of items by using a combo box, or select more than one item by using a multiple-select list box. You can also let users enter anything but validate the entry later against a database lookup table or a code table (Zetie 1995, 210–212). For more information about small sets, see Combo Box.

Some applications use keystroke restriction—in other words, the application validates each character as it is entered. This method has the advantage of immediate feedback. However, if the user can't see the list that the application is using *and* she makes a spelling mistake, which will prevent her from continuing, she can't tell what the error is and can't get out of the field. To avoid this problem, either make sure the user can see the relevant part of the list (as per the Microsoft Windows help indexes) or use keystroke restriction's more friendly cousin, auto fill. (See "Auto Fill.")

RECOVERY STRATEGIES   Users learn best by exploring; they will be inclined to explore if they know that the application will let them explore without causing unintended damage or that it will let them correct mistakes easily. One of the consequences of being able to explore is error—either user error (typing errors, format errors, and so on) or exception error (any action that is invalid in the current system state).

Most field edits are designed to prevent or catch user errors. However, exception errors are unpredictable because they are interactions of mode, context, and whatever has been done so far in the session. Some, in fact, are not really errors, just unfortunate combinations of circumstances—for example, the sales clerk cannot ring up an item because the barcode has no match in the inventory database. Most exceptions, therefore, cannot be prevented. The alternative is allowing a graceful recovery.

Zetie offers three principles that can help the developer design error-recovery strategies (1995, 222–228):

- *Principle of forgiveness.*   Make it easy to reverse unwanted actions. For example, offer multiple levels of undo and redo. In transaction processing, do not force users to commit database changes until absolutely necessary (perhaps by using temporary, local tables for partial saves and pre-commit saves).

- *Principle of confirmation.*   Make it hard to do irreversible damage. The simplest type of confirmation is the chicken switch: "Are you sure that you want to blow up the Moon? Yes, No, Cancel." However, confirmation at the point of closure, although necessary, doesn't cover the many possible levels of destruction. In a multi-user transactional-processing environment, for example, a mistake can have significant business costs. If a warehouse supervisor records a stock delivery, other agents may immediately begin accepting orders against that stock. If the warehouse supervisor made a mistake, the company may find itself with orders it cannot fill. The developer has to strike a balance between making it difficult for the user to make a mistake and obstructing correct actions unnecessarily. The key is the importance of the mistake (Zetie 1995, 227): How much will a mistake cost in rework or in actual cash? And how likely is it to happen?

- *Principle of failsafe.*   Make the default or easiest action harmless. Partly this means don't make Exit or Delete the default action. (Within reason: If the user is in a Delete state of mind, forcing her to reselect the Delete key and do a confirmation for each file or record is intrusive. Give her a method for turning off confirmation temporarily.) But failsafe also requires that work be saved temporarily somewhere—in automatically created backup files, in a change-control system, in wastebaskets that let you undelete files. Make sure that your users can change their minds.

AUTO FILL   Auto fill, a type of input transformation, is a good alternative to the popular but problematic auto skip. (See the "Auto Skip" section.) With auto fill, the program fills in the rest of the field as soon as the user has typed enough characters to match a previous entry for that field uniquely. For example, Quicken will fill in "U.S. Post Office" as soon as the user types "U." The advantage of this approach is that it doesn't slow down an inexperienced user (Snyder 1997).

To find candidates for auto fill, do some brainstorming. Test each field for possible "set" behavior. For example, does this field have a small defined set of entries (states or provinces)? Does the user have a standard set of entries that he can enter either all at once or as he goes along, like the vendors' list in Quicken?

If the users' current software has auto-fill fields, at least make sure that you have the same ones in the new software. But also look for additional possibilities—for example, say that the current software fills in the city and state automatically from the ZIP code. Extend this functionality by generating a delivery-point bar code for the address.

When you use auto fill, just make sure that it doesn't too tightly restrict users. For example, commercially available ZIP-code databases occasionally have missing or wrong ZIP codes. The data-entry clerk has to be able to override wrong addresses. Work with expert users to identify typical exceptions and problems.

From an object-oriented point of view, "an autocompletion text entry field should appear as a subclass of the generic text entry field." Finding good candidates in advance and "designing a class hierarchy [for them] will help insure behavior that is consistent and useful." (Collins 1995, 278).

RECALCULATION AND "FALSE" VALUES   Number-crunching applications (stock and bond analyses, accounting applications, spreadsheets) often have a "recalculation" problem, stated as follows: "As soon as the user changes one of *these* numbers (some crucial benchmark, fee, etc.), all the rest of the numbers are invalid. How do we prevent him or her from taking these bad numbers seriously?"

This problem is complicated by timing. In some applications, the entire set of fields is recalculated automatically as soon as the user moves to the next field. With automatic recalculation, most of the difficulty goes away. (The problem remains if the user's attention is lost momentarily or if the recalculation takes a while—she might forget that the numbers are invalid.)

In other applications, however, the cost of recalculating automatically is too high. For example, the calculation might require information from the server or has to be done on the server, which means network access and delays. Or perhaps users need to change more than one number and it doesn't make sense to recalculate until they've finished the entire set of entries.

The question is, how do you indicate to the user that a number is invalid or untrue pending a recalculation? The answer is, offer good feedback. Following are some of the possibilities. Make sure that you test your choices on users—an indicator that may seem obvious to you may be invisible to users.

- Make the other dependent fields unavailable until the recalculation is finished. This may be appropriate when fields are mutually dependent—in other words, a change in one field *must* change the other fields. For example, in a bond-analysis program, changing the price changes the yield and the spread; changing the spread changes the price and the yield; and so on. You can't change two of the three values at the same time.

- Indicate which mutually dependent field is "true" by changing its background color, font, or the border of the field. If the user enters a value in another dependent field, then that field becomes true instead and its appearance changes.

- Make the user type the new value or values into a separate command line (spreadsheet-style) or dialog box. This has the advantage of indicating that something out of the ordinary is happening.

- Change the false values to italic or a different color until the values are recalculated. This works for both automatic systems and systems in which the user must press a Recalculate button. Once the values have been recalculated, change the color or font back to normal.

- If the recalculation itself can take a long time, disable printing and data exporting (to prevent dissemination of bad values) during the calculation but let the user do other work in the meantime. Also provide him or her with a way to cancel the recalculation—a progress-indicator box with a Cancel Calculation button, for example.

When recalculations are instantaneous rather than slow, you have a different kind of problem. Daniel P. B. Smith describes it as follows: "What do you do as consecutive digits are typed into the field? That is, suppose the old value was 105 and you are typing in the new value, 100. As you type successive digits, the value in the window is, successively, 105, then 1, then 10, then 100. The calculation itself is virtually instantaneous, so it is completely feasible to recalculate the successive results for 1, then 10, then 100. Thus it is easy to have the display 'always tell the truth.' But the resulting appearance looks and feels weird, and I decided that was wrong. I decided the right thing to do was to delay recalcuation until the entry was 'complete,' continuing to display the values for 105 and then changing to the values for 100. This then compelled me to deal with the issues of knowing when the entry *is* complete (wait for the focus to change), and modifying the appearance to signify that 'stale' values are being displayed."

He added, "I continue to be astonished that such a familiar problem seems to have no well-accepted standard convention for its handling" (Smith 1997).

CODES FOR PAPER AND ONLINE FORMS If you need to use codes, keep in mind the following difficulties (Galitz 1989, 117–119).

On hand-written forms, these letters are often illegible: Y N V Z Q U G.

On forms and online, these pairs are often confused:

- I and 1
- and 0
- B and 8
- Z and 2

These codes are hard to type: YX, JS (vs. TH, IN).

INTERNATIONALIZATION OF DATA Different cultures have different calendars, different ways of presenting dates and times, different ways of indicating currency, different weights and measures, and different requirements for control characters.

The next few sections contain information about various data formats. However, these tables are designed to show the range of variations rather than every possible format. You might want to consult an experienced translator during the design phase for any exceptions or recent changes to the target-language standards. Note: The "See Also" section contains a list of internationalization resources.

CALENDARS   Some of the calendar systems used in different countries or industries are listed on Table 3.

TABLE 3

International
Calendar Systems

Civil or Business	
Arabic astronomical lunar calendar	A lunar calendar beginning on the first day of the month preceding Mohammed's journey from Mecca to Medina (July 16, 622 Gregorian); it measures the Era of the Hegira.
Arabic civil lunar calendar	A lunar calendar that retains the traditional method of calculating exact lunations for the user's location (Apple Computer 1992, 226).
Buddhist calendar	Countries using Buddhist calendars specify their year as the Buddhist era, which varies from country to country, as does the recognized birthdate of the Buddha (National Language Technical Center 1992, 4-1).
Hebrew calendar	A solar and lunar calendar that measures time from the traditional date of creation, which can be extrapolated to October 6, 3761 B.C. on the Gregorian calendar. A year can be 353 to 355 days long or 383 to 385 days long (Apple Computer 1992, 227).
Japanese imperial calendar	The same as the Gregorian calendar except that its year number is based on the year of accession of the current emperor. Since each emperor gives a name to his reign, the dates also include the name of the reign (Apple Computer 1992, 228).
Gregorian calendar	A solar calendar that measures time since the date accepted as the birth date of Jesus Christ. Used as the civil calendar in English-speaking and Western European countries and as a business calendar worldwide.
Professional	
Julian day	Astronomical day count. January 1, 1987, is Julian day 2,446,795.5, for example (National Language Technical Center 1991, 3-2).
Day number reference	YYDDD format. January 1, 2000, is 00001 (National Language Technical Center 1991, 3-2).

TABLE 4

International Date
Formats

Country	Format	Sample
Bulgaria	yyyy-*mm*-dd (months use roman numerals)	1998-XII-05
Canada, English	dd/mm/yy	05/12/98
Canada, French	yy-mm-dd	98-12-05
France	dd/mm/yyyy or dd.mm.yyyy	05/12/1998 or 05.12.1998
Germany	dd.mm.yyyy	5.12.1998
Japan, civil	yyyy.mm.dd	1998.12.05
Japan, imperial	*era* yy *year* mm *month* dd *day*	must be written in Kanji characters
U.S.	mm/dd/yy	12/05/98

Many of these calendars, or algorithms that can be used to switch from one to another, are supplied with localized versions of operating-system software.

DATE FORMATS The short-date formats are methods for writing the day, month, and year in numbers and symbols. (In long-date formats, the date is spelled out—December 5, 1998, for example.)

Date formats vary between different calendar systems as well as between countries and regions. Table 4 lists some short-date samples using December 5, 1998 as the date.

Note that some multinational organizations use long-date formats exclusively to prevent misunderstandings.

TIME Ways of presenting time of day also vary, although not as often as dates. Table 5 gives some examples (National Language Technical Center 1992, 4-8–4-9).

MONEY Currency has these characteristics::

- The symbol used to indicate the currency—for example, £ for British pound, ¥ for Japanese yen.
- Where the symbol appears in the number.
- The formats of the monetary fields themselves.

TABLE 5

International Time
Formats

Country	Format	Sample
Canada, English	hh:mm:ss	22:49:11
Canada, French	hh *h* mm *min* ss *s*	22 h 49 min 11 s
Sweden	*kl* hh.mm.ss	kl 22.49.11
U.S.	hh:mm:ss *a.m.* or *p.m.*	10:49 p.m. or 10:49:11

- How negative numbers are shown (see "Mathematical formats").
- Field sizes.

Table 6 lists some examples of monetary formats (National Language Technical Center 1991, 3–6).

Note that ISO 4217, Codes for the Representation of Currency and Funds, is a list of unambiguous, uppercase, three-letter codes for all national currencies. Although many countries call their currency "dollars," the ISO codes differentiate among them well: For example, the code for the U.S. dollar is USD, the code for the Canadian dollar is CAD, and code for the New Zealand dollar is NZD. For lists of international currencies (in a currency commodities application, for example), using these codes may be easier and less ambiguous than trying to use the national symbols.

Although localized operating-systems accommodate different currencies, you must remember to leave enough space in your fields. Some currencies use numbers that are up to four digits larger than what you'd need to express the same amount in U.S. dollars. For example, the equivalent of $10,000 is approximately 16,850,000 Italian lira.

TABLE 6

International
Currency Formats

Example	Country and Currency Name
$12,345.67	U.S. dollar
DM12.345,67	German mark
12 345,67 F	French franc
N$ 123,45-	Uruguayan nuevo peso, negative
123$45	Portuguese escudo

If the country uses brackets to indicate negative numbers, you must add another two characters, plus up to four more characters for the currency symbol, and two characters for delimiters (National Language Technical Center 1991, 3–6).

The international financial markets have their own peculiar formats for prices. Prices are often quoted in eights, sixteenths, and thirty-seconds, which may be displayed as fractions ($98^1/_8$), decimal numbers, or with hyphens and pluses to indicate various combinations of eighths, sixteenths, and thirty-seconds (98–15+).

MATHEMATICAL FORMATS   Although mathematics is an international language, it does have dialects. Here are some areas of difference:

Negative numbers   You may find a leading hyphen –10, a trailing hyphen 10–, parentheses (10), or square brackets [10] being used to indicate negative numbers. Remember to align numbers correctly:

123 456 789
[234 567 890] ← out of alignment

Names for large numbers   In the U.S., this amount—1,000,000,000—is a billion. In the U.K. (and Europe generally), this same amount is called a "thousand million" or a "milliard." A British billion is the same as the U.S. trillion—1,000,000,000,000. This difference is beginning to be erased in financial applications. (The international community is settling on the U.S. format.) However, if there is any possibility of error, make sure that you know what terminology your users are using.

Separators for decimals and thousands   Table 7 lists some common variations in decimal and thousands separators (National Language Technical Center 1991, 3–6; National Language Technical Center 1991, 5-3–5-4; Apple Computer 1992, 200; Microsoft 1993, 217–228).

Rounding conventions   Rounding conventions vary not only from one country to another but from one industry to another, and sometimes within industries according to convention.

In Switzerland, for example, legislation governs the rounding of monetary values. Instead of rounding up by 0.01, Swiss francs round up or down by 0.05. For example, according to the National Language Technical Center (1992, 5-2),

12.325 rounds down to 12.30

12.326 rounds up to 12.35

12.376 rounds up to 12.40

Another example: In the U.S. bond market, prices of primary-market Treasuries ("primary" means sold by the Federal government to brokers) are rounded to three decimal places, but secondary-market Treasury prices (from brokers to portfolio managers and other buyers) are rounded to six decimal places. Corporate, government agency, and municipal securities are truncated at three decimal places.

WEIGHTS AND MEASURES   Most countries use metric systems rather than the imperial system used in the U.S. and the U.K. Therefore, enabling weights and measures usually means accommodating metric weights, measures, and unit names or symbols. It may, however, include transforming numbers from one system to another in countries like the U.S. and Canada that use both metric and imperial measurement systems.

Also, some industries have their own systems. For example, U.S. land surveyors and engineers use an imperial foot divided into 10 rather than 12 segments. Paper manufacturers measure their paper by caliper

TABLE 7

International Mathematical Formats

Convention	Decimal	4 Digits Plus Decimal	More than 4 Digits	Used in
Comma, period	.123	1,234.56	12,345,678.90	U.S., English-speaking Canada
Apostrophe, period	.123	1'234.56	12'345'678.90	Switzerland
Space, period	.123	1 234.56	12 345 678.90	Greece
Space, comma	0,123	1234,56	12 345 678,90	French-speaking Canada, France, South Africa
Period, comma	0,123	1.234,56	12.345.678,90	Poland, Iceland, Brazil

thickness and weight. Font manufacturers use points, picas, and agates. Jewelers use carats. Some of these systems are local; others, to facilitate trade, are international.

Usability Tests

When you use auto fill, make sure that it doesn't restrict users. Users have to be able to override wrong information or add missing information. Work with expert users to identify typical exceptions and problems.

If the application will be internationalized (users can pick their own calendars, currencies, and so on, but most of the interface will be in English) or localized (all of the interface will be translated), do extensive testing with target users in the other locations.

See Also

Command Line; Field, Protected; Field, Required.

INTERNATIONALIZATION RESOURCES   For an overview on the internationalization of GUIs, see Fowler and Stanwick, *The GUI Style Guide* (1995). For help with internationalization programming, see Nadine Kano, *Developing International Software for Windows 95 and Windows NT* (1995), Ken Lunde, *Understanding Japanese Information Processing* (1993), the National Language Technical Center (IBM) *National Language Support Reference Manual,* Vol. 2 (1992), Bill Tuthill, *Solaris international developer's guide* (1993), Apple Computer *Guide to Macintosh Software Localization* (1992).

As well as programming structures and hints, these books also contain information on sorting orders, cultural differences, differences in calendars, money, weights and measures, and so on, from one country to another. If you're serious about internationalization, it is worth your while to get them all, whether they match your development platform or not.

Field, Protected

An area that displays data but that doesn't accept a cursor. Use protected fields to show system values, already saved values, or calculated values without allowing changes.

Good For

- Displaying read-only results of calculations or earlier entries (Figure 59).

Figure 59

Permanently protected field.

Protected Field

- Indicating and managing business and data-integrity rules (Figure 60).

Figure 60

Grayed-out, temporarily protected field in Windows 95.

Protected Field

Design Guidelines

Note that data-entry, required, and protected fields overlap. Required fields are a type of data-entry field, and protected fields can change from protected to entry, depending on which business or data-integrity rules are in effect.

There are two types of protected fields—text-entry fields that are changed dynamically between protected and unprotected modes to fulfill business rules; and read-only fields. Read-only fields can be changed dynamically as well to reflect changes in states. For example, you can use a read-only field to display the current directory path or the current date and time (Microsoft 1995, 162).

You can create read-only fields using a text label (if you can change labels dynamically) or a field set to not accept user input (false for user input).

VISUAL DESIGN FOR PROTECTED FIELDS To indicate a read-only field:

- Don't put an entry-area box around the text in a read-only field (Figure 59).
- Set the background color to the window's background (the client area).

To indicate that an entry field has switched to protected, either:

- Change the text to gray (Figure 60) and continue to show the entry-area box (the bounding box).
- Change the entry area to the background color (but maintain the bounding box). In Windows 95, the system itself changes the background color of the field to indicate the change (Microsoft 1995, 158).

FUNCTIONAL GUIDELINES Don't confuse the user:

- Don't let users select protected information if they can't copy or change it. (However, if they can copy protected information *and* you want them to be able to copy it, making it selectable is fine.)
- Make sure that read-only data really has to be read-only. For example, if a Windows 95 icon label is editable on the desktop, it should also be editable in the Properties box.

VIEW-ONLY VS. DATA-ENTRY WINDOWS Confusions   sometimes occur because designers have used the data-entry window as the view window—the layout and the fields are the same, but suddenly the user can't change any of the information.

Rather than trying to fix this problem in the documentation or training, try making separate versions of the window. Input and view are often such different modes that they require different layouts. For example, data-entry windows must match the entry form or script, while view windows should organize the data according to the user's interest in the information. See Window for information about the three types of windows.

On the other hand, you may want to rethink the divisions between inquire and update—a rigid differentiation may not actually be necessary in windowing systems.

BUSINESS RULES   Field protection is often used to enforce business rules such as "Only managers can approve a draw against a new account." Make sure that you capture the business-rule information in the requirements phase.

Usability Tests

Make sure that the customer really needs to protect the data. This information should have been captured in the requirements phase, but it's always good to check again.

Also, when you do usability testing, listen for questions that indicate that the users are lost: "Why can't I change this?"

See Also

Field, Entry; Field, Required.

Field, Required

An entry area that requires users to enter valid data.

Good For

- For databases, making sure that records contain complete or necessary information (Figure 61).
- For analyses, making sure that the entries are complete and probably valid.

Figure 61

One way of indicating a required field.

Design Guidelines

Note that data-entry, required, and protected fields overlap. Required fields are a type of data-entry field, and protected fields can change from protected to entry, depending on which business or data-integrity rules are in effect.

HOW TO INDICATE A REQUIRED FIELD   Feedback for required fields has three aspects:

Look—how are required fields distinguished from normal fields?

Timing—when are required fields distinguished from normal fields?

Behavior—what happens when required fields are not filled in?

The type of feedback you use depends on the user profile. If the users are mostly inexperienced (either because they use the application only occasionally or there is high turnover), then you want feedback to be obvious and immediate (within reason). If the users are experienced, then your feedback can be more subtle and unobtrusive. Use Table 8, Table 9, and Table 10 to pick the appropriate type of feedback for your user profile. The tables are organized from most to least obtrusive. (For more background, see Zetie, 1995, chapter 6, "Errors and Help.")

TABLE 8

Look of a Required Field

Type of Visual Distinction	Effect on Inexperienced Users	Effect on Experienced Users
Change background color of field.	Strong cue.[1]	Probably distracting.
Add "Required," an abbreviation (R or Req'd), or a symbol (⊠, ✱, ➜, for example) to the label.	Medium-level cue; easy to learn.	Not distracting, although the symbols may add clutter.
Change the color of the field text.	Invisible until the user starts to type.	Less distracting.
Change the color of the label.	Less obvious than changing the background of the field.	Less distracting.
Change the label font size or style (bold for required, medium for normal).	Changing type sizes or styles may be too subtle.	Too many fonts looks messy.
Change pointer when over required field.	No cue is visible when pointer isn't over field.	Less distracting.
Don't distinguish at all—instead, identify the required mode in status-line hints or tooltips.	Not much help for novices.	Use if *any* option is too distracting for experienced users.
Don't distinguish—however, put all required fields at the top of the window.	If the fields are at the top, the user is naturally inclined to fill them in.	Not distracting. However, putting all required fields in one place may break up logical groupings or a natural order.

1. One development team came up with a mnemonic for required fields: "A project I've been working on uses a blue background in the field itself to emphasize required fields. When the field was filled in, the color changed to white so that only empty required fields were emphasized .... I have to admit that I wasn't a big fan of color-coding required fields at first. However, one team member introduced the jingle, 'Do the blue' and the system users LOVE it. We also use an error message if a user clicks the OK button before he or she has 'done the blue'" (Motte, 1995).

Once you've decided on a visual cue, follow up with a behavioral cue. See Table 9.

When you notify users—before they enter the field, when they are in the field, or when they leave the field—is as important as *how* you notify them. Make sure that you match the feedback levels for look, timing, and behavior. See Table 10.

TABLE 9

Behavior of a
Required Field

Behavior Type	Advantages	Disadvantages
Forbid field exit until user enters value.	Instant feedback.	Very constraining—user may never get out of the field if she doesn't know what caused the error.
Forbid field exit but show explanation.	Explicit explanation is good.	Very modal and irritating to experienced users.
Disable the OK, Save, or Apply button until all required fields are filled.	Good for simple cases (for example, when a Logon button is disabled until user enters a password).	Bad when user can't deduce which *combinations* of fields are required.
Show alert when user selects enabled OK, Save, or Apply button: User gets an error message saying that highlighted fields must be filled in, and the required fields change color (or otherwise show themselves).	Strong feedback plus offers an explicit explanation for novices without distracting experienced users.	Not as obvious as enabling the button when all of the required fields are filled.

TABLE 10

Timing of
Notification

Timing Method	Effect on Inexperienced Users	Effect on Experienced Users	Notes
Always distinguish required fields.	Helpful.	Distracting.	Creates a stable display.
Distinguish on demand.	Must be documented; otherwise, users will never know about it.	Offers control.	Give the user a keyboard shortcut, preference-style setting, or a View menu option that turns the distinction on and off. Preference should be saved between sessions.
Distinguish only when validation fails.	Little feedback.	Unobtrusive.	Required fields are marked only when the user tries to leave the field or the dialog box.

DEFAULTS AND REQUIRED FIELDS If you are going to make a field mandatory, then add a default entry. Make sure that this default is automatically selected as soon as the user enters the field, so that it can be easily replaced if necessary.

Whenever possible, consider replacing required fields with combo boxes or drop-down list boxes.

HELP FOR REQUIRED FIELDS Add tooltips to your required fields; if you can't add tooltips, at least add a status-bar hint that says something like "Required" or "You must enter data in this field."

Provide field-level help to the required fields. See Online Help, Context-Sensitive, for details.

If you use error messages for required fields, add a help button or Details button to the message box. Put "Required" as the first word in the tooltip and online help panel. Offer business-rule help as well as formatting help (if necessary). Also have the cursor return to the required field when the error message appears. Do not delete the erroneous text, if possible. Instead, let the user modify it.

Usability Tests

Do not over-constrain. When testing prototypes, watch for and ask about signs of frustration.

Make sure that users can get all the information needed to fill in the required fields (perhaps on other windows) or, if they cannot, that they can save an unfinished window. Although much of the constraint information (logical or because of business rules) should be in your task analysis, subtleties may appear in the test phases.

See Also

Combo Box; Drop-Down List Box; Field, Data-Entry; Field, Protected.

Graph

A graphical method for displaying numeric and quantitative information.

Good For

■ Quickly showing relationships among data points (Figure 62).

Figure 62

A line graph.

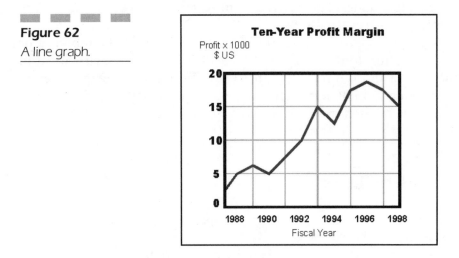

Not Good For

■ Showing details like the data points themselves.

Design Guidelines

Following are the most common types of graphs. Make sure that you select the right graph type for the data and that your format is correct. For example, many applications mistakenly use an area-chart format for line charts or a histogram format for bar charts. (For more information, see Fowler and Stanwick, 1995, chapter 7, "Charts and Graphs.")

Graph   81

CHANGES OVER TIME

Bar

Other names. Column

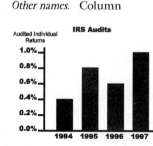

Good for *comparing or ranking a small number of values* (no more than 10 or 12).

Also useful when the data sets are so similar that they would overlap if shown as lines. By using a bar chart, you can visually separate the data sets.

The spacing between bars or sets of bars should be 1/2 the size of the bars.

Variations:

Clustered bar, zero-line

Line

Other names. Time series

Good for *comparing one set of values to another.* Also good for *displaying trends.*

Line graphs show interpolated points and slopes well.

Variations:

In finance, high/low/close (in commodities field, also called "bar"); candle charts

STATISTICS

Frequency polygon

Other names. Bell curve, mistakenly—bell curves are smoothed normal distributions.

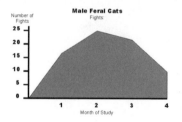

Good for *showing counts*—how many times something happened or how many times a number appeared. Shows frequency distributions (the count for each interval during which data were collected) as smoothed curves.

Variations:

See *Histogram.*

Histogram

Other names. Step

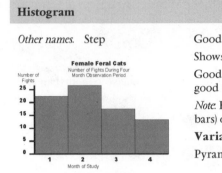

Good for *comparing counts.*

Shows frequency distributions as steps or bars.

Good when values fall into discrete sets and not good when they don't.

Note. Histogram bars always touch. Bars (or sets of bars) on bar charts do not touch.

Variation:

Pyramid histogram

Scatterplot

Other names. Scattergram, XY scatter

Good for *spotting clusters or out-of-range points.* Each data point is the intersection of two variables plotted against the two axes.

Variation:

Bubble chart

PROPORTION

Area

Other names. Surface, component part, belt, mountain

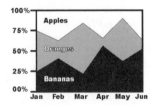

Good for showing *cumulative totals over time.* Each data set is added to the data set below it, so that the top edge of the top set is the sum of the data at any point on the timeline.

Totals can be numbers or percentages.

Graph   83

Pie

Other names. Circle, cake, sector

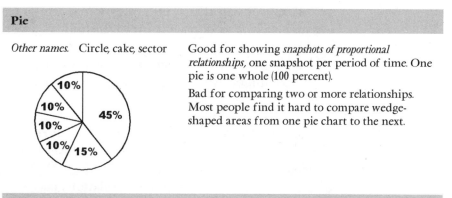

Good for showing *snapshots of proportional relationships,* one snapshot per period of time. One pie is one whole (100 percent).

Bad for comparing two or more relationships. Most people find it hard to compare wedge-shaped areas from one pie chart to the next.

Segmented bar

Other names. Stacked bar chart, sliding multi-component bar chart, population pyramid, butterfly chart, subdivided bar chart

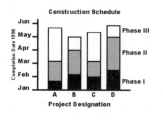

Good for *showing proportional relationships* (like pie charts) *over time* (like bar charts).

Use to compare parts of a whole—for example, how interest and principal equal total savings.

Do not include parts and the whole in the same bar. For example, don't stack interest, principal, and total savings on the same bar. The bar will be twice the height it should be.

Variation:

Paired horizontal bar chart (deviation bar chart)

COLOR ON GRAPHS Eight percent of men—one in twelve—have red-green color blindness. In other words, if you have 24 men in your office, two will have trouble separating red from green, either when the colors are next to one another or when the lights are dim. (Note that most individuals with color blindness see all colors of the spectrum, but simply can't tell the difference between two of them. For this reason, "color confusion" has replaced "color blindness" as the term of choice.)

What does this mean to your GUI? It means that using red and green lines as the default colors in your graphs, for example, is a bad idea. Every twelfth male user won't have a clue as to what the graph says. Using red and green borders to indicate which window has focus, as Motif does, is also a bad idea. Another bad idea is using red lettering on a black, brown, or green background, since all of these colors may blend into one another for users with color confusions.

However, say that you never use red and green in your graphs because, well, you don't like green. Instead, you use blue and orange, or red and blue.

It doesn't matter which colors you pick. Everyone without a color printer might as well be color-blind when he or she prints out that graph.

THE SOLUTION There are a variety of solutions to this problem. However, the bottom line is this: Use color as a secondary, not a primary, signal.

Use color to quickly show correlations between things (for example, all required fields have a blue border) or to indicate changes. For example, you could have a temperature gauge on which a virtual mercury bar changes color as the temperature gets higher. The height of the mercury would be the primary cue. The change in color would be the secondary cue.

Following this rule, then, you could revise a line graph as shown in Figure 63: One solid line, one broken line. (Remember that black and white are colors too—on a white background, a black line has more contrast than any color and vice versa.)

Figure 63

The right way to do a line chart.

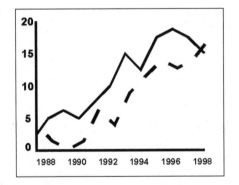

You can fix clusters of bars on bar charts by using various hatching and fill patterns. However, the results can become very busy (see Figure 64, "Poor").

For a two-bar chart, the best solution is one solid black bar (or white bar, depending on the background color), and one empty bar. For charts with more than two clustered bars, use shades of gray (Figure 64, "Good"). You can either use shades of gray or you can use colors with appropriate grayscale values. Every color has a grayscale value (its "dark-

Graph

85

ness," so to speak) as well as a hue (the "redness" of red). If you use colors separated by 20 percent differences in grayscale, everyone will be able to tell the bars apart.

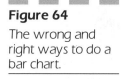

Figure 64

The wrong and right ways to do a bar chart.

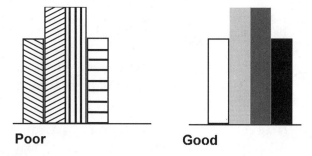

Poor   **Good**

The best way to check for grayscale is to create a grayscale chart, and then put your colors on the chart and compare them to the grays in low light or by squinting. If you've matched your color to the grayscale chart accurately, the color seems to fade into the gray. For a very low-tech approach, simply pick a few likely colors, fill in your bars, and squint. If the colors stay separate, then you've picked the right colors.

HOW TO CREATE A GRAY-SCALE CHART

1. Pick a program with a color or palette editor. Open the editor and either find or create a set of nine grays and one black separated by 10 percent differences in darkness. Use white for the background. The values for each gray are:

Gray	RGB Values	HSV Values
10%	26, 26, 26	0, 0%, 10%
20%	51, 51, 51,	0, 0%, 20%
30%	79, 79, 79	0, 0%, 30%
40%	102, 102, 102	0, 0%, 40%
50%	128, 128, 128	0, 0%, 50%
60%	153, 153, 153	0, 0%, 60%
70%	181, 181, 181	0, 0%, 70%

Gray	RGB Values	HSV Values
80%	204, 204, 204	0, 0%, 80%
90%	232, 232, 232	0, 0%, 90%
100% (black)	255, 255, 255	0, 0%, 100%

2. Draw a set of gray boxes on a white background, one color of gray per box, ranging from 10 percent to 100 percent (black).

3. Draw diamonds of all the colors you want to test.

4. Drag each color sample over the chart, squinting as you drag it. When the color and a gray box seem to match, you've found its gray-scale value.

5. Save the colors that are either 20 or 30 percent apart (separated by two or three boxes) and discard the rest.

Some colors, because of their brightness, maintain high contrast no matter where you put them on the grayscale. However, check the size. Small areas of yellow disappear against white. Red, if used for small dots or thin lines, shrinks away to nothing against a dark background. At the other end of the spectrum, avoid thin blue lines and text. Because of the structure of the eye and blue's wavelength, it is hard to focus on small blue objects.

SHOW UNDERLYING DATA POINTS   Make sure that users can access the underlying data. Here are a few methods:

- Let users switch between tabular and graph views with a pushbutton or tabbed dialog boxes.

- Let users toggle data points on and off with a check box (Figure 65).

Figure 65

Toggle data points with a check box.

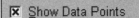

☒ Show Data Points

- If the user clicks on a data point or bar, show the underlying value (Figure 66).

Graph   87

Figure 66

Show the value
when the user
clicks the data point.

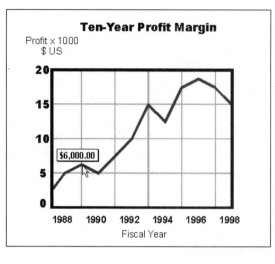

RECOMMENDATIONS FOR TITLES   For marketing or sales-oriented graph applications, find a way to let users put a message or point of
view in the title—let them emphasize the point of the data. For example, "Company Sales Trend" doesn't say as much as "Company Sales Up
in Northwest" or "Sales Down in Southeast." Provide a default title that
users can overwrite if they want.

RECOMMENDATIONS FOR LABELS   *State the units of measurement.*   Include the units in the X and Y axis labels. For example, if the
dependent variables are percentages, include "Percent" or "%" in the Y-
axis label.

Don't stack letters vertically.   When the left margin is too narrow for
the Y-axis label, the label should appear above the margin. If you cannot put the label there, don't stack the letters like this:

L
a
b
e
l

Most people read by recognizing the entire shape of the word, not
individual letters. When you stack the label, you force the reader to
puzzle out the word from the letters. You can, however, turn the label
sideways without causing as much of a readability problem.

Make labels clear.   Spell out all words. If space is very tight, abbreviate using only standard abbreviations or symbols. Check an abbreviation dictionary.

Try to avoid keys (legends) whenever possible.   Instead, put explanations on the bars, lines, or data points themselves. For example, rather than creating a key to explain what a set of bars means, label the bars directly by adding numbers to the data points or to the tops of bars.

If you do use a key, try to put it inside the graph panel, in a spot where there are no data. If you put it outside the panel, the eye is drawn away from the data. Do not box the key because then the box draws attention to itself.

Usability Tests

Obviousness.   Are the goals of the graph apparent? For example, if the graph is supposed to highlight out-of-range data points, can users spot them immediately? Is the title too generic—can the users recognize the use or contents of the graph from the title?

Affordances.   Do the users recognize the graph type and, if so, does it help them understand the data more easily?

Heuristics.   Do experts agree that you've formatted the data correctly? Check with people with expertise in statistics and mathematics.

Many industries and business domains have specialized types of graphs. As well as developing lists of subject-matter expert reviewers, it might help to collect standard reference works, even textbooks, in the domain for which you're developing graphs. Expect expert users such as stockbrokers and doctors to be visually literate and to prefer windows full of complex graphs and charts.

In addition, different cultures have different levels of visual literacy. Unlike mass-audience U.S. readers, for example, Japanese readers expect and can understand highly complex pictures, charts, and graphs (Kohl et al. 1993, 63–73). If you expect to internationalize your applications, check all graphical and data-analysis requirements with your international experts and marketing departments.

Mechanical.   Users often prefer to see preformatted graphs as their first experience with a graph program. Later, if they need to, they can fine-tune the display. Have you made it easy for the user to get an interesting graph the first time he or she uses the application (perhaps with a wizard, if the display or data are complex)?

See Also

Tables.

For examples of successful and failed charts, graphs, and tables from a variety of domains, see Edward Tufte's *Envisioning Information* (1990) and *Visual Display of Quantitative Information* (1983).

To avoid stepping into one of graphing's many pitfalls, see Darrell Huff's *How to Lie with Statistics* (1954), a slender book now (for good reason) in its fortieth edition.

Gene Zelazny's *Say It With Charts: The Executive's Guide to Successful Presentations in the 1990s,* is designed for people doing business presentations. The book explains what all of the major chart types are, how to use the various types correctly, and how to make them easy to read. Zelazny then goes a step further, and shows you how to create sophisticated and elegant charts from the basics.

Icon, Desktop

A picture used to indicate an application or an object (printer, wastebasket).

Good For

- Starting an application (Figure 67).

Figure 67
Application icon.

- Using an interface object, such as printing a document by dragging it to a printer icon (Figure 68).

Figure 68
Object icon.

Design Guidelines

The desktop icon not only identifies your application but it has a marketing and corporate identification function as well. A successful icon:

- Looks different from all other unrelated icons on the desktop.
- Resembles your corporate logo (or at least uses the same colors, shapes, and typefaces).
- Gives the users some idea of what it does or represents. For example, a word processing program's icon might include a pen, an accounting program might show a ledger, and so on.
- Is recognizable when it is no larger than 16 pixels square.
- Looks as good in black and white as it does in color.

Because desktop icons are a very important part of your company's corporate identity, make sure that the same professional artists and designers who designed your logo also design your icon (or oversee its design). This is not a job for amateurs.

Usability Tests

A desktop icon must be discriminable from all other desktop icons and should, if possible, indicate the type of software it represents (network tools, word processor, etc.). Use a paper-and-pencil matching test.

See Also

Iconic Label.

Iconic Label

A pictorial description of a tool or function that generally appears on toolbars and palettes.

Good For

- Identifying tools that require a mouse or pen to be effective. Drawing tools—paintbrushes, erasers, and so on—are typical examples (Figure 69).

Figure 69

Tool label.

- Identifying mouse shortcuts—for example, Save, Cut, Copy, Paste. Use standard images for these types of options (Figure 70).

Figure 70

Mouse shortcut for Save.

Not Good For

- Abstract functions for which it is difficult to find visual metaphors (for example, Sort). Use text labels instead.
- Functions that do not require or benefit from mouse use.

Design Guidelines

Most development packages contain sets of iconic labels that you can use for free. Take advantage of the most popular ones: Save, Cut, Copy, Paste, New, Open. However, other icons may not be very recognizable or standard. If you use these less well-known icons, make sure that they have tooltips and that you test them for comprehensibility. (See "Usability Tests" below.)

OFFICIAL SIZES The Windows 95 style guide suggests that you let users toggle the sizes of the toolbar buttons. These are the suggested sizes:

- 24 x 22 pixels and 32 x 30 pixels for the buttons themselves.
- 16 x 16 and 24 x 24 pixels for the picture labels.

The guide also contains a list of all Microsoft's common toolbar images and the official names of their functions (Microsoft 1995, 176–178). Other platforms have similar suggested icon sizes and uses; most development kits come with a basic set of iconic toolbar buttons. Reuse whatever you can.

WHAT REALLY WORKS Mullet and Sano (1995, 201–202) report that the toolbar icons described as most useful typically correspond to either concrete attributes of visible objects (font attributes, paragraph alignments, etc.) or to concrete system objects (printers and folders).

They add that it is difficult to develop visual representations that distinguish between similar functions (Save and Save As) or between controls that should probably look similar but have different behaviors (print a document, fax a document).

As visual designers, they argue for putting abstract commands and activities on menus, where you can use words to describe them, and putting only concrete settings and tools on toolbars and palettes.

This is the ideal solution. However, most development companies don't live in the ideal world but rather in the trade-off world. Although an idealist might find this solution messy, human-factors research indicates that buttons with both pictures and text labels are the best solution. See "Usability Tests" below.

HOW TO DESIGN AN ICONIC LABEL The first rule of icon design: Start designing on paper, not on the computer. Sketching on paper is faster. It's also easier to throw away the bad ideas when they're only on napkins and scrap paper.

Following are some hints for finding and developing the right images.

SHOW THE OBJECT (WHEN YOU CAN) Showing the object is probably the most direct way of communicating an idea. For example, to represent the idea of printing a file, make an icon of a printer. Or to represent deleting a file, show a garbage can or wastebasket.

If necessary, turn verbs into nouns. It is much easier to represent an object (a noun) than it is to represent an action (a verb) through pictures. For instance, rather than trying to represent the *action* of printing a document, it is much easier to show the *printer*.

USE A VISUAL ANALOGY   If you can't show the object itself, try to use a visual analogy.

Metaphor   Have an image stand in for an idea. For instance, say that you need an icon for a maintenance program. To condense a complex idea into a simple image, use a picture of a maintenance tool—a wrench, for example (Figure 71).

Figure 71
Possible
maintenance icon.

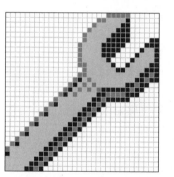

Litotes   A litotes (pronounced LIE-ta-tees) is a way of describing something by stating the negative of its opposite. For example, when you say "not bad" for "good," you're using a verbal litotes. A picture of a broken chain could be a visual litotes representing "freedom." Any image inside a circle with a slash through it is a litotes (Figure 72).

Figure 72
A litotes.

Synedoche   A synedoche (pronounced si-NEK-da-kee) is a metaphor in which a part represents the whole. For example, a chili pepper could represent a Mexican restaurant (Figure 73), the Golden Gate bridge could represent San Francisco, or the Eiffel Tower could represent Paris.

Figure 73
A synedoche.

Hyperbole   Hyperbole uses exaggeration to convey an idea. For example, you could use a bomb to represent danger, a bulging garbage can to represent a thrown-away file, or a remarkably steep incline to represent a hill (Figure 74).

Figure 74
A hyperbolic image.

MAKE SURE THAT A THREAD RUNS THROUGH THE BUTTONS When you're designing the pictures for toolbar buttons, simplify the process by finding a theme for the buttons (Figure 75):

Give the buttons an intellectual theme—for example, for a recipe program, "sort" could be represented by a sieve; for a banking program, it could be represented by a coin dispenser.

For models of good thematic design, look at the symbol sets developed for the Olympic Games and the symbols developed by Xerox Corporation for copier and office equipment.

Give the buttons a visual theme—for example, use only geometric shapes or only rounded shapes, or use a common color palette. Macintosh buttons use similar colors by default, since only 34 colors of the entire 256 color palette are available in ResEdit. Microsoft Windows 3.x provides only 16 colors.

Figure 75

A thread runs through a successful toolbar's buttons.

REUSE EXISTING SYMBOLS Many industries have their own iconographies—electricians have symbols for transistors and electrical lines, telecommunications workers have symbols for central offices and the public network (a cloud), network engineers have symbols for nodes, WANs, LANs, and so on. In the U.S., the American National Standards Institute publishes and/or redistributes national and international standards, including symbol sets. The symbol sets include everything from agricultural equipment and aircraft systems to electrical and mechanical systems to warning signs.

Use old-fashioned images. Traditional, simpler, images sometimes work better than new ones. For example, a skeleton key—not a modern button lock—is often used to represent locked or safeguarded information on Web sites. In the U.S., the most common image used for electronic mail is the rural mailbox, which is widely recognizable even though it is seldom seen in the cities where most users live (Horton 1994, 46–47).

IF ALL ELSE FAILS, FIND IDIOMATIC IMAGES Alan Cooper in *About Face* (1995) suggests that humans can learn and remember idioms ("beat around the bush" or "cool") very easily without relying on comparisons to known situations. Many idioms have no metaphoric meaning at all, he points out; the stories behind others were lost ages ago.

Although idioms must be learned, Cooper says, good ones only need to be learned once. It is quite easy to learn idioms like "politically correct" or "the lights are on but nobody's home" after a single hearing. It is also easy to learn how a scrollbar or a resize button works, he says, and as neither exists in the real world, they are clearly not metaphoric. They are idiomatic.

How do you create an idiom, then? Branding—marketing—advertising, he suggests. "Synthesizing idioms is the essence of product branding, whereby a company takes a product or company name and imbues it with a desired meaning. Tylenol is, by itself, a meaningless word, an idiom, but the McNeil company has spent millions to make you associate that word with safe, simple, trustworthy pain relief" (Cooper 1995, 59–60).

In terms of a user interface, then, an idiom is any image or action that is striking enough to learn quickly and that has a reasonable affordance. (A scrollbar that closed documents, for example, wouldn't make sense and would therefore be hard to learn.)

AT THE END, SIMPLIFY THE DESIGN Once you have an icon or set of icons that everyone likes, simplify it (Figure 76). See how many elements (colors, lines, shapes) you can remove without "breaking" the icon.

Figure 76

A good design, and a too fancy design.

Usability Tests

The issues in testing iconic labels are:

- Whether users understand the meanings of the pictures immediately (ease of learning).
- Whether they remember the meanings readily, once learned (memorability).
- Whether users can discriminate between similar pictograms or similar ideas.
- How long it takes them to become proficient and whether they graduate to doing complex or sophisticated tasks (Horton 1994, 302).

Ease of learning is especially important when you're writing for casual or inexperienced users. Test using a paper and pencil matching test.

Memorability is most important when you're writing for experienced users. If your user group will use the product daily, you can use "nonsense" pictures (a yellow triangle, a green square, etc.), provided that the icons are visually distinct from one another.

Some pictures may be hard to recognize no matter what you do to improve them. The solution is not to beat your collective heads against the wall, trying to find the best image. Rather, add tooltips. Many researchers have repeatedly found that images combined with text works better than images alone or words alone.

See Also

Icon, Desktop; Palette; Toolbar; Tooltip.

Keyboard Shortcuts: Mnemonic, Accelerator

A mnemonic is a programmer-defined keyboard shortcut consisting of the Alt key and one character. A mnemonic must be visible before the user can invoke it. Mnemonics are indicated with underlines in the labels of the menu options, pushbuttons, and other GUI components for which they are defined.

An accelerator is a function key (F1, F2, etc.), a [Ctrl] key or ⌘ key sequence, or a keyboard key marked with a function name (for example, Help or Delete). Accelerator keys are always available—unlike mnemonics, they don't have to be visible to be used.

Good For

- Users with disabilities that make mouse use difficult.
- Accessing commands and operations quickly, by bypassing the graphical (mouse-oriented) user interface (Figure 77).

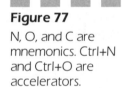

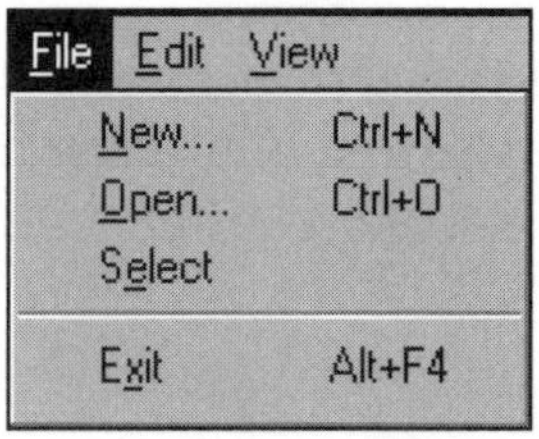

Figure 77

N, O, and C are mnemonics. Ctrl+N and Ctrl+O are accelerators.

- When a mouse is unavailable—for example, on trading floors and in manufacturing clean rooms—or too irritating to use—for example, on laptop computers.

Not Good For

- Novice computer users. (Graphical interfaces, by making important options and activities visible, are better for users who have never used a computer before.) Mnemonics and accelerators are, relatively speaking, hidden functionality.

Design Guidelines

Define mnemonics and accelerators for users who work faster without the mouse: power users, users of earlier command-line systems, touch-typists, and laptop users who don't want to use the built-in trackball or touch-pad.

DEFINING MNEMONICS   Keyboard shortcuts take advantage of "body" or kinesthetic memory, which comes into play when you learn to type, ride a bicycle, or drive a car. This kinesthetic memory is the reason that touch-typists dislike interfaces in which too much functionality is tied to the mouse—you can't memorize the mouse's location the way you can memorize keyboard positions. Keys are always in the same place. The mouse pointer rarely is.

Figure 78

Mnemonics on pushbuttons.

Platform guidelines require mnemonics (or the equivalent) for all menu options. Some mnemonics are already defined in the platform specifications. Most guidelines also suggest adding mnemonics to push-buttons.

The rules for defining mnemonics are as follows (IBM 1992, 344–349; Microsoft 1995a, 33–34; OSF 1993, 5-3–5-4):

- Mnemonics are combinations of Alt and single characters.

- The program accepting the mnemonic must be case-insensitive.

- When focus is on the menu or menubar, the user just presses the mnemonic letter or number. If focus is anywhere else, he or she must press the special key (in Windows, for example, Alt) plus the mnemonic.

- The label must contain the character to be used as the mnemonic *unless* there are no characters in the label (pictures can be used as labels) or the labels will change (on lists of open windows, for example). In either of these situations, number the labels and use the numbers as the mnemonics.

■ As long as the label does contain characters, the mnemonic character must be underlined, except in language environments in which underlining is unavailable.

■ For all systems except OSF/Motif: When a mnemonic is not part of the label but instead is a number or other code, put the number or code flush left in front of the label (at the fourth space) and underline it. Do not include parentheses or periods. For Motif, put a letter mnemonic in parentheses *after* the label (OSF 1993, 5-3). Numbers go in front of the label.

■ Avoid using the same letter more than once on any individual pulldown menu. (The problem with using the same mnemonic twice is that the user has to stop to think about which one she wants.) If, nevertheless, you reuse a letter, the first keypress goes to the first item on the menu; when you press it again, it goes to the second.

■ You can use the same letter more than once on *different* pulldown menus or on a menu and a submenu. In other words, you can use F for *File* on one menu, and F for *Film Stars* on another. The items are differentiated from one another by the titles of the menus themselves—say, [Alt]-[F] for *File* menu plus [F] for *File* versus [Alt]-[T] for *Talent* plus [F] for *Film Stars.*

■ All duplicate menu items should use the same mnemonic. For example, if *Save* shows up on two menus, both *Saves* should use the same mnemonic.

Table 11 is a decision tree for selecting letters. In addition, there are two high-level rules:

1. Find the five to seven most important options in the entire menu system and assign their mnemonics first. (These five to seven options will also get accelerators.) The reason for this is the chunking rule: You can remember only five items at a time, plus or minus two. Since users are likely to memorize only five to seven mnemonics (or only five to seven at a time), it is best to make the most important options the most memorable.

2. If the option has a traditional mnemonic, use it.

TABLE 11

Picking
Mnemonics

Default: Use the first letter in the word or phrase.	
If	**Then**
That letter is already used.	Use the first consonant or the most interesting consonant.
If	**Then**
The first or most interesting consonant is already used.	Use the first letter of the second or third word in the phrase.
If	**Then**
There is only one word.	Use any letter.
If	**Then**
The label contains no letters or the letters will change.	Use numbers in front of the label. Start with 1 and end with 9.
If	**Then**
The label uses a non-Roman writing scheme (Kanji, for example) but a Roman keyboard.	Prefix the label with a Roman letter and use that letter as the mnemonic.

You might also let users redefine the mnemonics to suit themselves—for example, typists who memorized the old Wordstar keys (in international markets where Wordstar is still popular) might want to redefine your keys to match.

DEFINING ACCELERATORS Certain key combinations are reserved for system-wide accelerators—[Ctrl]-[C], for example, has come to mean "copy" in nearly every environment. Users automatically have access to the system accelerators unless your program prevents it. Defining new accelerators for important application functions is encouraged but not required.

The rules are:

■ Accelerators are function keys, Ctrl or ⌘ key combinations, or named keys on the keyboard. Note: The IBM guidelines say, "Use the Alt key only to provide access to mnemonics," then list a number of nonmnemonic uses for the [Alt] key (IBM 1992, 315). However, that stricture seems to be a "guideline" rather than a "requirement." Just something else to keep in mind.

- Don't use the accelerators that are already defined in the environment for application-specific operations. In other words, don't use [F1] or the [Help] key to open a tutorial.

- Define accelerators only for high-frequency functions. Find the five to seven most often-used options in the entire menu system and assign accelerators to them (if there isn't a system-defined accelerator already).

- On option labels, use a plus sign (+) between the key names to indicate that a user must press two or more keys at once—for example, use Ctrl+F4, not Ctrl-F4.

- Remember that function-key shortcuts are easier to localize than modifier-plus-letter shortcuts. Since no name or letter is associated with a key, no translation is required.

- Avoid using punctuation character keys in accelerators if you expect to internationalize your application. International keyboards have different punctuation characters. Also, if you select a letter primarily because of its mnemonic association (for example, Ctrl+B for bold), you may have to change it to fit a particular language. (Microsoft 1995a, 418).

For the standard accelerators on your platform, refer to the guidelines for your current environment.

Usability Tests

To decide which accelerators to define, find the five to seven options used most often. Test experienced users, not novices.

For the most accurate results, use a usage or keystroke-capture program. Do the analysis by playing back the sessions and counting the number of accesses.

Note that accelerators, although *shown* on menus, do not *work* on menus. For example, pressing Ctrl+P while the File menu is open doesn't let users access the Print dialog box. Users new to GUIs may have trouble with this idea—"It's right there on the menu! Why won't it work?"

See Also

Command Line; Menu, Pop-Up.

Label

A description, usually text but sometimes pictorial, of fields, buttons, and areas of windows or dialog boxes.

Good For

- Indicating expected content for fields (Figure 79).
- Indicating the purpose of a button or other control.

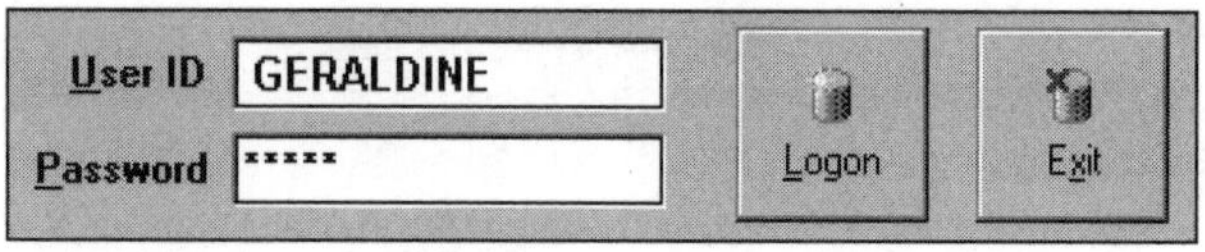

Figure 79

Typical field and button labels.

Not Good For

- Showing detailed instructions. Offer instructions using tooltips, status-bar messages, or context-sensitive online help.

Design Guidelines

Following are some general guidelines on window and dialog-box layout. Labels, although not as important as the fields and buttons themselves, are nevertheless the most visible items on most windows.

MAKE LABELS MATCH TASKS In "The Cognitive Walkthrough Method" (1994, 112), Nielsen and Mack suggest that users often follow a "label-following" strategy. They will select an action if the label matches the description they have in mind for the task. For instance, a user who wants to print a document might select an action with the label "Print" or "Document" (or an icon that shows a printer or document).

REDUCE COMPLEXITY Reduce complexity not necessarily by eliminating information but by organizing it. Following are some guidelines.

ORGANIZE THE INFORMATION Put the most often entered or referenced information at the top, and the least often used information at the bottom or in dialog boxes.

CREATE FUNCTIONAL GROUPS OF INFORMATION Create groups of information by putting, for example, names and addresses at the top, billing information in the middle, sales data at the bottom. Break up the groups by putting them in boxes or by separating them with blank lines or rules. If there are no functional breaks, then break the screen every five to seven rows (Galitz 1994, 78). See Figure 80 and Figure 81 for a demonstration.

Figure 80

Unaligned fields on a window makes the window look complicated.

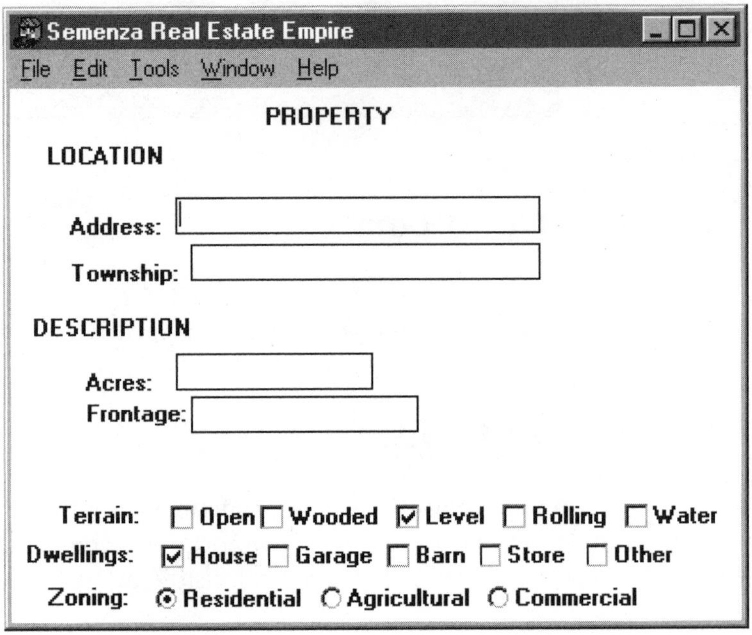

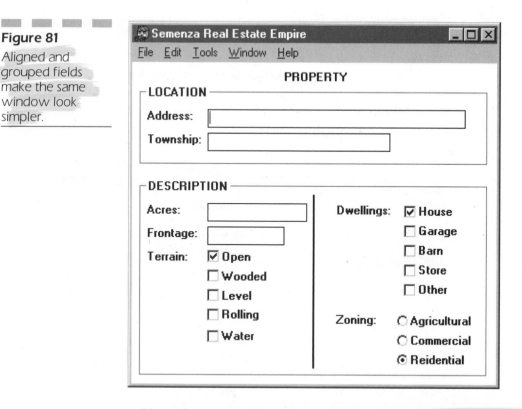

Figure 81

Aligned and grouped fields make the same window look simpler.

Note that you might want to group all required fields at the top of the window or dialog box, even though this might break up your functional groups. See Fields, Required, for more information.

ALIGN FIELD LABELS Figure 80 and Figure 81 contain exactly the same fields, but Figure 80 looks much more complicated. Minimizing the number of columns and rows—the number of alignment points, in other words—is one of the best ways to reduce window complexity. Figure 81, the revised version, is about 50 percent simpler.

PROVIDE ONLY NEED-TO-KNOW INFORMATION If the user is looking for price relative to yield, then show her price and yield at the top of the window. Information about the company issuing the stock, the number of shares outstanding, the broker recommending the stock, and so on, can go at the bottom of the window.

PUT NICE-TO-KNOW INFORMATION IN DIALOG BOXES When space is tight, separate need-to-know from nice-to-know information. For instance, a lab analyst needs to know whether a test result was positive or negative—therefore, this information goes on the main window at the top left. However, he might also like to know the statistical likelihood of a false positive using this batch of reagent, this level of humidity, and so on. This information can go in a separate dialog box.

POSITION BUTTONS CORRECTLY Put buttons related to the entire window at the bottom of the window. Put buttons related to sections of the windows inside those sections.

HOW DENSE IS TOO DENSE? Some early guidelines suggested keeping screen densities to under 25 percent—in other words, only 25 percent of the window should actually contain fields or displayed information (Galitz 1994, 83). Studies support these recommended densities. For example, NASA researchers found that densely packed screens (70 percent full) took an average of 5 seconds to scan, while sparsely filled screens (30 percent full) took only 3.4 seconds. By improving the labeling, clustering related information, using indentation and underlining, aligning numbers, and eliminating unnecessary characters, the researchers reduced task time by 31 percent and errors by 28 percent for inexperienced users. Experienced users did not improve their task times, but they did become more accurate. A study of telephone operators found that maintaining a 25 percent density and suppressing redundant family names reduced search times by 0.8 seconds per search (Schneiderman 1992, 318–319).

However, expert users (stockbrokers, air traffic controllers, and so on) prefer denser displays because more information per screen means fewer computer-related operations. Since these users are familiar with the data, they can find what they need even on a screen with 80 or 90 percent densities.

The key to the density mystery may be Jared Spool's breakdown of applications into "core" and "ring": A core application enhances the user's core competencies. For example, an engine analysis system enhances a car mechanic's core competencies. A ring application—for example, a parts locator program—helps with tasks outside the mechanic's core competencies. A core application can and should be as dense as necessary, since their users will be spending a lot of time with it and will want to have as much information available as possible. Since, on the other hand, users will use ring applications only occasionally, they will need all the help they can get—not just white space and careful grouping but built-in templates and wizards to get them over the learning hump quickly (Spool 1996a, 1–3).

See also Cooper's breakdown of applications into sovereign, transient, daemonic, and parasitic (1995, 151–170).

Conclusion? On core applications, concentrate on reducing overall complexity rather than density. On ring applications, reduce both density and complexity.

You can measure density by counting the total number of characters on the window and dividing by the total number of characters available on the window. This number was easier to calculate on character-based screens, which were always 80 characters across and 26 lines deep (minus a few lines for status bars and other screen apparatus). However, you can count the number of characters on the window by typing "1234567890123 . . ." across the top and down the side. For the total, multiply the horizontal and vertical counts (Galitz 1994, 72–73).

USE ABBREVIATIONS CAREFULLY If you have to create a visually tight window (a form-based data-entry window, for example), you may need to abbreviate.

Studies of abbreviation methods have found that truncating words is the best method for creating abbreviations. Unless a standard and well-known abbreviation exists—for example, DOB for date of birth, SSN for Social Security number—truncate words.

Avoid making up abbreviations, because people have different ideas about the "natural" abbreviation for any one word—"meeting" might be "mtg" or "meet," for example (Galitz 1989, 115).

Keep in mind, however, that you can end up with the same abbreviation for more than one word. Here are two more methods for shortening terms:

- Contract words to the first and last letters, delete vowels, and use phonic puns—for example, FX for "effects," XQT for "execute." (If you are going to internationalize your application, note that puns in one language rarely translate well to another. Sometimes puns don't translate between two versions of English—E-Z Add reads as "easy add" in American English but "ee-zed add" in British English.)

■ Use the abbreviations in commercial abbreviation dictionaries. This strategy may help users who move often between jobs in the same industry.

WHAT LABELS SHOULD LOOK LIKE   Field labels should be a word or phrase followed by a colon and a space:

Label: Data

Microsoft says to put a colon at the end of the text: "Not only does this help communicate that the text represents the label for a control, it is also used by screen review utilities" (Microsoft 1995, 162).

WHERE TO PUT LABELS   Put labels for columns above the column. For example:

Names: Birthdays:
Lucy   10/06/53
Sally   11/03/51
Mud   12/05/58

Put labels for individual fields in front of the fields. For example:

Price: 123.45   Yield: 6.78

Don't put labels *above* individual fields—as well as using two lines per field instead of one, the labels tend to become visually detached from their fields:

Price: Yield:
123.45   6.78
Spread: Benchmark:
10 bp   TSY10Y

JUSTIFICATION   Labels should be as close as possible to their fields, yet line up vertically in unobtrusive but organized columns. The best way to fulfill both requirements is to justify the labels and the fields separately.

In general:

■ Left-justify the labels.
■ Left-justify alphanumeric data.
■ Align decimal numbers on the decimal point.

- Right-justify whole numbers (since there is no decimal point).

- To figure out the spacing for labels, find the longest label and add one space between it and its field or other component. Left-align the rest of the fields with that first field.

HOW TO WRITE LABELS   Labels can't just look good—they should read good, too. Recommendations:

- Use symbols—$, #, %—only if all users will understand them. Remember that "all users" may include international users. Some symbols will not be on all keyboards.

- Try to use short, familiar words—"Cut" instead of "Reduce," for example. As well as being more readily understood, short words tend to be more punchy and authoritative. However, keep in mind that a long, familiar word is better than a short, unfamiliar one (Galitz 1989, 74–75).

- Try to use positive terms, which are generally easier to understand than negative terms. For example, use "Growing" instead of "Not Shrinking."

- When comparing objects, use the "more" rather than the "less" dimension if you have a choice—"longer" instead of "shorter," "bigger" instead of "smaller" (Galitz 1989, 74).

- Don't stack letters to label a column or a table:

  C
  o
  l
  u
  m
  n

  Since most readers read words whole, not one letter at a time, the stacked style is difficult to read. Instead, put the label above the column or table or turn the entire word sideways.

- For better readability, don't break words between lines.

- Show abbreviations, mnemonics, and acronyms without punctuation. Periods and other punctuation marks take up valuable window real estate without adding anything to readability.

HOW TO CAPITALIZE LABELS   The Windows 3.1 style guide calls for headline-style capitalization for labels of more than one word. The Windows 95 and OS/2 guidelines call for sentence-style capitalization for labels. Note that, for menus, pushbuttons, and tabs, Windows 95 requires headline-style capitalization (Microsoft 1995, 387–388).

Sentence style.   Capitalize only the first letter of each label. For example, *Save as.* Exception: Capitalize any proper noun that appears in the label. For example, *About BoschDraw.*

Headline style.   Capitalize every word in the label except articles (a, an, the); coordinating conjunctions (and, but, or, for, nor); and prepositions (at, by, in, to, from, with) unless they are the first or last words in the label (Chicago 1993, 282–283). For example, *Save As.*

Avoid using all capital letters in titles. All-uppercase text causes problems. First of all, uppercase letters take up more room than lowercase letters. A title that breaks into two lines when it is all uppercase will often fit on a single line when it is in upper- and lowercase.

Secondly, all uppercase is hard for non-programmers to read.[3] Reading studies indicate that:

- People get their cues from the tops of letters.
- Capital letters give them fewer cues than lowercase letters.

See which of these two samples you can read more easily:

LOW PRICED DEVICE BESTS IBM DISPLAYS

Publisher to drop copy protection

EXPANSION RATES BETWEEN ENGLISH AND OTHER LANGUAGES   If you intend to internationalize your software, expect labels and other text to require more room in the new language. For example, "Apply" in English is "Appliquer" in French. See Table 12.

Note that, the shorter the text, the more room you may need (National Language Technical Center 1991, 2–4).

To accommodate internationalization and localization, put all label text in resource files. See the "See also" section below for some good reference books.

---

3. Developers who've been writing in all uppercase for many years read uppercase as easily as most people read mixed case text.

	Number of characters in English	Extra space required for other
TABLE 12 Expansion Rates Between English and Other Languages	Field labels, menu options	
	up to 10 characters	100–200% (20 to 30 characters)
	11 to 20 characters	80–100% (31 to 40 characters)
	Messages, onscreen instructions	
	21 to 30 characters	60–80% (34 to 54 characters)
	31 to 50 characters	40–60% (43 to 80 characters)
	Online help, documentation	
	51 to 70 characters	30–40% (66 to 98 characters)
	over 70 characters	30%

Usability Tests

To test labels, ask the test participants to find an item and see whether they pick the right field. For unsuccessful choices, ask them what label they would use. Change the labels between tests until most users pick the right field.

You might also test the time required to find information. Develop a set of "reasonable" timings, then give participants a list of items to find. Time them with a stopwatch. Revise the order and groupings until most participants can find the items within your reasonable time-frames.

Note that experienced and inexperienced users will have very different times. If your application is a core application, use experienced participants. If a ring application, use occasional or novice participants.

See Also

Field, Entry; Field, Protected.

For an overview of the internationalization of GUIs, see Fowler and Stanwick, *The GUI Style Guide* (1995). For help with internationalization programming, see Nadine Kano, *Developing International Software for Windows 95 and Windows NT* (1995); Ken Lunde, *Understanding Japanese*

Information Processing (1993); the National Language Technical Center (IBM) *National Language Support Reference Manual*, vol. 2 (1992); Bill Tuthill, Solaris International Developer's Guide (1993); and Apple Computer's *Guide to Macintosh Software Localization* (1992).

As well as programming structures and hints, these books also contain information on sorting orders, cultural differences, differences in calendars, money, weights and measures, and so on, from one country to another. If you're serious about internationalization, it is worth your while to get them all, whether they match your development platform or not.

List Box, Multiple-Selection

A scrollable list from which users can select more than one item.

Good For

- Letting users select more than one item from a long and possibly dynamic list (Figure 82).

Figure 82

A multiple-selection list box. (From HotDog Pro, Version 2.097, from Sausage Software, Australia).

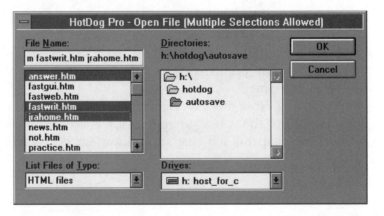

- As an alternative to check boxes, especially if the options will change often or be translated.

■ By using selection summary boxes (Figure 83), showing multiple selections.

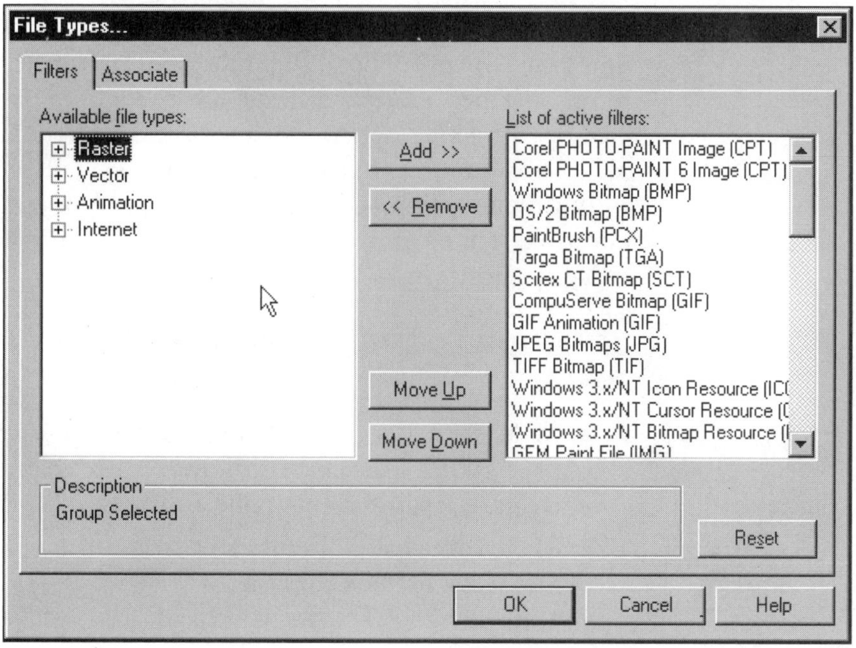

Figure 83

A selection
summary box.

Not Good For

■ Situations in which space is limited. You may need to rethink the function. See "Design Guidelines" below.

■ Situations in which users may need to enter new items. Use a combo box instead (but combo boxes are single-select components) or add data-entry functionality to the list box.

■ Situations that could be done better graphically. For example, if users need to select states or provinces, it might be better to let them select them from a map rather than a list.

Design Guidelines

The more items you can display at the same time, the faster users will be able to select the right item. This is the advantage of multiple-selection list. However, because multiple-selection lists take up so much room, it is best to restrict their use to large or system-wide functions (like opening files) where obviousness is a virtue; and to keep them in dialog boxes rather than on main windows. You wouldn't usually want a multiple-selection list as a data-entry component in most database applications, for example. Combo boxes are usually better choices in data-entry applications.

BEHAVIORAL GUIDELINES   Leavens suggests the following (1994, 286–288):

■ Make sure that users can make discontiguous selections, not just contiguous. In other words, make sure that they can select items that are separated from one another.

■ Make sure that all items can be viewed horizontally. Too often one sees a list box that isn't wide enough for the complete path and file name. Test the widths of your lists *in the field,* not just in your office.

■ Before you specify or start to develop a long list box, make sure you know the limits of your development package. If the built-in multiple-selection list accepts only 200 items, say, you can't use it (at least not without modification) for a list of ZIP or postal codes.

MAKE THE USER'S CHOICES OBVIOUS   After users select more than one item, how do they know what they've selected? If the entire list appears on the screen—if there is no scrolling, in other words—all the selections appear as well. No problem. But when the list is longer than the list container, then the user needs better feedback.

Two options are the selection summary box (see Figure 83) and checkbox/list box component (Figure 84). Not only do the check boxes indicate the selections, but they also show users that multiple selection is possible.

Figure 84

Check boxes in a
multiple-selection
list box.

Hint: On a scrolled list, because some selections will not be visible, add a label that says how many items were selected.

MAKE THE MULTIPLE-SELECTION OPTION OBVIOUS Developers often assume that users will know how to select more than one item (generally with the Shift and Control keys or with sweep-select). This is not necessarily a good assumption, especially with inexperienced users. If your user profile shows that users aren't familiar with windowing systems or the application *and* that training may be spotty or nonexistent, add an obvious selection indicator or a tooltip. Note the hint in the title bar in Figure 82. (It would, however, be better to have the hint just above or next to "File Name.") Also see Figure 84.

HOW TO ORGANIZE LISTS Once you have a list, how do you organize it so that users can find the items they want? According to Kent Norman (1991, 133–134), there are eight ways to organize information, as described in Table 13. These styles are not mutually exclusive—you can use all of them in a single application.

ALPHANUMERIC VS. CATEGORICAL ORDER The list of organization styles (with the exception of random) falls into two parts—alphabetic, numeric, and chronological orders versus frequency, sequence, and semantic orders. If we call the division "alphanumeric versus categorical," is there any advantage of one over the other?

It seems that when users are looking for an *exact word or label*, alphanumeric order is fastest. For example, if you ask a test participant to find "Shiitake mushrooms," she'll find it quickly on an alphabetized list of foods, like the one in Figure 85.

However, when users are looking for an *answer to a question* (or a command leading to a particular outcome), categorical order is fastest, followed by alphabetical order, then random order (Norman 1991, 135–137). If you ask a test participant to find "mushrooms, Japanese," he'll find "Shiitake mushrooms" faster on a categorical list (Figure 86).

TABLE 13

Organization Styles for Lists

Organization Type	Explanation	Examples
Random	Not recommended, although random order (or what appears to be random to an uninitiated observer) is sometimes unavoidable.	Icons on a desktop.
Alphabetic	Use when the items can be meaningfully alphabetized and scanned. Also use alphabetical order when no other type of organization springs to mind.	A list of typefaces: *Arial, Helvetica, Times Roman.*
Numeric	Use for items that are associated with numbers.	Baud rates, type sizes, numbers of copies, and so on.
Chronological	Use for items that are most effectively organized by date or time. You can sort by age or in standard cognitive order.	Age: E-mail messages from newest to oldest, articles in a news service from oldest to newest. Cognitive order: January through December.
Sequential processing	List items according to their likely order in a process or according to a cognitive ordering of items.	Process order: *Open Picture, Modify Picture, Save Picture, Close Picture.* Cognitive order, from large to small: *Galaxy, Cluster, Star, Planet, Moon.*
Semantic similarity	Order items in terms of some semantic dimension, such as impact, reversibility, potency, and so on. Items that are most similar are next to each other on the list.	Emphasise styles ordered by impact: *Normal, Underlined, Italic, Bold.*
Frequency of use	Okay for "last n used" or "last n saved" lists. Can be problematic for other	The four most recently used files on *File* menus.

Table 13 *(cont.)*

Organization
Styles for Lists

Organization Type	Explanation	Examples
Frequency of use	Okay for "last n used" or "last n saved" lists. Can be problematic for other situations since frequencies change when users become more expert, and in data-entry tasks, when demographics change. If frequency order is the only suitable order, then log usage to find actual frequencies. Or let users change the default themselves.	The four most recently used files on *File* menus.
Standard or custom	The platform guidelines suggest certain menu options in certain orders. Although all of these suggestions may not be suitable for your application, use them when you can. Standardization reduces the number of decisions during development and helps users cross program boundaries more easily.	*File, Edit, View,* and *Help* menus.

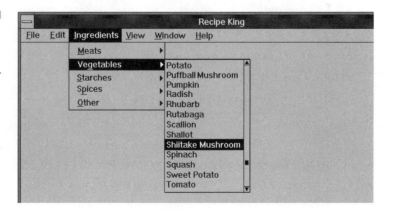

Figure 85

Searching an
alphabetized list.

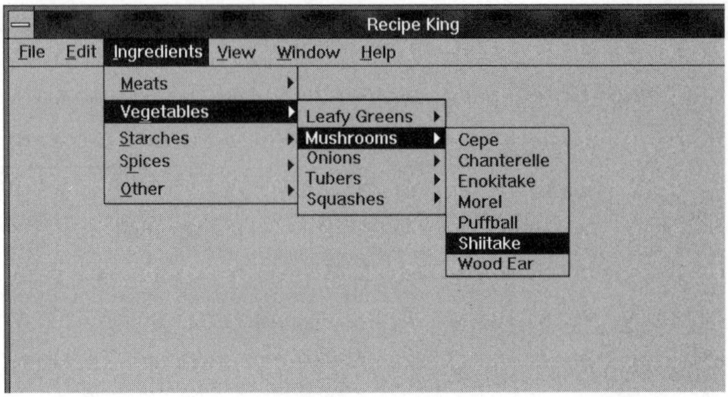

Figure 86

Searching a
categorized list.

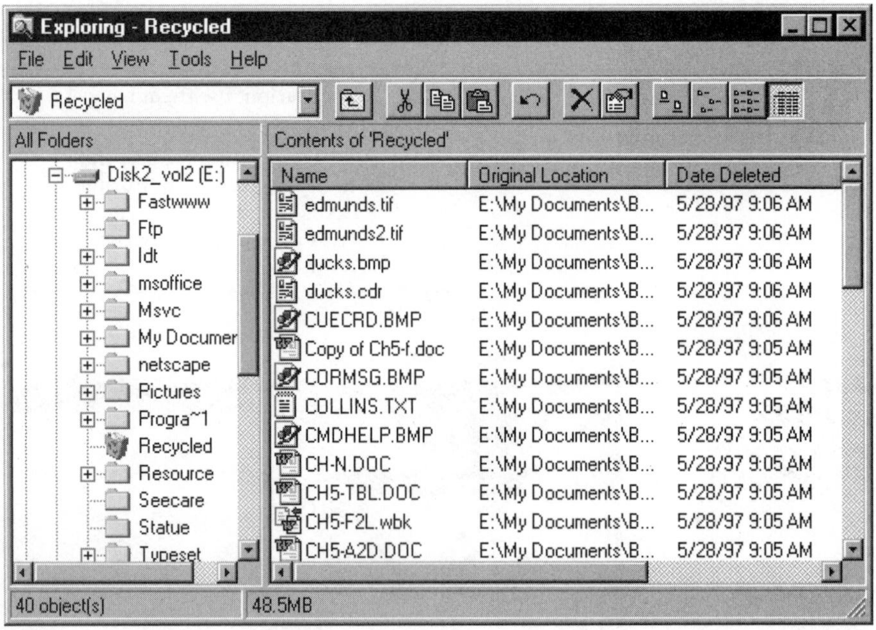

Figure 87

Clicking a column
heading ("Date
Deleted," for
example) toggles
the list between
ascending and
descending order.

However, users' needs change. Let them rearrange the list or columns so that whatever they now feel is the most important information is at the top. This is usually done by turning column headings into sort toggle buttons. See Figure 87 for example.

SEARCHING LISTS ELECTRONICALLY In addition to developing reasonable orders for the application's list, you might want to let users search them electronically. Try using:

■ Filters such as alphabetical buttons—if the user clicks R, the list jumps to the R items.

■ Search fields—the user types in a match or partial match and the application jumps to the closest match (Figure 88).

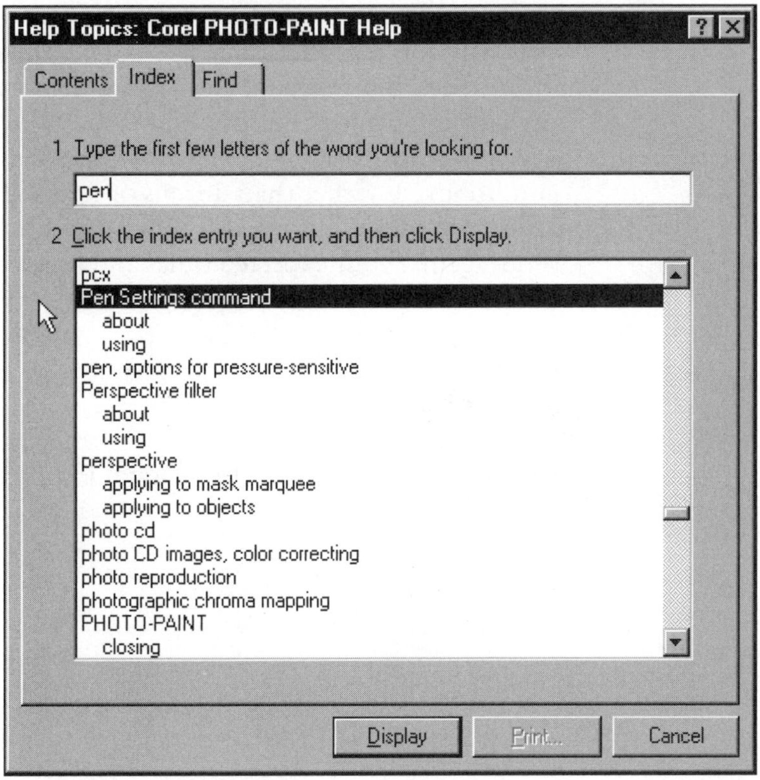

Figure 88

Search option for a multiple-selection list (in this case, a help index).

SORTING ORDER FOR MULTIPLE COLUMNS When you have a long list of items broken into two or more columns (type styles and sizes, for example), sort the list up and down, not side to side across the columns.

INTERNATIONAL SORTING SCHEMES Your alphabetical lists will stop being alphabetical as soon as you localize your software, not just because the words change but also because sort orders, especially for accented letters, vary dramatically between one language and the next. Also, ideographic languages such as Chinese don't have alphabetical orders (they don't have alphabets). If your software will be sold internationally, don't depend heavily on alphabetical order.

Usability Tests

Check affordances.   Make sure that the test participant knows he or she can select more than one item at a time.

Check sort orders.   Do the test participants seem to spend a lot of time scrolling up and down the lists? Make a set of expected timings before you start the test, then time the participants. If they don't meet your time expectations, you may need to add a dynamic "change sort" option, perhaps by turning the column headings into sort toggle buttons.

Find out whether you need a search option or filter.   Do your lists contain hundreds rather than dozens of items? Do the participants spend a lot of time scrolling up and down the lists? Again, check actual task times against your expected times and revise the interface until most of the participants hit the time expections.

See Also

Check Box; Combo Box; Drop-Down List Box; List Box, Single-Selection.

List Box, Single-Selection

A scrollable list from which users can select only one item.

Good For

- Making the user select one item from a list of six or more items (Figure 89).
- Can be used as an alternative to radio buttons.

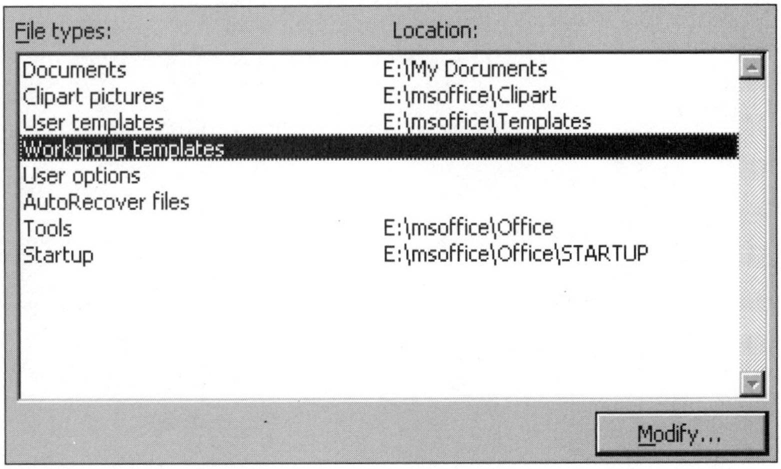

Figure 89

A single-selection list box.

File types:	Location:
Documents	E:\My Documents
Clipart pictures	E:\msoffice\Clipart
User templates	E:\msoffice\Templates
Workgroup templates	
User options	
AutoRecover files	
Tools	E:\msoffice\Office
Startup	E:\msoffice\Office\STARTUP

Modify...

Not Good For

- Situations in which the list is not yet complete or well-defined. Use a combo box instead, since combo boxes let users enter new items when necessary.
- Situations in which space is limited. Use a drop-down list box instead.

Design Guidelines

Since single-selection and multiple-selection list boxes look very much alike, provide some clue that users can select only one item from the list at a time. For example, put something like "Select one of [these items]" in the label.

Leavens suggests the following (1994, 286–288):

- Make sure that all items can be viewed horizontally. Too often one sees a list box that isn't wide enough for the complete path and file name. Test the widths of your lists *in the field*, not just in your office.

- Before you specify or start to develop a long list box, make sure you know the limits of your development package. If the built-in multiple-selection list accepts only 200 items, say, you can't use it (at least not without modification) for a list of ZIP or postal codes.

Usability Tests

Make sure that users never have to add items. Ask experienced users for advice before designing the list box and watch test participants carefully for signs that items are missing from the list.

See Also

List Box, Multiple-Selection; Radio Button.

Menubar

On main and secondary windows, the area containing the labels of the
drop-down menus.

Good For

Showing the high-level structure of the application (Figure 90).

Figure 90

Sample menubar.

File	Edit	View	Image	Effects	Mask	Object	Special	Window	Help

Design Guidelines

The rules for menubars are:

- Don't put pushbuttons on menubars. Menubar labels should go
  to menus, not activities or dialog boxes.

- Don't put pushbuttons in a row at the top of a window, especially
  on Web pages, which do not yet have clear conventions about
  what goes where. A row of buttons at the top of a frame may look
  like a menu and thoroughly confuse users.

- Menubar names (the titles of the drop-down menus, in other
  words) should be no more than one word. The reason is that the
  titles aren't visually separated enough. Until you actually select a
  menu title, you can't see the edges of the underlying widget.
  Therefore, a title of two words looks like two menus.

DO YOU NEED THE FILE MENU?   Note that the platform guidelines recommend—sometimes insist—on specific sets of top-level menus.
However, some applications don't need every menu. The rules are:

- Provide the platform's recommended menus, in the order shown,
  if your application provides any of the choices listed in the platform guidelines pull-down menus. However, most usability experts advise against one-item menus and suggest adding single
  items to the next most logical top-level menu.

■ If your application contains options that don't fit on any of the standard menus, add application-specific top-level menus to the left of the Help menu.

■ Help is the last (or on the Macintosh, next to last) item on every menubar.

The *File, Edit, Format,* and other menus are meaningless for applications without user files—for example, a game, a collection of financial calculators, a set of telecommunications analyses. In these cases, put the list of the most important options in the first position. For example, if the application is a set of calculators, then the first menu is *Calculators* and the drop-down options are the names of the calculators.

VARIATIONS AND EXCEPTIONS   Instead of one top-level menu-bar, OS/2 has two bars on each window—the top bar contains the system menu and window-sizing buttons, and the second contains a standard set of menus.

TASKBAR   Windows 95 has a moveable and reconfigurable taskbar that appears on the desktop. Since it is always visible, it lets users switch quickly from one open application to another. Another visibility advantage is that minimized applications become buttons on the taskbar rather than icons lost behind other windows.

Note that, because the taskbar is shared across applications, Microsoft asks that you carefully follow their guidelines and conventions when you set up your application to use it (Microsoft 1995a, 25).

WINDOW CONTROL MENUS   Windows 3.x applications have window control menus (indicated with a space-bar or hyphen icon). The window control menu in a Windows 95 application is indicated with an icon (Figure 91) that represents either the application or the type of data the application saves or uses (for example, a document icon for a word processor). If the user clicks on the icon, the window's shortcut menu appears (Microsoft 1995a, 96–98).

Figure 91

Windows 95 title-bar control-menu icon for Corel Photo-Paint.

Apple has its environment-control "Apple" menu as the left-most item on the menubar. The Apple icon brings up the list of all items that users put in their *Apple Menu Items* folder—usually cross-application tools like alarm clocks, network access, and games (Apple 1992, 98).

MENUBAR LAYOUT   Use three spaces between titles. Leave one space in front of the first title and at least one space behind the last title. Note: Your development environment probably does this for you automatically.

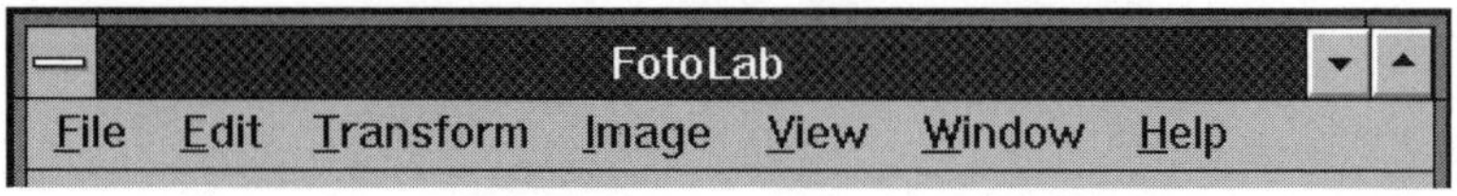

Figure 92

Spacing on menubars.

HIDE THE MENUBAR?   Drawing, desktop publishing, and other visually oriented applications should let the user remove the menubar temporarily so that she can use or see the entire screen.

Other applications (games and CD-ROMs) should not show the menubar unless the user asks for it.

The usual method for hiding the menubar is to put a "hide" option on the View menu, and when the user hides the menubar, having the application accept Escape to show the menubar again.

However, some users may stumble on this method of operation only by mistake—in other words, the menu disappears and the panicky user hits every key on the keyboard until one finally works. Leaving a cue on the window—a little button at the lower right corner, perhaps?—is much friendlier.

Usability Tests

Test that the menu labels match the user's conceptual model. Use a paper and pencil test.

HIDDEN MENUBAR FUNCTIONALITY   If the user can remove the menubar from the screen, can she get it back again? If the menubar does not appear by default, can the user figure out how to access it? See if the users can hide and recall the menubar:

- Without prompting.
- With prompting.
- Only after training.
- Only if mentioned in job aids, online help, or printed documentation.

Share the results with your training and documentation departments.

An invisible menubar should be *nice to have*, not *necessary to have*. Make sure that this is true.

See Also

Menu, Drop-Down.

Menu, Drop-Down

A list of application-related activities and settings that opens downward and, if there are submenus, usually to the right and down (cascades), when accessed with the mouse or from the keyboard.

Good For

- Accessing secondary tasks. (In a drawing application, drawing is the primary task; saving the drawing, although very important, is a secondary task.)
- Selecting settings that affect the entire application or window. See Figure 93.

Figure 93

New, Open, Close,
Save, and Save As
(and most of the
other items) are
secondary tasks.
Page Setup,
however, is a
settings option.

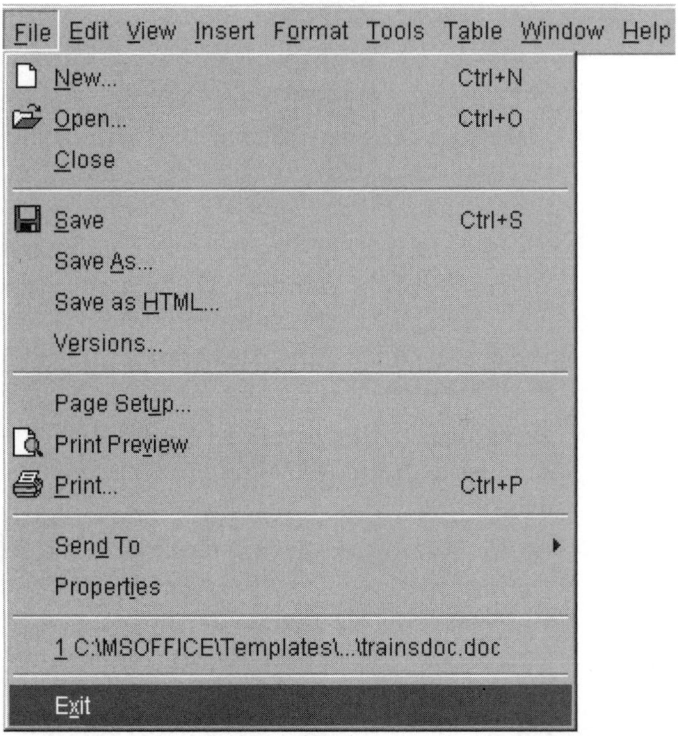

File	Edit	View	Insert	Format	Tools	Table	Window	Help

☐ New...	Ctrl+N
☞ Open...	Ctrl+O
Close	
💾 Save	Ctrl+S
Save As...	
Save as HTML...	
Versions...	
Page Setup...	
📄 Print Preview	
🖨 Print...	Ctrl+P
Send To	▶
Properties	
1 C:\MSOFFICE\Templates\...\trainsdoc.doc	
Exit	

Not Good For

- Tasks or settings that are more naturally handled using a mouse (picking a drawing tool, for example).

- Situations in which the user might want to pick more than one option at a time (for example, setting text both bold *and* italic). Drop-down menus close up as soon as the user either selects the desired option or moves off the menu, which means that the user has to keep reopening the menu for every option she wants to use.

- Situations in which the user might want to interact with other parts of the application while a menu is open. Since menus are modal, users can't do anything when a menu is open except select an option or cancel the menu. For alternatives, see "Tear-off menus" below.

Design Guidelines

To design drop-down menus correctly:

■ Make sure that the width of the menu is the width of the longest label on the menu, not the title of the menu on the menubar (titles are usually very short).

■ Leave three spaces in front of all menu labels. The first space separates the label from the left edge of the menu, the second contains checkmarks, checkbuttons, or radio buttons when needed, and the third separates the occasional checkmark or button from the label itself.

■ Remember to designate a keyboard shortcut for each option. See Keyboard Shortcuts: Mnemonic and Accelerator for more information.

■ Accelerator key names are flush-left on the first *tab* after the name of the longest option label. Don't use spaces to align accelerators—spacing is irregular in proportional typefaces (Microsoft 1992, 87). See Keyboard Shortcuts: Mnemonic and Accelerator for more information.

■ For accelerators, use the key name as it is printed on its key cap. For example, use "Ctrl," not ^. Keyboards, unfortunately, vary. For example, some keyboards say "Del," others say "Delete," and some say both. Keyboards attached to Unix workstations often have both [Return] and [Enter] keys, which sometimes do different things and sometimes don't. If this variability causes a problem, find the most standard or the newest computer in the office and standardize on that one.

■ The ellipsis indicator (for panels or dialog boxes) follows the label. Do not add spaces between the label and the ellipsis. Also, don't add spaces between the periods in the ellipsis (this is often done in typesetting).

■ The triangle indicator (for submenus) is always flush right. Leave one space between the triangle and the right edge of the menu.

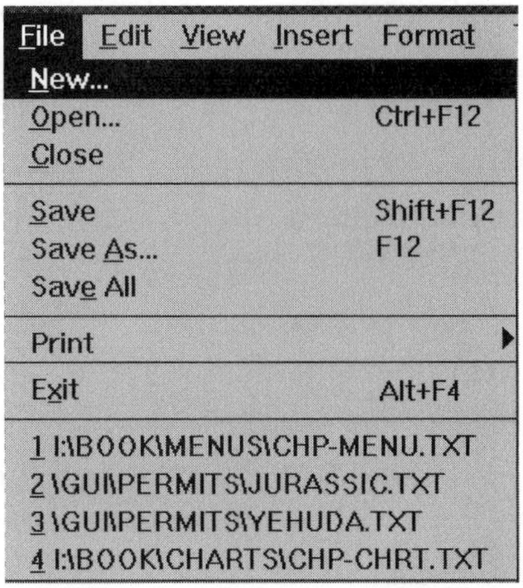

Figure 94

Correct drop-down
menu design.

```
 File   Edit   View   Insert   Format
 New...
 Open...                        Ctrl+F12
 Close
 Save                           Shift+F12
 Save As...                     F12
 Save All
 Print                                   ▶
 Exit                           Alt+F4
 1 I:\BOOK\MENUS\CHP-MENU.TXT
 2 \GUI\PERMITS\JURASSIC.TXT
 3 \GUI\PERMITS\YEHUDA.TXT
 4 I:\BOOK\CHARTS\CHP-CHRT.TXT
```

■ Don't show a submenu immediately—incorporate a brief pause. This pause keeps the submenu from flashing open and closed when a user runs the cursor over the submenu option (Microsoft 1992, 86).

■ Use reverse video to indicate that an option is selected.

■ If your system has dynamic menus, note that users learn the positions of items on menus very quickly, sometimes within one session. Although individual items may not always be accessible, their positions should remain constant—graying them out is better than deleting them and closing up the list. Maintain absolute positions, not just relative positions (Norman 1991, 140, 169–170).

■ When your system has a variety of security levels, do remove *unavailable* options from menus. In other words, if a user doesn't have access to particular options, don't show them on her copy of the menu. (For some people, a grayed-out "Top Secret Files" option is a challenge, not a restriction.)

Your development environment probably takes care of many of these design issues for you.

MENU OPTION TYPES   Drop-down menus contain options of various types (listed below), plus type indicators and keyboard shortcuts. The main types of options are:

Action.   A command; an option that does something without asking for additional user input. *Save* is a common action.

Dialog box or palette.   A collection of settings organized in a dialog box.

Settings or toggles.   Individual settings and toggles. Use when there are too few settings to make a dialog box worthwhile.

Submenu.   A second or third level on a drop-down menu. For example, a Fonts option on a Format menu might lead to a submenu of typefaces and sizes. Submenus are also referred to as "cascades" and "hierarchical menus."

Other, less common, types of menu items are:

Files.   A list of the last four to six files opened, usually accessed from the File menu if there is one.

Graphics.   Pictures of selectable patterns or drawing tools.

Windows.   A list of all open windows, usually numbered.

INDICATING OPTION TYPES   Each of these types of menu options—command, dialog box or panel, setting, and submenu—has its own symbol (provided that you consider null a symbol). See Table 14, Option Type Indicators.

LABELS FOR MENU OPTIONS   Once you've defined the menu bar, you can define the names of the options on the drop-downs. Here are the main issues:

- Following the specifications for your environment.
- Creating unambiguous names.
- Capitalizing well.

CREATING UNAMBIGUOUS LABELS   Using the option-type symbols (triangle, ellipsis, and so on as shown on Table 14) is necessary but not sufficient, since many users neither know the symbols nor care about them. However, you can reinforce the symbol with the right *type* of

TABLE 14

Option Type
Indicators

Option Type	Symbol	Sample
Actions (commands)	none	Save All
Dialog boxes (requests for more input)	. . . immediately after option name (use 3 dots, not ellipsis character)	Save As...
Settings (checkbuttons)	pushed-in button, checkmarks	√ Align Left
Submenus (cascades)	right-pointing triangle, flush right	Print ▶
Indicator for applications running in background (Macintosh only)	diamond (can also use alert box and sound)	◆ PrintMonitor
Indicator of mixed case or partial setting—for example, part of the text is italic, part is roman.	dash on Macintosh, grayed or blanked sample on Windows 3.x and Windows 95	Style — Plain Text ⌘T / — Bold ⌘B / Italic ⌘I / — Underline ⌘U / Outline

word (noun or verb) or phrase (see Table 15). Correct wording helps users know what to expect when they choose a new option.

Here are some helpful hints:

If the option opens a window, match the window's name

Whenever a menu option opens a window or dialog box, make sure that the menu label matches the window or dialog box label. For example, if the dialog box says "Radio Station," the menu label should say "Radio Station."

This is such a natural, completely obvious rule that it hardly requires mentioning. However, one sees mismatches all the time. The problem is

TABLE 15

Matching
Word Types to
Option Types

Word Type	Option Type
Actions	Use verbs (*Save, Copy*) or verb phrases (*Find File*). The commands should fit into a sentence like "Save my file" or "Copy the data" (Apple Computer 1992, 58).
Dialog Boxes	If the purpose of the option is an action, and a dialog box or panel exists only to set parameters for the action (for example, *Save As* or *Find*), follow the Actions rule—use a verb or verb phrase.
	If the purpose of the option is to bring up a panel, then name the option after the panel—for example, *Spelling* to bring up the spelling panel (NeXT Computer 1992, 108).
Submenus	If a submenu brings up a menu of actions, use the target of the actions as the label of the submenu. For example, a text-editing submenu might be called *Document* and the submenu options might be *Open, New,* and *Save.* The options can then be read as *Open Document, New Document, Save Document* (NeXT Computer 1992, 109).
Settings	Use an adjective or adjectival phrase—for example, *Bold, Italic, Underlined.* The action is implied. Setting labels should fit into a sentence like "Change this text to bold" (Apple Computer 1992, 58).

design drift compounded by proofreading failures. The menu and window labels probably did match in the beginning, but the names of the dialog boxes and windows changed over time, and no one proofread the interface to look for mismatches.

Don't repeat the menu title in the menu option   For example, on a *Report* menu, you don't need to say *Format Report, Generate Report, Print Report*, and so on. *Format, Generate,* and *Print* are enough.

Take advantage of the menus' titles   Try creating phrases or sentences by putting the title and options together as sentences. For example, on an *Insert* menu, you could have Insert *Picture*, Insert *Box*, Insert *Text*. Or you can use a verb and an adverb—the options on a *Sort* menu might be *Alphabetically, Numerically, In Reverse Order.* The resulting sentences would be *Sort Alphabetically, Sort Numerically,* and *Sort In Reverse Order* (NeXT 1993, 130–131).

Use parallel construction   Here are non-parallel labels: *Print, Execute a Program, Disk Eject.* Here are parallel labels: *Print a File, Execute a Program, Eject a Disk.* The non-parallel version isn't terribly wrong, but it gives a bad impression—it looks as if the developer just threw the menu together and didn't take the time to neaten it up (Norman 1991, 142).

Don't be too consistent   A large publishing firm had just suffered the delivery of an expensive accounting system from a large and famous auditing firm. On the main menu were "Name Maintenance," "Title Maintenance," "Account Maintenance," and so on. The woman who demonstrated the system said, exasperated, "These don't lead to maintenance! Most of the submenus let you add, inquire, *and* maintain. And some of them only let you search." The consistency in the text hid major (and legitimate) differences between modules. The neatness was confusing because the system itself wasn't.

If the label contains a phrase, put the key word first   The key word is usually a verb—in other words, the command itself. *Open File* is easier to grasp than *File Open; Show Ruler* is easier than *Turn Ruler On* (Norman 1991, 142).

Don't abbreviate or truncate menu labels   The reasons are:

- Some users won't recognize the abbreviation. Or they may recognize it, but assign the wrong meaning. For example, on Wall Street, the abbreviation "MTG" means "mortgage," not "meeting." "Tick" cannot be truncated and used to stand for "ticker" because "tick" is a word with its own meaning ("the smallest unit used in trading a stock or a bond").
- Some abbreviations don't translate, even from one form of English to another. For example, a menu option called "EZ Add" reads nicely as "Easy Add" in the U.S., but as "Ee-ZED Add" in the U.K.
- GUIs are expandable. You don't *have* to abbreviate.

Use the singular, not the plural   Default to the singular unless the word you need for the label is a plural—for example, "Graphics" or "Telecommunications."

Put menu labels in resource files   Use resource files for ease of translating and for ease of rewriting. It's far too much work to find and change each menu label imbedded in the interface code.

Repeat labels when uniqueness is not a virtue   The platform guidelines agree: Do not repeat options on more than one top-level menu. If you want to give users more than one way to access a particular function, create pop-up menus or toolbars.

In a system with only one menu bar and one set of menus, this is a reasonable rule. However, some applications have more than one menu bar (for the "Create" part of the application and the "Runtime" part, say). In cases like these, use the same labels for the same functions. For example, the printing option should be called "Print" and should use the same mnemonic no matter where it appears.

CAPITALIZING LABELS   You can use either of two methods, provided that you use the chosen method consistently. However, the headline style is more common. Only the IBM OS/2 guidelines show sentence-style labels.

Sentence style   Capitalize only the first letter of each label (unless a proper noun—a product name or person's name—appears in the label). For example, *Save as.*

Headline style   Capitalize every word in the label except articles (a, an, the); coordinating conjunctions (and, but, or, for, nor); and prepositions (at, by, in, to, from, with) unless they are the first or last words in the label (Chicago 1993, 282–283). For example, *Save As.*

Here are the rules for capitalizing hyphenated (compound) words in headline style:

- The first part of a compound word is always capitalized.
- The second (or third or fourth) part is capitalized unless it is an article, a preposition, or a coordinating conjunction—for example, *Run-in Text.* There is one exception: If the compound comes at the end of the label, its final section is always capitalized, no matter what part of speech it is: *Text Run-In.*
- If the compound word is actually a prefix plus word, the second (or subsequent) part is never capitalized: *Re-save, Re-map* (Chicago 1993, 283).

PROOFREADING FOR CROSS-MENU CONSISTENCY Make sure that menus are consistent. It is easy enough, during one of the interstices of the programming day (while the network is down or the designers are off arguing about something) to check the menus against one another. If you make a print-out of each one as you finish it, you won't need access to the computer. .

Also, the technical writers and editors may be willing to accept this task. Eliminating inconsistency on a dozen menus, say, can add a few hours to a writer's schedule. Documenting the inconsistencies, on the other hand, can add *days*. Ergo, justification for asking for a writer's help.

HOW TO GROUP OPTIONS   All of the platform guidelines suggest organizing categorical items into logical groups, and then separating the groups into sets of no more than four or five items each (Figure 95). Separate the groups with lines (each environment provides some sort of separator line).

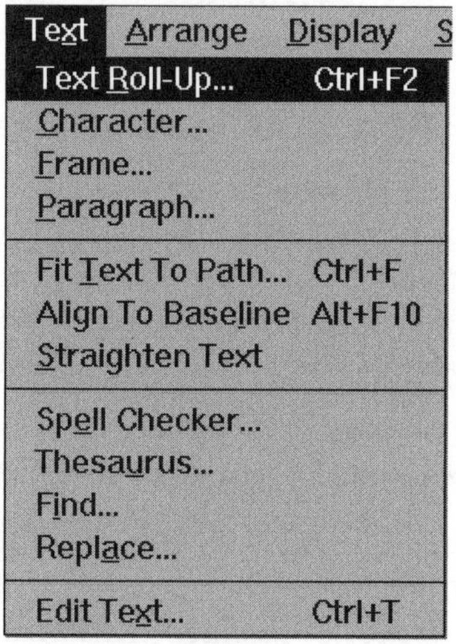

Figure 95

Breaking long lists into shorter lists.

Text	Arrange	Display	S
Text Roll-Up...		Ctrl+F2	
Character...			
Frame...			
Paragraph...			
Fit Text To Path...		Ctrl+F	
Align To Baseline		Alt+F10	
Straighten Text			
Spell Checker...			
Thesaurus...			
Find...			
Replace...			
Edit Text...		Ctrl+T	

Recommendations for lines:

■ Don't use a line as a first or last component on the menu.

■ Make sure that there are at least two options in each group (in other words, don't put lines above and below a single option).

■ Use lines to separate lists of checkbuttons or radio buttons from the rest of the menu options.

■ Don't separate groups with subtitles (by using dimmed items, for example)—people might mistake them for commands (Apple Computer 1992, 63).

DEFAULT OPTIONS   Pick the most commonly used option, unless it is dangerous (defined below), as the menu's default option. In most environments, the first option on a drop-down menu is a default option—if the user opens a menu and presses [Enter], she automatically selects the first option simply because the first option is automatically highlighted. In Windows 95, the default option is shown in bold text (Microsoft 1995a, 138).

DESTRUCTIVE OPTIONS   Options like *Quit, Exit, Close Connection,* and *Delete All,* even when easily reversible, should never be default choices. They should never be first on drop-down menus, either, because if no other default has been defined, the first option on a menu becomes the de facto default option.

DEPTH AND BREADTH

Menu search is a problem because target items are in a sense, hidden under successive layers of vague clues. Consequently, the user has to spend a lot of time peeking under the shells to find the pea. Large memory demands are placed on the user to remember where things are buried in the menu structure. Breadth, however, allows the system to lay the cards on the table, so to speak.

—Kent Norman in *The Psychology of Menu Selection,* 1991, p. 223.

In 1982, J. W. Tombaugh and S. A. McEwen found that when users were searching for information, they were very likely to choose menu items that didn't lead to the desired information and, on a high proportion of searches, tended to give up without locating it (Norman 1991, 204). In reaction to this sorry state of affairs, researchers asked this question: Does the depth to which menus are nested affect users' ability to use a program? The answer was yes, it does.

A study by Kiger (described in Norman 1991, 203) found that a menu hierarchy (or tree) with no more than two levels and no more than eight items on each submenu (called 8^2) was rated highest for speed, accuracy, and subject preference (Figure 96). A four-level menu with three items per submenu (4^3) was the next best style. A deep, narrow tree of six levels with two items on each (called 2^6) was the slowest, least accurate, and least preferred version (Figure 97). Other studies confirmed that a low number of levels (two to three) and an intermediate level of choices (four to eight) resulted in faster, more accurate performance (Norman 1991, 213).

Figure 96

8^2 menu

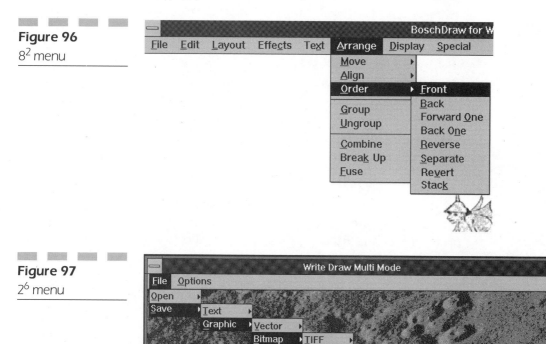

Figure 97

2^6 menu

Nevertheless, the issue may not be so simple. "For lists of linearly organized arrays, such as numbers, alphabetized lists, letters of the alphabet, and months of the year, one should increase breadth to the maximum practical level," says Norman. In other words, users can easily find a month or a font size in an ordered list. Distributing months across *Winter*, *Spring*, *Summer*, and *Fall* submenus, just to fulfill the depth rule, would irritate users very much.

However, Norman goes on to say, "it may very well be that the depth versus breadth tradeoff issue is really misplaced, and that the transcending issue is that of effectively revealing menu organization to users, while reducing the number of frames and responses required to locate target items" (1991, 213).

In other words, offer as many drop-down menus at the top and as many items at the bottom of each drop-down or submenu as possible. A wide number of the choices *at the top* helps the user guess where he might find an item. Once he knows he's on the right track, more choices *at the bottom* is better—now he can just scan the list to find the one he wants.

FILE AS THE FIRST MENU?   Although all of the platform style guides show File as the first menu, Edit as the second menu, View as the third, and so on, you don't have to follow the standard if your application has none of those things. In fact, the style guides say that you don't have to use File, Edit, and so on, if they don't make sense for your application.

Then how do you decide what your menus are? The key is: Put the most important or most often used choices in the first menu, then the next most important choices in the second menu, and so on. The Help menu is the one exception, since it always goes at the end, either because it's unimportant (because your application is so well built) or because users can find it there easily.

TEAR-OFF MENUS   Drop-down menus generally disappear as soon as the user selects an option or clicks outside the menu. However, sometimes menus are more useful if they stay around.

Some environments have methods for turning menus into temporary panels, called "tear-off" menus or "pushpin" menus—when you push the pin in, the menu stays posted (Sun Microsystems 1990, 287–289). Tear-off menus typically contain tools, patterns, colors, and other items that users select repeatedly.

Advantages of tear-offs over permanent toolbars and palettes are:

■   Relative impermanence—you post them when you want them posted, remove them when you don't.

■   No real estate. Since you don't have to reserve space for a permanent palette, you can create a larger workspace. (The tear-off panel floats on top of the graphic or document wherever the user drops it.)

On Macintosh systems, a user can detach a tear-off menu from the menu bar by putting the cursor on the menu's title, pressing the mouse button, then dragging the menu three pixels away from the menu bar (Apple 1992, 92–95). There is nothing to indicate whether a menu can be torn off or not.

In Motif systems, the tear-off point is a button that looks like a dashed line: ----------- This button appears on the menu itself, just above the part of the menu that can be torn off. The user can post the menu where it is, just below the menu bar, or drag the menu to another spot on the window (OSF 1993, 9-126–9-127).

The Microsoft Windows 3.x and 95 guidelines say nothing about tear-offs or other menu-panel hybrids, but clever developers can create them nevertheless.

DIFFERENCE BETWEEN CHARACTER-BASED AND GUI MENUS   In character-based systems, the main menu was used to select either primary applications (*Word Processor, Database, Spreadsheet*) or different modes within a primary application (for example, *Inquire, Update, Add New*).

In GUIs, however, menus let users *modify* the current application— open a different file, switch between drawing and text modes, change settings, cut and paste within the current file, and so on. To select primary applications, users now use desktop icons.

AUDIO MENUS   Audio menus are usually associated with phone systems, but software designers are beginning to create virtual phones on the desktop. Microsoft released a Windows Telephony Software Development Toolkit (TAPI SDK) in November 1993.

Also, keep in mind that many software developers are using audio tools to make sure that their menus are accessible to blind and partially-sighted users, as well as for other users whose eyes must be elsewhere than on a video screen.

The guidelines for creating audio menus are:

USE DELIMITERS   Use the # symbol to delimit data entry when the entry may have an indeterminate end-point—for example, when the system is asking for a check number or personal identification number. (A time-out can also be used as a delimiter.)

If the data entry has a known end-point (when the caller enters a Social Security number, for example), don't ask for the # delimiter. However, don't penalize a caller for pressing # when he or she doesn't have to.

ALLOW INTERRUPTS Let the caller end or interrupt the current activity and skip to the next activity by pressing # or the number of an item on the next menu (allow type-ahead, in other words).

BE SENSITIVE TO CALLERS LACKING HIGH-TECH VOCABULARIES
When you write your messages, keep in mind that some customers won't know the name of the # key. Also, the name changes from country to country. In the U.S. and Canada, it is usually called "pound," but it may also be called "hash" or "sharp" (the musical sharp). In Sweden, it is called "brädstapel," meaning "pile of sticks" (ISO 1993, 40).

Another problem is that, although anyone who uses a computer is comfortable with the idea of "entering" a number, the millions of people who don't use computers won't know what you are talking about (Gardner-Bonneau 1992, 223).

Note that there is consensus on the name of the * key—it's called the "star" key (Schumacher 1992, 1053).

KEEP MENUS SHORT Since sound does not persist, audio menus are constrained by short-term memory. (You can't go backwards on an audio menu unless you repeat the recording.) For this reason, menus should contain no more than four items at a time.

KEEP OPTIONS SHORT State options in language short enough to suit expert users but clear enough for novice users. Finding the right mix requires usability testing.

USE "GOAL-ACTION" FORMAT FOR MESSAGES Put the goal first and the action second. In other words, say "To forward a call, press 6," not "Press 6 to forward a call." The caller is listening intently for the thing she wants to do, not for the meaning of a particular button (Schumacher 1992, 1053).

WEB AND MULTIMEDIA MENUS If you need information about the Okefenokee Swamp, why not look for it on a map? If you need to set the time, why not use a clock?

Kent Norman (1991) says that nonlinear menus (menus that aren't lists, in other words) have two advantages. First is that visual recognition and spatial memory are powerful tools for locating items. Graphical representations such as maps, color wheels, and the periodic table of the elements are already well tested and well understood in the noncomputer world, so you might as well use them in the computerized version.

The second advantage is that nonlinear menus (especially round ones) can speed up selection time by reducing mouse travel (Norman 1991, 309–310). Selecting a color from a color wheel, for example, can be a tiny movement from the center point to the desired color.

On multimedia systems, the main menu may be a picture that is a collection of hotspots (also called "anchors" or "triggers"). When you touch a point on the picture, you go to a section of an online book (hypertext), a photo, an audio clip, or a video clip. For example, Figure 98 shows the opening window for a CD-ROM book about the Statue of Liberty. When the standard arrow cursor moves over a hotspot, the cursor changes shape and an outline appears. If the user clicks anywhere inside the outline, she goes to the part of the book containing information about that part of the restoration.

When the trigger is part of the visual object, you normally have to indicate that it's a trigger. One possibility is to distinguish the triggers visually from the rest of the drawing. For example, you can use a deeper shade of the drawing's main color to indicate the trigger. Or you might render triggerable mechanical parts in three dimensions, leaving the untriggered parts of the drawing in two dimensions. Or you can put dotted lines around trigger areas, as in Figure 98.

Another common method of indicating triggers is to change the cursor shape. For example, you can change the cursor from an arrow to an ear to indicate "audio output here," or a video-camera shape to indicate "video here" (IBM 1992, 16–17).

In games and educational programs, however, there may be no trigger indicator—the user must find the triggers by exploring. For example, in Brøderbund's *Arthur's Teacher Trouble* and *Grandma and Me*, many items in each panel are "live." When you click the cursor on a starfish in *Grandma and Me*, the starfish jumps up and leads nearby shells in calisthenics. In *Arthur's Teacher Trouble*, when you click on the science lab's door, a green puddle leaks out from underneath the door, goes "bloop, bloop," then goes back inside. There are no predefined paths, nothing is highlighted; everything is a surprise—a perfect learning tool.[4]

Figure 98

Statue of Liberty mega-icon or picture menu.

Usability Tests

To make sure that you're using the user's terminology for tasks, do a paper and pencil test on the menus. For example, you can easily test menu options with a simple paper and pencil quiz. If your test participants don't make the right connections, then you know you have more work to do on the design.

---

4. Brøderbund, 500 Redwood Blvd., Novato, CA 94948-6121.

To find out how users would group functions, do a sorting test. See Appendix B for details.

See Also

Keyboard Shortcuts; Menubar; Menu, Pop-Up; Pushbutton.

For more on organizing lists, see "How to Organize Lists" in List Box, Multiple-Selection.

ADAPTIVE TECHNOLOGIES, AUDIO   For information about audio technologies for computer hardware and software, contact the National Technology Center, *American Foundation for the Blind*; 11 Pennsylvania Plaza, Suite 300, New York, NY 10001; 212/502-7600.

The Trace Research and Development Center at the University of Wisconsin offers software, telephone communication devices, and computer-access software. Contact: Trace Research & Development Center, University of Wisconsin-Madison, Room S-151 Waisman Center, 1500 Highland Ave., Madison, WI 53705; voice 608/263-2309; TDD 608/263-5408.

Librarians and teachers will find Ruth A. Velleman's *Meeting the Needs of People with Disabilities: A Guide for Librarians, Educators, and Other Service Professionals* useful (1990, ISBN 0-89774-521-3). The book is available from The Oryx Press, 4041 N. Central Ave., Suite 700, Phoenix, AZ 85012-3397.

VOICE MESSAGING AND TELECOMMUNICATIONS   The Microsoft Telephone Software Development Kit (TAPI SDK) is available from the Internet. Download the file via remote ftp: on the browser's "Go To" command line, type ftp://ftp.microsoft.com/developr/TAPI/. For contents, see README.TXT.

The Human Factors and Ergonomics Society has a *Communications Technical Group*, which consists of approximately 350 people working in telecommunications firms, universities, consulting firms, and manufacturers. For more information, contact the Human Factors and Ergonomics Society, P.O. Box 1369, Santa Monica, CA 90406-1369; voice: 310/394-1811.

Two controlled-circulation periodicals from the same publisher contain information about voice messaging:

- *Computer Telephony.* describes the world of phone-computer hybrids—phone and fax boards in computers, computerized voice processing applications, speech recognition and text-to-speech applications, voice processing standards, and so on.

- *Teleconnect,* which publishes articles on automated attendants, call and voice processing systems, telephony applications, and hardware of all kinds.

Contact *Teleconnect* and *Computer Telephony* at 12 West 21st St., New York, NY 10010; voice: 212/691-8215.

For international voice-messaging specifications, see ISO/IEC 13714:1995, "Information technology—Document processing and related communication—User interface to telephone-based services—Voice messaging applications." The Internet address for ISO is www.iso.ch.

Menu, Pop-Up

A context-sensitive menu accessed by pressing the secondary mouse button.

Good For

- Expert computer users who want shortcuts (Figure 99).

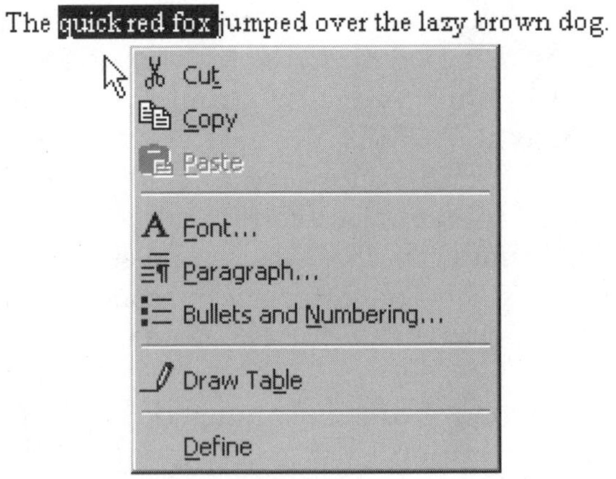

Figure 99

Word 97 pop-up menu.

The quick red fox jumped over the lazy brown dog.

- ✂ Cut
- 📋 Copy
- 📋 Paste

- A Font...
- Paragraph...
- Bullets and Numbering...

- Draw Table

- Define

■ Minimizing mouse travel by making options available at the current pointer or cursor location.

■ Accessing properties of selected objects.

Not Good For

■ Options that appear nowhere else in the system.

■ Novice computer users who are unaware of pop-up menus.

Design Guidelines

Pop-up menus appear when the user moves the cursor over a hotspot or hot area (defined by the developer) *and* presses the secondary mouse button (usually the right button). Although a cursor change can be used to indicate that a pop-up exists, the development guidelines are silent about whether an indicator is required or not.

Rules for pop-up menus vary among platforms. Following are the areas of agreement and disagreement.

TITLES   The Motif guidelines call for a title placed at the top of the menu and separated from the menu elements by a standard separator (OSF 1993, 6–41). The Windows 3.x and Windows 95 guidelines, on the other hand, do not show titles on pop-up menus (Microsoft 1992, 76, 79; Microsoft 1995a, 126–131).

RECOMMENDED MENU OPTIONS   The IBM OS/2 guidelines suggest three groups of items on a typical pop-up: *Help* and *Open* as the first group, clipboard choices as the second group, and application-specific choices as the third group. The third group can also contain choices such as *Undo, Print,* and *Clear* (IBM 1992, 192–193).

Motif recommends that you put options such as *Properties* (set properties), *Cut, Copy, Paste, Undo, Select All,* and *Deselect All* on your pop-ups (OSF 1993, 6-27–6-30).

The Windows 3.x guidelines have no recommended list of options, although *Undo* and *Properties* options are mentioned as typical (Microsoft 1992, 77).

The Windows 95 guidelines say that the contents of a pop-up menu are supplied by the object, container, or any combination of the two. For example, they say that the pop-up menu for a file in a folder can include transfer commands (Cut, Copy, Paste, and other specialized Paste commands). Transfer commands are properties of the container rather than the file itself (Microsoft 1995a, 127).

ORDER OF OPTIONS The Windows 95 guidelines suggest the following:

- Put the object's primary commands first (for example, Open, Play, Print), other commands supported by the object or its context, and the What's This? command (if supported).
- Put the transfer commands next.
- Put the Properties command, if available, last (Microsoft 1995a, 127).

ACCELERATORS AND MNEMONICS If the development environment doesn't offer keyboard access for pop-ups, show neither mnemonics nor accelerators. In environments with keyboard access, show the same accelerators and mnemonics on a pop-up menu as you use in the top-level drop-down menus.

However, keep in mind that accelerators defined for the primary menus will work anyway, whether or not they appear on the pop-up menu. Probably for this reason, the Windows 95 guidelines suggest that you simplify the interface and not include the accelerator labels ("Ctrl+S") on the pop-up options (Microsoft 1995a, 129).

SUBMENUS In general, adding more than one level of submenus defeats the purpose of a pop-up, which is supposed to be an easy-to-manipulate mouse-based shortcut. The Windows 3.x guidelines say that one level of submenus is acceptable, but two or more are not (Microsoft 1992, 77).

INVISIBILITY IS A PROBLEM Make sure that:

- The options on the pop-up are high-frequency functions.
- The users know the menu is available.

■ The options also exist on the main menus or on other more visible components—since some users may never notice the pop-up menus, they may never find these additional options.

Usability Tests

Observe carefully to see whether users are likely to find the pop-up menus:

■ Without prompting.

■ With prompting.

■ Only after training.

■ Only if mentioned in job aids, online help, or printed documentation.

Share the results with your training and documentation departments.

See Also

Menu, Drop-Down.

Message Box

A specialized, often modal, usually moveable, type of dialog box used to present information or warnings and ask questions.

Good For

- Asking for a user response.
- Explaining an error.
- Confirming a potentially dangerous choice.

Not Good For

- Messages for which no response is needed. If the application doesn't require a response, use a status-bar message instead.

Design Guidelines

Many error messages say things like, "Invalid input. User must type xxxx." Why can't the program, if it knows what the user must type, just enter xxxx by itself and save the user the tongue lashing? Instead of demanding that the user find a file on disk, introducing the chance that the user will select the wrong file, have the program remember which files it has accessed in the past and allow a selection from that list . . . .

Undoubtedly, [these solutions] will cause more work for programmers. This doesn't bother me a bit . . . . It is the programmer's job to satisfy the user and not vice versa. If the programmer thinks of the user as just another input device, it is easy to forget the proper pecking order in the world of software design.

—Alan Cooper, *About Face: The Essentials of User Interface Design*, p. 432.

The most important guideline for messages and message boxes is, Try to design them *out* of the software. If you, as the developer, can figure out what has to be done at some point in the program, then have the software do it. If the users can cope with uncertainty in particular fields ("I don't have the invoice number but I can fill it in later before we ship"), then the software should accommodate uncertainty as well.

Also, Cooper points out that too often the software stops dead so that a message box can report normalcy. If something has happened that was supposed to have happened, he says, never report this with a message box. Instead, put the message in the status bar. Save message boxes for events that are outside the normal course of events (1995, 144).

PICK THE RIGHT TYPE OF MESSAGE According to Microsoft, there are three types of messages: information, warning, and critical.

An information message (Figure 100):

- Provides information about the results of a command.

- Offers no user choices. The user acknowledges the message by clicking an OK button.

- Uses an "i" icon.

Figure 100

Information message box.

A warning message (Figure 101):

- Alerts the user to a condition or situation that requires a decision and input from the user.

- Lets the user back out of an irreversible action (a "chicken switch").

- Can be written as a question.

- Uses the exclamation-point icon.

Figure 101

A warning
message.

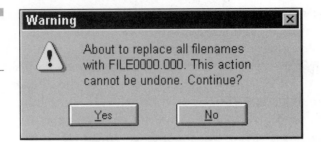

A critical message tells the user about a serious problem requiring intervention or correction before work can continue (Microsoft 1995a,
210–212). Windows 95 uses a red X icon (Figure 102); Windows 3.x and
other platforms use a stop-sign icon.

Figure 102

A critical message.

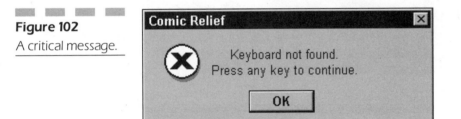

However, the lines between information, warning, and critical tend
to blur as soon as you sit down with a list of real messages. Many developers find themselves splitting their lists between information messages and error messages.

Error messages can, theoretically, be either warning (semi-modal—
the user might be able to work around it) or critical (modal—all work
stops until the problem is resolved). However, except in situations
where failure has extremely high costs (like space missions), your application should never take itself so seriously that it stops the application
dead. Oh, the printer is offline? Well, then, let the user know and
switch to the next printer in the queue. No printers in the queue? Let
the user know about it and retreat into the background until a printer
comes back online.

In short, you can expect to use the information message (with its "i"
icon) and the warning message (with its exclamation-point icon) most
often, and the critical message rarely.

- Use the information message when you need simple user confirmations—"OK, gotcha."
- Use the warning message when you need a more complex response—"Yes, No, Cancel the Search."
- Use the critical message when hardware is broken or missing—"Error code 0: Computer not on. OK."

WHAT GOES IN THE TITLE BAR   The platform standards agree: At a minimum, put the application name in the title bar of the message box. If the message is generated from a particular document, spreadsheet, record, or other item, include that item's name as well.

The reason is that the application or situation that generated the message may not be visible—it may be minimized, it may have come from the network or from a background process, it may be hidden behind other windows or documents, and so on.

The message itself should be the first line inside the message box. See "Write Messages Right" below for details.

USE RESOURCE FILES   Put all messages in resource files. Don't embed text in the dialog boxes themselves. The reason for resource files is that they make changing text relatively easy. But why would you change text? There are at least three reasons:

Changes in corporate terminology.   The name of the software will probably change between alpha and release; approved names of objects may change; even the company name may change.

Corrections.   Usability tests often lead to changes in terminology. Changing embedded text requires opening every affected file, finding the text, changing it, recompiling, retesting—in other words, time and money. If the text is in resource files, however, human-factors personnel, technical writers, and entry-level programmers can change it without inadvertently damaging underlying code.

Internationalization and localization.   As soon as you translate an interface in which all text is embedded, you have two versions of the program to support, one of them in a language you may not know. See the next section for more information.

MAKE SURE THAT YOU CAN INTERNATIONALIZE   In addition to keeping messages in resource files, internationalization has other requirements, as follows.

BE CAREFUL OF NEGATIVES   Native English speakers find sentences like this difficult to understand (non-native speakers find them impossible):

Wrong: Are you sure that you don't want to save the file?

How are you supposed to answer this? By reversing the sense: Yes, I don't want to save the file. No, I do want to save the file.

Right: Do you want to discard the file?

The answer is then either "No, I don't want to discard the file" (this should be the default "safe" answer) or "Yes, I do want to discard the file."

Also, English questions phrased in the negative may be answered in unexpected ways in other languages. For example, a positive response to a negative question in French is not "oui" but "si":

«Vous n'êtes pas malade?» «Si, je suis malade.»

("You're not sick?" "Yes, I am sick.")

AVOID CONCATENATED STRINGS   A common method for creating customized messages is to embed variables in strings of text (Kano 1995, 46–47). For example, instead of writing, "The hard disk drive has crashed," "The scanner has become disconnected," "The floppy disk drive has crashed," "The hard disk drive has a boot error," and so on, you might write:

MSG=The %1 has %2.

where the first variable could be "hard disk drive," "scanner," or "floppy disk drive," and the second variable could be "crashed," "become disconnected," or "a boot error."

But this message becomes difficult to translate because the %2 variables are different parts of speech. In English, you can use "has" as:

- An indicator of a not-so-distant past tense.
- A past-tense indicator and part of a verb phrase.
- Meaning "owns" ("the drive owns or suffers an error").

However, there is no reason to believe that a similar substitution would be possible in any other language.

Here is another straightforward string substitution (as long as you stick with English):

> Your mission is to shoot down this bomber before it reaches our %t and destroys it. You will start near the %t. Engage the %b bomber when it approaches.

If, however, you were to translate this phrase into a language with different word forms for different genders, you would have to substitute more than locations (%t) and bomber names (%b). As Steve VanDevender says in *The (Much-Requested) Translation Manifesto*, "Where in English we have one accusative possessive article 'our,' German has 'unseren' used with masculine nouns, 'unsere' used with feminine nouns, and 'unser' used with neuter nouns [as well as] separate articles used with different grammatical cases—like 'der/die/das' used where we would use 'the' before a subject [and] 'des/der/des' used where we would use 'of the'" (VanDevender 1993, 3).

In the sample above, then, the *our* and each *the* would have to be tested and set to the correct form, or the substitutions would have to include the correct *our* or *the*. Instead of *before it reaches our %t*, the phrase would be *before it reaches %t*.

Also, don't construct messages from *parts* of words or phrases. For example, concatenating *Mon, Tues, Wednes,* and so on, to *day* works well in English, but not in French—lundi, mardi, mercredi, jeudi, vendredi, samedi, and dimanche—or German—Montag, Dienstag, *Mittwoch*, Donnerstag, Freitag, Samstag, and Sonntag (National Language Technical Center 1991, 2–8).

USE MESSAGE NUMBERS   There are at least five reasons to show message numbers or identifiers:

1. If the system gets completely fouled up, the number may be the only information that appears on the screen. As long as the documentation lists the numbers with the messages, users will at least be able to find the message by number.

2. The text of messages may be similar or the same, especially when translated into other natural languages.

3. Messages written for end-users often lack the level of detail that professional troubleshooters need. Without the number, a cus-

tomer service representative may have difficulty communicating exactly what the problem is to the developer. With the number, on the other hand, the developer can figure out almost immediately what "flavor" of error this is.

4. If your application will be internationalized, the numbers help translators track messages and panels throughout the translation process. The online messages are often translated a year or two earlier than the documentation. Once the documentation is ready to be translated, the translators can simply copy the original translation of the message into the documentation, provided that they can tell which message is which—ergo, the message numbers.

5. Customer support can use the numbers to provide help to international users. A U.S. service representative may know the English version but be unable to read French or German. The number, however, crosses language boundaries (Uren, Howard, and Perinotti 1993, 20–21).

USE THE RIGHT BUTTONS   Here are guidelines for user-response pushbuttons. See Pushbutton for more on pushbuttons.

- If the message is informational only (the user simply has to acknowledge that he or she has seen it), use OK or Continue.
- If the message is a question, use Yes and No, not OK and Cancel.
- If the question has a third option (an "if, then, else" structure), use Yes, No, and Cancel (or other appropriate button). However, be specific about what you're canceling. In a message like, "Do you want to exit without saving this formula?" Cancel would mean "cancel this message box" or "don't exit"—but then what? It would be better to use Yes, No, and Return to Formula rather than Yes, No, and Cancel.

For error messages, include a help button or, in Windows 95, additional details. For what to put in help or a details panel, see "Do error messages in three parts" below.

For alignment (left, right, center), follow your platform guidelines.

WRITE MESSAGES RIGHT   Messages must be both informative and provide a solution to any identified problem. Beyond those two criteria, there are a handful of other standards and suggestions, as follows.

Figure 103

Offer guidance by being explicit.

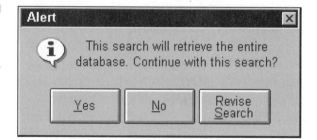

BE POLITE Politeness means letting the software take the blame rather than throwing the blame back at the user. For example, Figure 104 shows a typical "impolite" message.

Figure 104

A standard impolite message.

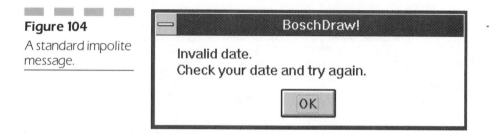

Figure 105 shows the same message, rewritten to shift the blame to the software.

Figure 105

The corrected (and more specific) message.

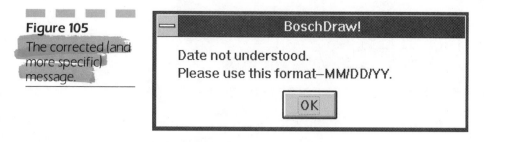

Politeness is important because it is emotionally neutral. In other words, since the user doesn't feel blamed, she is neither intimidated nor angered by the problem and just carries on. The more emotionally neutral business software is—the more that the software fades into the background—the more satisfying it is to users. (This also explains why humor and personalizing the computer fail to appeal to business users—anything that draws attention to itself shoves the task into the background and makes users lose track of where they are in the task.)

An interesting side effect: Putting more thought into the style of a message seems to force developers to be more specific about the cause of the problem. The result is a more useful message.

CLEAR MESSAGES AUTOMATICALLY   Remove the message automatically whenever your application can determine that the error has been corrected. For example, if the printer sent an "out of paper" message to your application but now sends a notice that the paper tray has been refilled, remove the alert message. Don't wait for the user to do it.

USE THE "GOAL-ACTION" FORMAT   Put the problem or goal first and the action second—see Figure 106 and Figure 107.

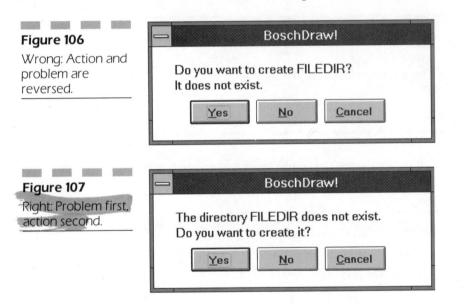

Figure 106

Wrong: Action and problem are reversed.

Figure 107

Right: Problem first, action second.

If you have to write hazard or caution warnings, always put the nature of the hazard first and the consequences of ignoring the hazard second. Then state how to avoid the hazard (Fowler and Stanwick 1995, 145–150). The "See Also" section below contains more information on hazard messages.

USE CHRONOLOGICAL ORDER If the user has to do first one thing, then another, write the message in chronological order—see Figure 108 and Figure 109.

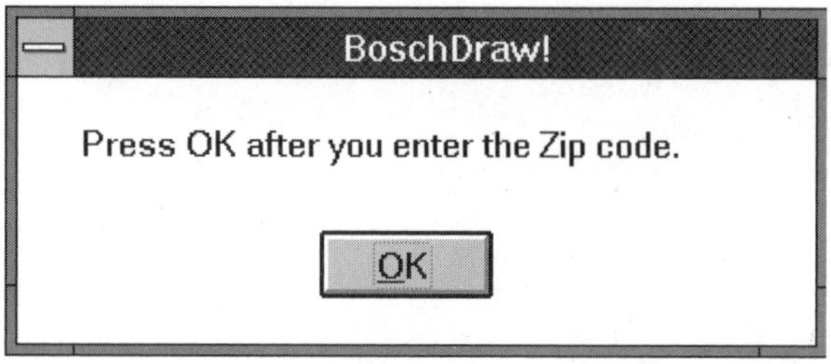

Figure 108

Wrong way to write a message. Some users will press OK before entering the ZIP code.

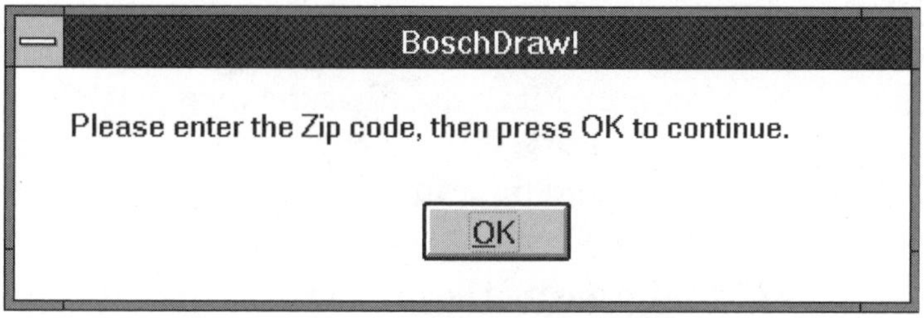

> **BoschDraw!**
>
> Press OK after you enter the Zip code.
>
> [OK]

Figure 109

Right way to write the message.

> **BoschDraw!**
>
> Please enter the Zip code, then press OK to continue.
>
> [OK]

ALIGN THE TEXT CORRECTLY Put the information or warning icon leftmost in the box, then start the text about a quarter inch to the right of the icon. Left-align the message text. Do not indent the first line of the message, paragraph style—see Figure 110 and Figure 111.

Figure 110

Wrong alignment—text should not be indented. According to the Windows 95 guidelines, the OK button should be centered.

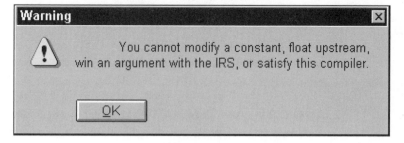

> **Warning**   [x]
>
> ⚠   You cannot modify a constant, float upstream,
>   win an argument with the IRS, or satisfy this compiler.
>
> [OK]

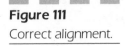

Figure 111

Correct alignment.

The buttons go at the bottom, aligned as per your platform's guidelines.

DO ERROR MESSAGES IN THREE PARTS Use the three-part diagnostic style:

1. *Message.* Make sure that the message describes the problem in terms the user can understand (for nontechnical audiences, avoid jargon) and in terms that actually describe what the problem is. Some corporate standards require error-message numbers as well.

2. *Explanation.* The most likely explanation of the problem, followed by the next most likely explanation, and so on through all possible explanations. (IBM's hardware diagnostics include actual "likelihood" percentages based on the service representatives' experiences in the field.)

3. *User Response.* Suggested actions or user responses, again ranked by likelihood.

The error message and ID number, plus the most likely explanation and suggested action, should appear in the error-message dialog box. The additional explanations and details can go into a "Details" panel, on-line help, or printed documentation.

AVOID INADVERTENT DESTRUCTION Once you've rewritten your messages to the standards described above, here is one more: People often do not read the messages, at least not more than once. Rather, they recognize the message (and the problem) from the shape of the words and, based on a mere glance, just clear it.

If two messages look very much the same, the user may end up clearing the wrong message. Therefore, after you've considered everything else, try to make dissimilar messages look different, especially when the results of mistaking one for another could be catastrophic.

Also check the default response carefully. Note that, in Figure 112, the destructive "delete" message has "No" as the default choice while the "archive" message (Figure 113) has "Yes" as the default.

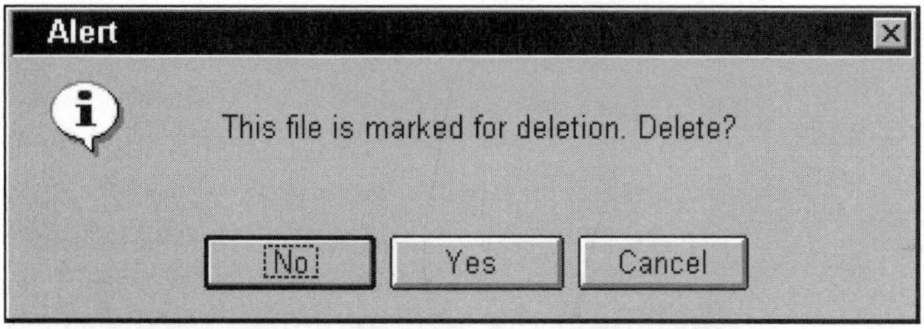

Figure 112

Although this message looks very similar to the one in the next figure . . .

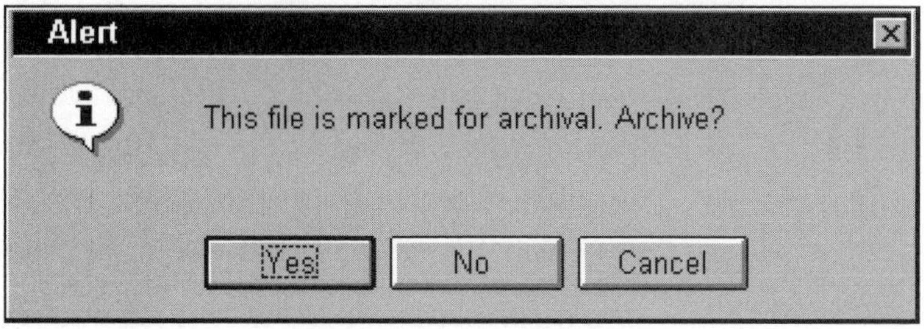

Figure 113

Users are protected from error by the different default buttons.

Usability Tests

Ask a technical writer or editor to review messages for:

- Consistent terminology—for example, Yes and No instead of OK and Cancel if that's what you agreed upon.
- Syntax—see "Write Messages Right" above.
- Layout—for example, make sure that all messages are left-aligned if that is what your style guide calls for.
- Grammatical and spelling errors.

Don't overdo confirmation and acknowledgment messages, especially modal ones. If possible, test your messaging strategy on experienced users as well as new users using low-fidelity or high-fidelity prototypes.

If your software will be used in countries other than the one in which you are writing the software, try to test in these countries. If you can't afford it, at least ask interested parties (your sales force, for example) to look at your messages. Even when two countries use the same language, there can be misunderstandings. For example, in Great Britain, "billion" generally means one thousand million. In the U.S., it means one hundred million. (Note, however, that international financial corporations often standardize on the U.S. style.)

See Also

Online Help, Status-Bar Messages.

For information on designing warning sounds, see chapter 4, "Messages," in Fowler and Stanwick (1995, 150–153).

For information on hazard messages and signs, see Fowler and Stanwick (1995, 145–150). Also (in the U.S.) see the American National Standards Institute (ANSI) publications on hazard and safety signs:

- *Safety Color Code*, ANSI Z535.1-1991 ($35.00)
- *Environmental and Facility Safety Signs*, ANSI Z535.2-1991 ($35.00)
- *Criteria for Safety Symbols*, ANSI Z535.3-1991 ($35.00)
- *Product Safety Signs and Labels*, ANSI Z535.4-1991 ($35.00)

For more information or to order these publications, contact American National Standards Institute, Attn: Customer Service, ANSI, 11 West 42nd St., 13th Floor, New York, NY 10036; voice 212/642-4900; http://www.ansi.com.

Online Help, Context-Sensitive

Help that appears automatically when the user presses F1, Shift-F1, or clicks a help icon. The user doesn't have to go to the help menu. (Reference help, on the other hand, usually does require loading from a menu.)

According to the Microsoft Windows 95 specifications, context-sensitive help is "What's This?" help. What's This? help is actually expanded tooltips (a good idea, according to some usability experts—see Tooltip). In fact, tooltips and What's This? help are functionally interchangeable.

In other environments, context-sensitive help is simply help for individual screen components.

Good For

- Finding out what a screen component is or does (Figure 114).

Figure 114

Windows 95
"What's This?" help.

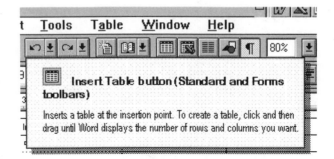

- Checking the field-edit rules or finding out what the acceptable entries are (Figure 115).

Figure 115
Quick reference
box from
Framemaker 3.0.

FrameMaker Help			
Moving in a table			
To move to:	**Press:**	**To move to:**	**Press:**
Next cell, selecting all text in cell	Tab, Esc t m n	Cell above	Esc t m u
Previous cell, selecting all text in cell	Shift-Tab, Esc t m p	Rightmost cell in row	Esc t m e
Cell below, selecting all text	Ctrl-Alt-Tab	Leftmost cell in row	Esc t m a
Cell above, selecting all text	Ctrl-Alt-Shift-Tab	Top cell in column	Esc t m t
Cell to the right	Esc t m r	Bottom cell in column	Esc t m b
Cell to the left	Esc t m l	Top-left selected cell	Esc t m s
Cell below	Esc t m d	Text column containing table	Esc t l (uppercase i)

Figure 115

Quick reference box from Framemaker 3.0.

Not Good For

- How-to and procedural information. Use procedural help instead.
- Background and overview information. Use reference-style help or printed documentation instead.

Design Guidelines

PROBLEMS WITH CONTEXT-SENSITIVE HELP   Don't rely too heavily on context-sensitive help. It has these limitations:

- Neither tooltips nor What's This? help (so far) let users link to on-line help windows if they need more information. And they are likely to need to: Usability experts say that most users want to know "How do I do this?" rather than "What is this?" Of course, you can write whatever you want in What's This? panels—for example, you *can* explain how to do something instead of just saying what the component is.

- If your specification calls for context-sensitive help *only* (every screen component must have its own context-sensitive help panel), where do you put the overviews? How do you tell users how to do operations that cross window boundaries? How can you do *any* task-oriented or goal-oriented help? You can't, at least not without a kludge—for example, deciding that the parent window's context-sensitive help will be a task overview.[5]

- Most readers will not be able to imagine a context-only help system, but they do exist. If someone in your organization starts to argue for context-only help, remind them that users need at least three types of information—descriptive, procedural, and background—and will be unhappy if you give them only one.

- Some items don't need any help. If your OK and Cancel buttons behave consistently, for example, a user doesn't need to know much about them. Writing about self-evident components gets silly.

WHEN DO YOU NEED IT?   You probably need context-sensitive help less often than you might think. First of all, most help is procedural, and secondly, mass-market applications usually don't have to worry about field edits and business rules. (Tax and accounting software are exceptions.)

If you have a database application, you probably do need context-sensitive help for the fields. Nevertheless, think about using more descriptive labels or automatic (but unobtrusive) tooltip or status-bar messages instead of help. Even the best online help is hidden, whereas labels, tooltips, and status-bar messages are either visible or readily made visible. Also, using combo boxes or drop-down lists for as many entry areas as possible helps users avoid errors and precludes the necessity for help.

For applications with extensive business rules and data-entry requirements—for example, real-estate or insurance contracts—consider using artificial-intelligence techniques rather than help. In other words, if the person entering the information picks one type of contract, the system fills in most of the boilerplate automatically and carefully checks the variable information. You'd still include a help system, but it would explain the underlying business rules.

---

5. A prime example of this atomization problem: Because of the structure we chose for this book, you can't get the whole story of online help without reading all three online-help sections, plus the sections on wizards, status-bar help, and tooltips.

ACCESSING CONTEXT-SENSITIVE HELP On Windows 3.x systems, pressing F1 usually opens the help system at the contents page and Shift-F1 opens context-sensitive help. The Help icon usually behaves the same as Shift-F1. On Windows 95 systems, both Shift-F1 and the Help icon open What's This? help.

Figure 116

The Help icon in the Windows 3.x environment.

Many users don't use or don't notice the Help icon and many don't know that Shift-F1 is supposed to bring up context-sensitive help. In fact, they often go straight to the help menu and select the Search option. However, this is a reasonable strategy since many systems don't have extensive or consistent component-level help—when the user asks for component-level help, she often gets higher-level help anyway.

Note that you can't count on training or marketing materials to let users know help is available. In a system the authors worked on, more than 1,000 panels of context-sensitive online help were accessible with a right-mouse-key click. Two years into the project, we discovered that most of the company's employees didn't know there was context-sensitive help. Although we believed that end-users knew about it, none of us was sure that they did.

Usability Tests

MECHANICAL ISSUES   See if the test participants try to use the context-sensitive help. If they do, determine first whether the interface, rather than the help, needs to be fixed.

Also see how users access help—do they press F1 or Shift-F1, access the Help menu, press the help icon, or none of the above? If they don't know they can get context-sensitive help, you might want to add instructions to your training classes and "Getting Started" manuals.

Do users get what they expect? For example, if a user presses Shift-F1 in a dialog box, is she looking for help on the box or on a component in the box? Is she puzzled if she gets help sometimes on the box and sometimes on a component? If inconsistency seems to be a problem, you might want to develop rules about which child components get their own help panels, and then retest on users.

BUSINESS ISSUES   Use a talk-aloud protocol to find out what domain or business-rule questions the test participants have about the application. Include the identified topics in the online help.

Also find out what task information the user needs. Tasks with more than one step or that require more context should go into procedural help, but short tasks (for example, "To check a word, highlight it and press the spell-checker button") can stay in the context-sensitive help.

See Also

Online Help, Procedural; Online Help, Reference; Status-Bar Messages; Tooltips.

For information about hypertext, see Online Help, Reference.

Online Help, Procedural

Any help that contains procedures and how-to information (the second part of the help triumvirate of description, procedure, and background).

Good For

■   Quickly learning a procedure.

Not Good For

■   Naming or describing screen components. Use context-sensitive help, tooltips, and status-bar descriptions instead.

■   Background and overview information. Use reference-style help or printed documentation instead.

Design Guidelines

There are two styles of procedural help, passive (Figure 117) and active (Figure 118).

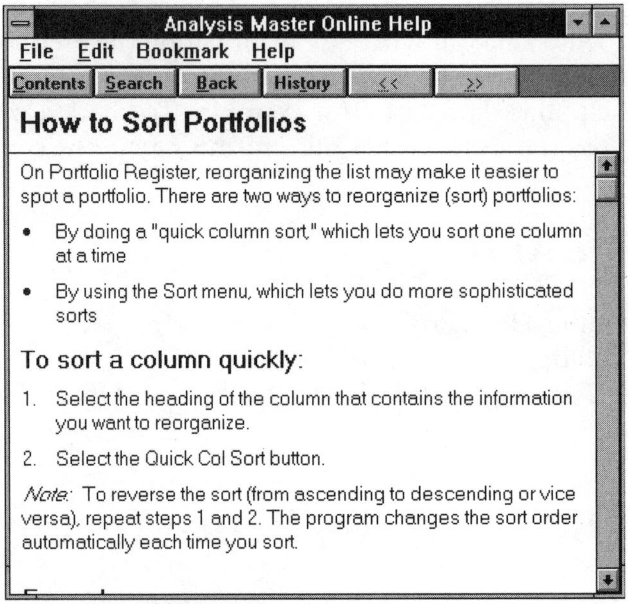

Figure 117

This help window explains how to sort a list.

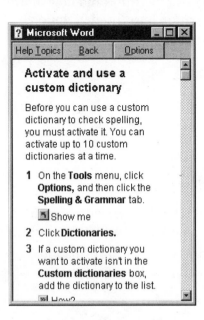

Figure 118

This active help window shows you how the procedure is done. Note the "Show me" button. This button probably saves at least a page of text.

Usability experts and technical communicators have found that active help is far more effective (and more interesting to create) than passive help. The Windows 95 development platform comes with tools that make developing active help relatively easy. See Boggan, Farkas, and Welinske, *Developing online help for Windows 95*, for details (1996).

MAKING EXPLORATION SAFE   John Carroll (1992), Carl Zetie (1995) and other experts on documentation point out that human beings learn by exploration. A successful interface allows safe exploration through feedback, affordances, and error recovery.

Good screen design shows users the main path. Good help catches explorers before they fall over cliffs and puts them back on track.

You will know that you have succeeded if a significant number of novice users become experts—it means that your interface made it easy and safe to explore.

WHAT PROCEDURAL HELP LOOKS LIKE   In Windows 3.x, procedural help often appears as "cue cards"—pop-ups that appear automatically when the user accesses a dialog box or other task-oriented component. It also appears in standard help windows.

In Windows 95, procedural help often appears in secondary help windows. These windows are smaller (often because they replace text with "Show me," "How?" and other interactive buttons), and contain highly structured text. (See "How to Write a Procedure" below).

In other environments, procedural help is differentiated from reference topics not by window type but by title ("How To" or "Example") and by having numbered steps.

SIZE OF HELP PANELS   Procedural help panels should contain only as much information as fits on an index card. If the user has to scroll or page down, the help topic is too big.

This may seem severe, if not impossible. However, development companies have found that if a procedure is hard to document, it is probably too complicated and should be re-engineered.

Also, users generally read only as much as they need to find out how to do the next step (User Interface Engineering 1996, 6). The implications:

- Design the help panel so that each step is easy to spot.

- Edit the text to the bone.

HOW TO WRITE PROCEDURES Title, introduction, step number, action, and feedback are required. Also helpful are examples, warnings, and notes. Table 16 provides descriptions of each part, in the order in which they should appear.

COACHES AND CUE CARDS Scott Boggan and his co-authors describe "coach help" as sequences of help topics that walk users through the steps that make up a task (Boggan, Farkas, Welinske 1996, 97). Users work with the application's regular interface (as opposed to wizards, which provide a simplified interface—see Wizard). Also, coaches, unlike tutorials, are a productivity tool—instead of working on canned examples as they would in a tutorial, users work on their own tasks (Boggan, Farkas, Welinske 1996, 100).

Figure 119

Task-oriented help from Microsoft Word for Windows 6.x.

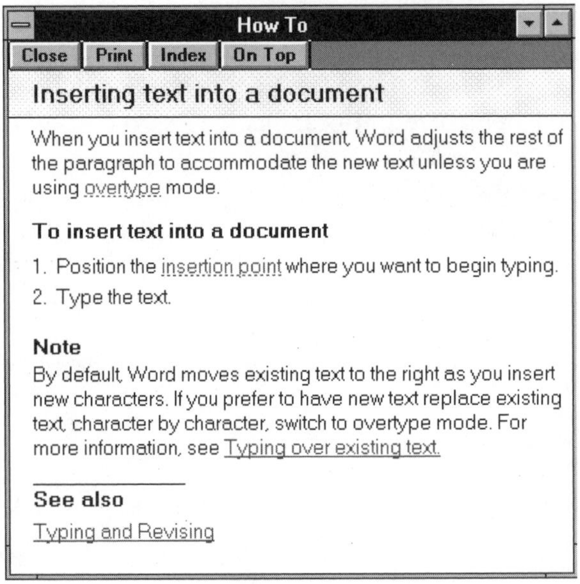

The helpfulness of coaches depends on how well their authors have identified their users' goals. User Interface Engineering tested coaches, done as cue cards (Figure 120), in four different programs and found that there was often a mismatch between what users needed and what the cue cards gave them. For example, one application told users how to open a file, but the users never read it because they already knew how to open files. Another cue card told users how to import a file, but missed the obvious (in retrospect) next step: how to view the import-

Procedure Part	Description
TABLE 16 Parts of a Procedure	
Title	"How To" is always a good start for task-oriented help (Figure 120). Note: The Windows 95 guidelines suggest "To [do whatever]" as the procedure's title *and* introduction.
Introduction	Provide easily scannable one-line introductions or headings. Users read the instructions faster and make fewer mistakes if you describe the goal or endpoint. For example: To process a work order:
Warnings	Put warnings and cautions *before* the step. *Note:* If the program or equipment could be redesigned so that the warning is no longer needed, you should change it. Always check with your legal department about requirements for warnings.
Step numbers	Number steps if there are more than one. Don't number a one-step operation. Use 5 to 7 steps (or less) per procedure
Action	*One* action per step. "One action" is what the user would define as a complete action, and this varies with experience. For example, a novice user might see "Type your login name and press [Return]" as two actions. An experienced user would see it as a single action. Start the step either with an imperative verb (Press F1) or with a trigger word such as To, If, or When: To start the motor, turn the key. If you want to save the file, select Save. If you want to quit without saving, select Cancel.
Feedback, Error Recovery	Include feedback statements: 5. Select OK. You're returned to the main menu. The feedback ("You're returned to the main menu") helps the reader orient herself in the operation and acts as error recovery information.
Examples	Use examples and counter-examples. Example: Ms. Marks has been a customer for 8 years and has had one warning notice in that time. Her payment history is good. Counter-example: Mr. Jones has been a customer for 1 year and has had two warning notices. His payment history is not good.
Notes and tips	A note can either be embedded in the step or fall below it. Notes contain "nice to know" information.

ed records (User Interface Engineering 1996, 6). Mismatches like these can be resolved with early usability testing of interface and help prototypes.

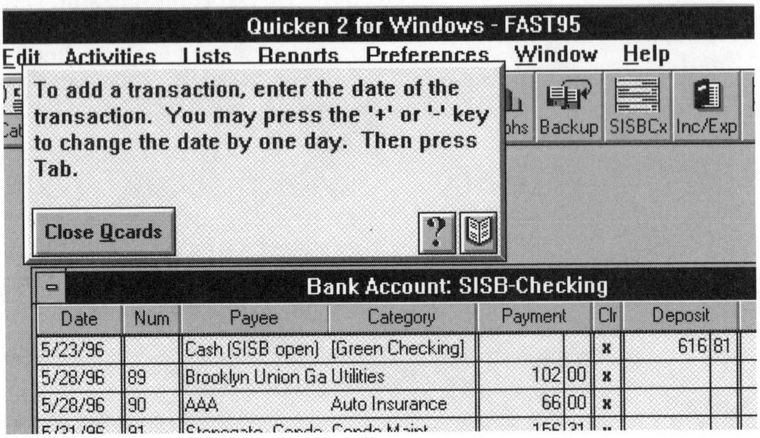

Figure 120

A cue card (called "QCard") from Quicken 2 for Windows.

Make sure that users can turn off automatic cue cards. Novice users often feel put-upon; experienced users find them irrelevant and interfering.

Usability Tests

Use a talk-aloud protocol to find out what task-oriented questions the test participants have about the application. Include the identified topics in the online help.

Also see Appendix A, "Usability Tests," in this book; *Managing Your Documentation Projects* (Hackos 1994, chapter 20); and *Human Factors for Technical Communicators* (Coe 1996) for types of usability tests appropriate for online help.

See Also

Online Help, Context-Sensitive; Online Help, Reference. For information about hypertext, see Online Help, Reference.

Online Help, Reference

Any help that contains background or "nice to know" information (the third part of the help triumvirate of description, procedure, and background). Reference help is often the paper documentation or actual reference books in electronic form.

Good For

■ Finding out what is going on behind the scenes (Figure 121). Learning more about the business context.

Figure 121

Reference help explains what's happening behind the scenes.

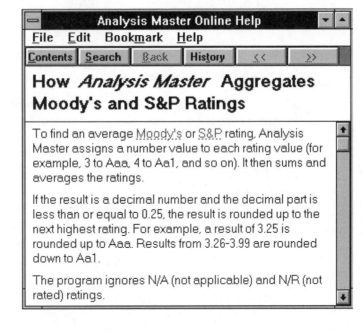

■ Accessing technical information quickly. Examples:

— Checking syntax for programming commands.

— Looking at troubleshooting flowcharts and procedures.

Not Good For

■ Procedural or context-sensitive information.

Design Guidelines

Reference help should be used only as a backup for printed documentation. Users generally don't like to read long sections of text online. However, having the reference text online has two advantages:

■ Users can often search the entire text for answers to questions rather than be forced to depend on the paper document's index (although a professionally done index can be an extremely valuable tool).

■ The online book is always handy, whereas a printed book may stray from the user's shelf (although online books may disappear from disk drives and networks).

Just make sure that users can print out desired sections of online manuals—text is often studied on commuter transportation and in other venues.

RULE OF THUMB   Put online what is done online, put on paper what is done off-line (away from the computer).

For example, setting up a computer or installing a piece of software is definitely an off-line project. Until the computer or software is set up, the user can't access any online instructions. (A possibly apochryphal story says that Apple Computer once started their online setup instructions with, "Remove the computer from the packing box ....")

But detailed domain information probably also falls into the off-line category. The concepts behind certain types of accounting practices or new structured programming techniques, for example, are best studied off-line. However, online help can and should state which of two formulas the program uses for an accounting procedure. It can and should include code samples that programmers can copy into their own applications.

Technical communicators have developed a variety of analysis and development techniques for task-oriented online help, including chunking, minimalist documents, and Information Mapping. Get professional help.

HOW TO WRITE COMMAND-REFERENCE HELP In general, use the same format as the development system or environment with which your users are familiar. For example, if you're documenting an API for C++ programs, match the style of the printed C++ documentation.

However, if there is no good model or if you feel the model is insufficient, *Developing Online Help for Windows* contains a useful section on command topics (Boggan, Farkas, Welinske 1993, 56–61).

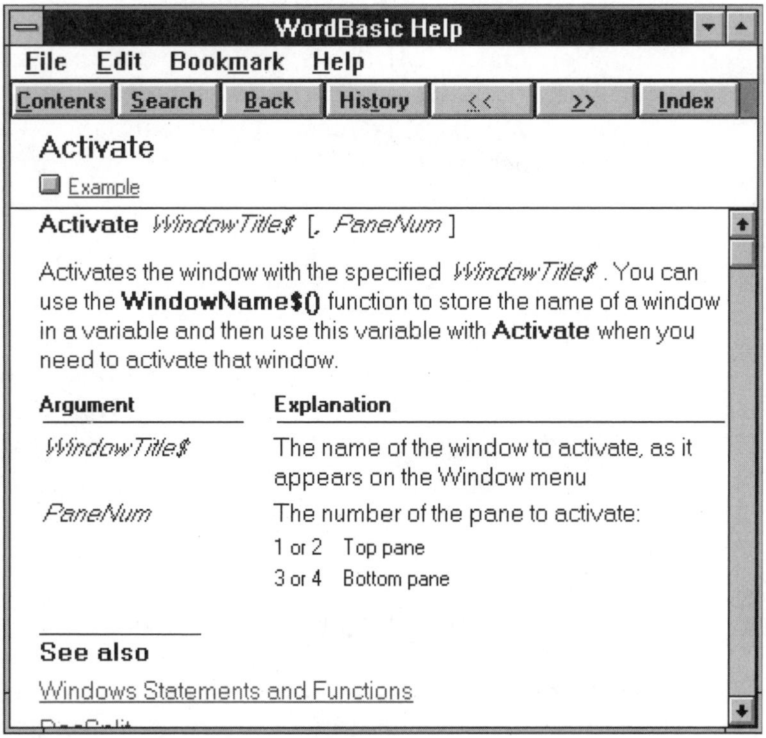

Figure 122

Word Basic help in an "API documentation" style (from Microsoft Word for Windows 6).

Hint: Include code samples that users can copy into their own programs and adjust for their own purposes.

HYPERTEXT GUIDELINES Hypertext is good for jumping to another piece of information (site, page, paragraph, etc.). In help systems, hyperlinks are indicated with underlines and sometimes also with a color change. Color is good as a secondary signal, but keep in mind that colored lettering has less contrast than black and white lettering. For best visibility, the colored words should be a larger point size or bolded.

(Your choices may be constrained by your help development system, however.)

In Web browsers, text links are usually indicated with underlines. Graphics can be used to create hyperlink pushbuttons. However, the linking methodology is the same—the graphic file's name is surrounded with a cross-reference instruction.

In either case, since underlines now mean "link," don't use underlines for anything *but* links. If you use an underline for highlighting (instead of italics, for example), users who try to select it, unsuccessfully, will think the "link" is broken.

Note that HTML (Web-based) help does not, so far, support pop-up information, definitions, or notes. Instead, links take users to a completely new page, frame, or browser instance. Then they have to get back somehow. As HTML help matures, pop-ups will no doubt be added to the toolkits.

Usability Tests

See Appendix A in this book, as well as *Managing Your Documentation Projects* (Hackos 1994, chapter 20) for types of usability tests appropriate for online help. See also *Human Factors for Technical Communicators* (Coe, 1996).

HYPERTEXT TESTING   Test that users recognize the underline and color change (if any) as indicating a hyperlink.

Test that users can find their way back to their starting points. Hypertext systems such as Web browsers or online help systems have navigation buttons (Home, Back, History, and so on). See if users use those buttons without prompting, and what other strategies they devise to move through the document (use a "talk aloud" protocol).

Test help strategies: In many help systems, links can bring up either entirely different pages or short definition boxes that stay up only as long as the user continues to press the mouse button. The link indicators may or may not look different. Your technical writers can develop a layout strategy that prevents surprises—for example, they may define a rule that "any link in the body of the text is a definition; any link in a See Also section jumps to another topic."

See Also

Online Help, Context-Sensitive; Online Help, Procedural; Status-Bar Messages; Tooltips; Wizard.

Palette

A specialized, non-modal, movable dialog box containing mouse-accessed tools.

Good For

▪ Quickly accessing related operations that are primarily done with a mouse or pointing device—for example, drawing circles, erasing, and filling areas with color (Figure 124).

Figure 123

Palette from RightPaint by ICOM. Note the clever in-context draw and erase buttons—the pencil point and the eraser.

Not Good For

■ Operations that are done more efficiently from the keyboard.

Design Guidelines

Palettes usually float in the window, often at one side. They can normally be repositioned to move them out of the user's way. Otherwise, they are functionally the same as toolbars. (For more design hints, see Toolbar.)

Palettes usually require many pictorial labels for the buttons. See Iconic Label for detailed design information.

HIDDEN FUNCTIONALITY   If you let users change palette button settings by holding down or doubleclicking on a button (Figure 124), make sure that users know the feature exists. Alex Leavens tells a story onhimself:

> In my icon editor, ICE/Works, there is a series of tools you can adjust the settings of, such as the Pencil tool. You do this by double-clicking on the tool, which brings up a dialog box where you adjust the tool's features. However, if you never double-click on a tool, you probably don't know this feature is available. In earlier versions of the program, I didn't have a menu method of accessing these tool setting features. As a result, people kept asking me to put in features that already existed. Finally, I got wise, and put in menu entries for these features, too, so people just browsing the menu structures could find them. (1994, 59)

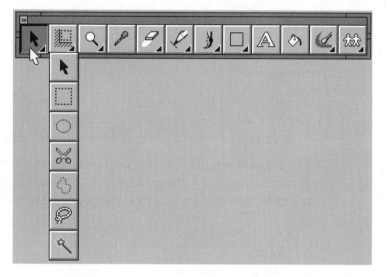

Figure 124

A set of pick tools dragged out of the CorelDraw "pick" palette button. Note the triangular indicators on the buttons that have additional settings or options.

If you want users to fly along in your application, make everything visible and make it visible in more than one way. As Jared Spool of User Interface Engineering has said, "The more different ways you can get the most important functionality to your users, the more likely they'll find it to use" (Spool 1995).

GROUPING BUTTONS   Horton (1994, 132) suggests grouping palette buttons (or icons in general) into meaningful categories and subcategories. He offers some guidelines, based on experience:

- *Involve users from the start.*   Ask them to help you pick the categories and subcategories. Let them suggest names for the buttons. (See Appendix A for information about sorting tests.)

- *Group by task.*   Create categories based on user tasks rather than the software's architecture.

- *Be practical.*   Don't be pedantic. If a button appears to fit into more than one group, duplicate it.

Usability Tests

Collect usage information on menu items, palette buttons, and toolbar buttons:

- Often-accessed menu items may be good candidates for toolbars.
- Often-accessed dialog boxes (or menus) that contain settings or groups of related tools may be good candidates for palettes.

Note that when half the users often access the dialog boxes or menus and half never access them, consider creating dialog boxes or menus that can be turned into palettes by tearing them off.

See Also

Iconic Label; Toolbar; Tooltip.

Pointer

A picture on the desktop that shows the mouse's location. (Think of the pointer as an icon for mouse movement.)

Good For

- Indicating where the current keyboard input focus is (Figure 125).

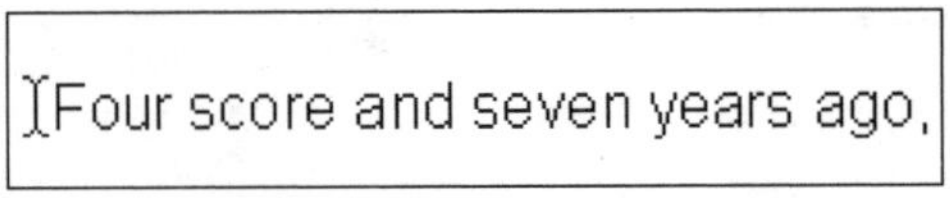

Figure 125

Text pointer in a document.

```
I Four score and seven years ago,
```

- Providing feedback on the current mode (Figure 126).

Figure 126

Wait pointer.

Design Guidelines

Pointers have two feedback functions:

- Indicating where the mouse is by appearing on the desktop at a particular location.

- Indicating the current mode by changing the pointer shape.

Changing the shape "has the great advantage that it cannot be overlooked by the user; the visual indication appears exactly where the user's attention is focused" (Zetie 1995, 177).

Pointers have three basic styles, matching the three basic modes:

- Arrow pointer for general control mode. (No other mode is in effect.)

- Specialized pointers for action modes—for example, the I-beam pointer for text-editing mode, an eraser pointer for erasure mode, and so on.

- Watch or hourglass pointer for system-busy or "wait" mode (for waits of less than 5 seconds).

The development platforms and kits offer standard pointers for system-busy, general control, and many common action modes. Use these pointers whenever possible instead of creating your own. For cross-platform comparisons, see Marcus (1995, 224) and Fowler and Stanwick (1995, 70–75).

HOT SPOTS   Pointers have two components: a visual representation (arrow, question mark, and so on) and a hot spot. The hot spot is an area inside the pointer that marks the exact location on the desktop that will be affected by the user's next mouse action (Microsoft 1995a, 31).

If you design your own pointers, place the hot spot in one of these two locations:

- At the upper left corner of the image. If you create an atypical pointer (a dinosaur or a banana, for example), point the head or top of the image to the upper left and put the hotspot in the image's head or topmost point (Figure 127).

■ Where the user would typically expect it. For example, the hot spot for a cross-hair pointer is logically at the intersection of the two lines (IBM 1992, 378).

Figure 127

The hotspot is on the fish's nose.

In short, the hot spot should "feel" obvious. Put the hot spot at the tip of an arrow, not at the blunt end. Put the hot spot on the vertical member of an I-beam pointer, not off to one side or at the bottom or top.

Note that "wait" and "do not" pointers may have default hot spots, but these hot spots do not have any effect.

DESIGNING POINTERS   Following are recommendations for pointer images:

1. Make sure the pointer is visible at all times, contrasts well with the background, and is big enough to locate and see easily. If there is more than one window or dialog box on the screen, make sure the pointer is on top of all of them.

2. Display only one pointer on the screen at a time. (You can have both a cursor and a pointer, however.)

3. The shape of the pointer should give some hint as to its purpose (much as an icon does).

4. The shape should be easy to see and recognize. Users may be unable to understand the pointer if the image is too small and the details are too fine or if the image is not familiar enough (see Figure 128).

Figure 128

Good and bad "wait" pointers.

5. Avoid visual clutter. A pointer is a small element on a large screen. If you cram too much detail into a tiny space, the users won't be

able to figure out what they are looking at. A watch is fine for a wait pointer, but if you include a sweep second hand, day and date function, and a moon-phase indicator, there is probably too much clutter for a successful pointer. See Figure 129.

Figure 129

Clutter in a pointer.

Good   **Poor**

6. Reuse images. If you use a picture of a pencil to indicate the drawing tool on a palette, use the same picture for the pointer.

7. Once an image is defined, do not use the same image for more than one purpose.

8. Do not create new shapes for already defined standard functions. Use your platform's standard pointers whenever possible.

9. Maintain the pointer's size in all screen locations and while it is moving. When you define a number of pointers with different shapes, keep their sizes similar.

10. Do not make the pointer or cursor so large that it obscures screen objects. Note that you can remove the pointer once the user has started working with the object. For example, Microsoft's Intelli-Type Manager lets users set an option that makes the pointer disappear as soon as the user starts typing. It reappears when he or she touches the mouse.

11. If you create animated pointers, make sure that they don't distract the user or restrict his or her ability to interact with the application. On client-server systems, animation can be a problem if it causes a lot of network traffic.

TOO MUCH FEEDBACK If the window contains many different modal areas and the pointer changes as the mouse crosses each area, the pointer will seem to flash when the user travels across the screen quickly. Microsoft suggests adding a timer to the pointer so that the shape changes only if the user pauses for a set period of time (Microsoft 1995a, 394).

WARPING THE POINTER: ARGUMENTS FOR AND AGAINST
"Warping the pointer" means automatically changing the location of the pointer based on some system action—for example, whenever the user opens a new dialog box, putting the pointer on the dialog box's default button.

The Motif guidelines argue against this behavior: "Warping the pointer is confusing to users, and reduces their sense of control. Also, warping the pointer can cause problems for users of absolute location pointing devices (like graphics tablets). Graphics tablets map pointer device locations to absolute screen locations; so, if the pointer is warped, the pointer loses synchronization with the pointing device, making some screen locations impossible to reach" (OSF 1993, 2–10).

Reducing users' control of their systems is something to be avoided. On the other hand, having the pointer jump into the current dialog box can be a time-saver for users who prefer to avoid the mouse (touch typists, for example). The key is to ask your users which they prefer—let them try warped and unwarped pointers and select the interaction they like better. If the results are mixed, let users turn the warping on and off.

Usability Tests

When you create pointers, make sure that users recognize the shapes (for example, "pencil") and uses ("drawing"). You can run paper and pencil tests in the early design phases.

Make sure that the pointers stand out from the backgrounds, don't flash, and are sized consistently, even when you change the shapes. Give users navigational tasks and watch for problems and difficulties.

If you warp the pointer, test user reactions.

See Also

Cursor; Iconic Label (for help picking the right image); Progress Indicator (for situations in which the user must wait).

Progress Indicator

Pointers and messages used to offer feedback for ongoing processes.

Good For

■ Indicating delays of more than five seconds (Figure 130).

Figure 130
Typical wait
pointers.

■ Showing progress toward a goal (Figure 131).

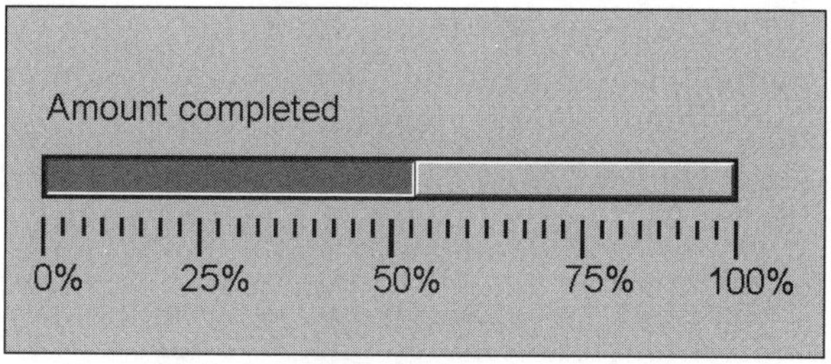

Figure 131
Progress-indicator
bar.

Amount completed

0%   25%   50%   75%   100%

■ By adding a pushbutton, letting users stop or pause the operation
and regain control of their systems.

Not Good For

■ Delays of less than five seconds. Use system-busy pointers for delays of one to five seconds.

Design Guidelines

Research indicates that, while people can adapt to working with slower
response times, they are generally dissatisfied with software response
times of more than two seconds (Schneiderman 1992, 288).

The reason is that humans can hold information in short-term memory for no more than 10 to 15 seconds at a time. As response time stretches beyond 10 to 15 seconds, remembering what you were trying to do becomes increasingly difficult, possibly because the set of steps in short-term memory has been disrupted and must be reloaded (Galitz 1994, 432)..

However, acceptable response times differ by the type of task:

- Typing, cursor motion, or mouse selection: 50–150 milliseconds.
- Simple tasks such as scrolling or browsing: less than 1 second.
- Data entry and data searches: 1–4 seconds.
- Complex tasks such as calculations, saving documents or records, and logging on or initialization: 8–30 seconds (Schneiderman 1992, 297; Galitz 1993, 50).

Whenever a process takes more than one second, show a wait pointer (Figure 131). Wait pointers are good from one to five seconds. After five seconds, however, users think that the system is hung and will try to cancel the operation. If the process normally takes more than five seconds, add an elapsed-time message, a percent-complete message, or a progress-indicator bar (Galitz 1994, 433–434).

ELAPSED-TIME MESSAGES When the user needs to know exactly how long a process will take ("Do I have time for a cup of coffee?"), add an elapsed-time message. For example:

Expected backup time: 20:10 minutes
Elapsed time: 08:48 minutes

Or:

Time remaining: 11 minutes

These messages can appear in the status bar or in their own message dialog boxes.

PERCENT-COMPLETE MESSAGES If other methods of showing progress are too slow, too memory-intensive, or too complicated for a particular application, use a simple percent-complete message, updated every few seconds. For example:

20% complete

These messages can appear in the status bar or in their own message dialog boxes.

RECORDS-PROCESSED MESSAGES   An alternative to the percent-complete message when the total number of records is unknown is "number of records processed." In large databases or high-volume network transactions, you can't calculate a percentage because you don't know how many records are in the set (not without wasting a lot of time looking for end-of-file markers). But you can at least provide an incremental frequency count so that users know that the system is working.

PROGRESS-INDICATOR BAR   A progress-indicator bar is a long rectangular bar (horizontal or vertical) that starts out empty but is filled as the operation proceeds (Figure 132).

Using a color or shade of gray, fill a horizontal bar from left to right. Fill a vertical bar from bottom to top (like a thermometer or like pouring water in a glass).

For readability, avoid putting text (other than a percentage) inside the bar.

STATUS BAR OR DIALOG BOX?   Progress indicators usually appear in their own message dialog boxes, but they can appear in the status bar. To decide between the two locations, consider how modal the process is. If it is running in the background, it rarely takes much time, or it is not very important, then use the status bar. Printing in background, for example, can be effectively tracked using the status bar.

If, on the other hand, the process requires regular attention, uses many system resources, or prevents users from accessing other parts of your application, you probably want to use a dialog box. Installation programs, for example, require dialog boxes.

TITLES   According to the Bellcore Design Guide (1994, 5–9), the rules for a progress-indicator dialog-box title are:

Common User Access	parent window name—action or situation
Motif	action or situation only
Windows	application name

INTERRUPTING A PROCESS   As a designer, one of the most polite things you can do is to let users break out of a time-consuming process:

- To interrupt the process, use Pause and Resume buttons.
- To end the process and return the window or data to its original state, use a Cancel button.
- To stop at the current point in the process, but retain any changes that may have been made so far, use a Stop button (Bellcore 1994, 5–139; Marcus 1995, 227).

WHEN IT REALLY TAKES A LONG TIME   If an operation is very time-consuming, try these suggestions:

- Consider breaking the operation into subtasks and providing progress indicators (plus interruption pushbuttons, if possible) for each subtask (Galitz 1997, 556).
- Support multi-tasking: Do not block access to other applications on the desktop and try not to block access to other processes within your own application. Note: If you allow multi-tasking within your application, you might want to indicate that a process is running in background using your platform's "background processing" pointer—for example, an arrow pointer with a small hourglass to the right (Microsoft 1995a, 30).
- When you allow multi-tasking or background operations, display a notification message when the operation is finished.

Usability Tests

During high-fidelity prototyping or acceptance testing, listen for comments indicating that the participants think the system has hung (the progress indicators appeared too slowly) or that nothing happened (the progress indicators came and went too quickly). The timings you chose for the appearance of the system-busy pointer and the progress indicators may be wrong.

For very long operations, watch for "the waiting dance"—users start tapping their fingers, humming tunelessly, rolling the mouse back and forth. Also listen for statements like, "Ah, the computer's back.... I don't remember what I was doing." The dance and the memory failure both indicate that the wait was too long. Try breaking the process into subtasks or allow multi-tasking.

See Also

Pointer; Status Bar.

Pushbutton

A control that starts an action or opens or closes a dialog box.

Good For

- Starting frequent or critical actions. Pushbuttons show users what actions they can take (Figure 132).

Figure 132

A set of pushbuttons from the Compuserve Information Manager toolbar.

- Navigating between windows and dialog boxes (Figure 133 and Figure 134).

Figure 133

Internal navigation: The buttons on the right close this dialog box and open others (except for Add>>, which opens an expanding panel).

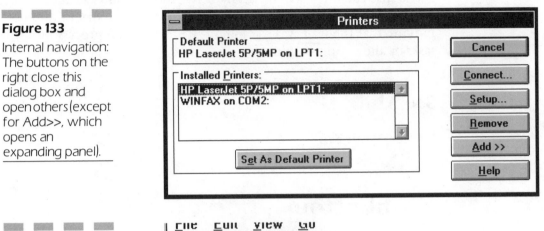

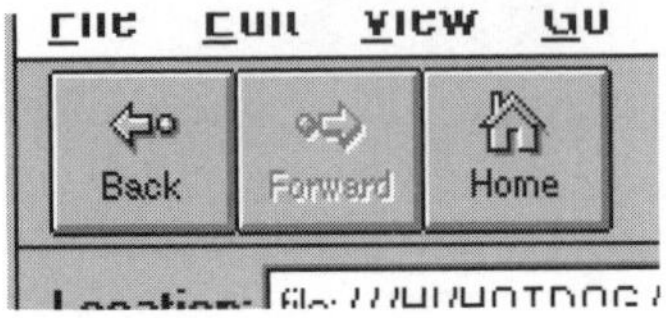

Figure 134

External navigation: These Netscape pushbuttons let users move from one Internet location to another —from one side of the world to the other, in some cases.

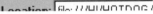

Not Good For

- Setting individual parameters—use radio buttons or check boxes instead.
- Options that affect the entire application. Put these options on menus.

Design Guidelines

Pushbuttons are used for small numbers of commands or actions. They are attached to a specific dialog box or section of a window. When pushbuttons are used on palettes and toolbars, they usually have pictorial labels. See Iconic Label for more information about these types of labels.

LABELING PUSHBUTTONS   In general, a word label should be either a verb describing the action (Save) or a noun that matches the title of the dialog box or window that the pushbutton opens (Paragraph Format).

In *The Cognitive Walkthrough Method,* Nielsen and Mack say that users often follow a "label-following" strategy. They will select a button or menu option if the label matches the description they have in mind for the task (1994, 112).

For instance, a user who wants to print a document is more likely to select a pushbutton with the label "Print" or "Document" (or a picture of a printer or document) than one with the label "More" or "Output."

KEYBOARD SHORTCUTS   Most of the platform guidelines suggest adding mnemonics to pushbuttons. See Keyboard Shortcuts: Mnemonic and Accelerator for details.

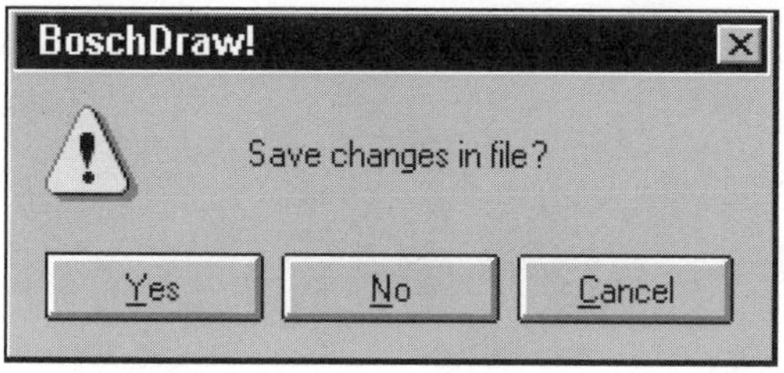

Figure 135

Mnemonics on
pushbuttons.

Also make sure that users can navigate between buttons with tabs, especially in intensive data-entry applications. Data-entry operators are generally touch-typists who prefer the keyboard to the mouse.

ACTION INDICATORS

Act up	When a pushbutton starts an action, use no punctuation or special characters
Open . . .	When a pushbutton opens a dialog box, use an ellipsis after the button name
Expand >>	To indicate that the dialog box expands, label the pushbutton with two right angle-brackets

See Dialog Box, Expanding, for more information about expanding dialog boxes.

DEFAULT PUSHBUTTON   Choose one pushbutton on the dialog box or window as the default—if the user presses Enter, that pushbutton is invoked. Make the most important or common action the default. For example, Print would be the natural default on a Print dialog box (Weinschenk, Jamar, and Yeo 1997, 192–193). Do not use a potentially destructive option (Delete, for example) as a default, even if it is the most common or important action, *unless* you test it very carefully with users.

Indicate the default pushbutton using your platform's guidelines. For example, the Windows 95 guidelines require a bold outline (Figure 136) around the button (Microsoft 1995, 184). After the pushbutton has been pressed once, Microsoft also adds a broken-line border inside the box.

Figure 136

"Find Next" is the default button in this dialog box.

Changing the default   You can change the default button as the user interacts with the window. If the user picks a button that isn't the default, this button can become the default until the user selects another pushbutton or until she selects an entry field, a radio button, or other component, at which point the default returns to the original pushbutton.

No default pushbutton   Some applications or sections of applications use Enter for other purposes. If the entire window uses Enter for other purposes—for example, a form-based data-entry application in which users move between fields using Enter—then do not define a default button. If part of the window uses Enter for other purposes—multiline text fields, for example—then temporarily remove the default outline from the pushbutton. Once the user has moved out of the component, you can restore the default aspect to the button (Microsoft 1995, 184).

CAPITALIZATION   The Windows 3.1 style guide calls for headline-style capitalization for labels of more than one word. The Windows 95 and OS/2 guidelines call for sentence-style capitalization for labels. Note that, for menus, pushbuttons, and tabs, Windows 95 requires headline-style capitalization (Microsoft 1995, 387–388). See Label for more information.

SIZING PUSHBUTTONS   In general, use the same size for every pushbutton in a related group of pushbuttons. For example, if the button labels are OK, Cancel, and Find Flights…, make all three pushbuttons as wide as Find Fonts….

  If there are many buttons and their sizes vary dramatically—for example, OK, Set, Fly vs. Cancel, Find Flights…, and Register Flights…—create two sizes. This strategy gives you approximately the right size for all buttons without creating too many sizes, which tends to be distracting (Weinschenk, Jamar, and Yeo 1997, 184–185).

INTERNATIONALIZATION AND PUSHBUTTON SIZES   If you are going to internationalize your application (or even if you think it might change often for some reason), put the labels in resources files. Let the buttons resize themselves dynamically—labels will expand by 30 to 200 percent when translated from English into nearly any other natural language. See Label for more information.

  When you can, create or use buttons that resize themselves dynamically. For buttons that cannot be resized automatically, keep their dimension data in a separate resource file. Then the dimensions can be modified as needed without forcing you to recompile the program (VanDevender 1993, 5).

Watch the vertical letter size   Another potential pitfall is vertical letter size (Figure 137). In many languages, the accents on uppercase letters rise above the usual ascender line and descenders fall below the usual descender line. Make sure that you leave enough *vertical* room to accommodate non-Roman lettering systems (Apple Computer 1992, 24).

Figure 137
Vertical font
boundaries.

Highest ascent

Ascender

Base line

Descender

Lowest descent

POSITIONING PUSHBUTTONS The rules for locating pushbuttons and other controls are:

1. Pushbuttons that affect only part of the dialog box should be located inside that part, at the bottom or right side (in countries where text is read from left to right).

2. Put pushbuttons that affect the entire dialog box (OK, Cancel) at the bottom or right side of the dialog box.

3. Whenever possible, place buttons in this order: affirmative buttons used to save any changes and leave the dialog box (OK); negative buttons to cancel changes and leave the window (Cancel); buttons unique to that window (Weinschenk and Yao 1995, 11). For a set of horizontal buttons, OK is at the left and the unique buttons are at the right. For a set of vertical buttons, OK is at the top and the unique buttons are at the bottom.

4. Whether the pushbuttons appear at the bottom or the right depends on the flow of movement through the dialog box. For example, if users will move horizontally through entry areas, put the buttons to the right. If they will move vertically, put the buttons on the bottom. See Figure 138 and Figure 139.

Pushbutton

193

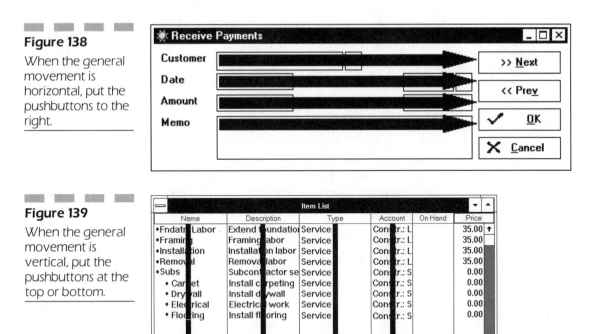

Figure 138

When the general movement is horizontal, put the pushbuttons to the right.

Figure 139

When the general movement is vertical, put the pushbuttons at the top or bottom.

In an expanded dialog box, position pushbuttons wherever they were positioned in the unexpanded version. In other words, if the pushbuttons appear at the bottom of the unexpanded dialog box, put Close and any additional buttons on the bottom of the expanded pane.

ALIGNMENT If you have a set of vertically arranged pushbuttons, left-align them (make sure they're all the same width). See Figure 139.

For horizontally arranged pushbuttons (Figure 140), the various platforms have different alignment rules:

- *Windows 95.* Right-justify.
- *Windows 3.x and Motif.* Center.
- *OS/2.* Left-justify.

What if you develop for more than one platform? Here is Bogo Vatovec's approach (1997):

> Our application is being developed for Motif and Windows 95/NT environments. Both style guides are very different so it is really difficult to follow both. We took the King Solomon's approach by agreeing that a GUI running in Motif must not break explicit Motif guidelines. If it doesn't, we choose between NT and Motif, using the ones that are better. Therefore, we do not break any explicit rules but still try to find the best of both. In cases when we really disagree with an explicit rule, we vote. In general, we are more inclined to follow Windows 95 guidelines as there are more and more users using Windows 95 and Motif is slowly becoming old.

RULES FOR GROUPING   Galitz suggests grouping pushbuttons as follows (1997 331–332):

- Order pushbuttons logically—for example, by frequency of use, sequence of use, or importance.
- Keep related buttons grouped together. However, to avoid activating potentially destructive buttons by mistake, separate them from frequently selected buttons. (Mouse slips are fairly common.)
- Always put the same buttons that appear on different windows in the same locations. For example, don't put OK and Search in that order on one dialog box, then Search and OK on another.
- For mutually exclusive options, do not use one pushbutton with a label that toggles. Instead, use two pushbuttons with labels clearly describing the two actions. (See Check Box for a discussion of this problem.)

What if your platform is the Internet and your buttons represent different hierarchical levels? Here is one solution:

> The standard we've adopted is that the buttons are arranged in order of application hierarchy. Therefore, the button on the far left represents "Home" or the highest level back and the button on the far right represents the next level down. (Left side equals going backward and right side equals going forward.) (Ruby 1997)

Number pads   Note that there are two types of number pads: telephone and calculator. Telephone pads have 1, 2, and 3 at the top and 0 at the bottom. Calculator pads have 7, 8, and 9 at the top and 0 at the bottom.[6]

Occasionally you see an application in which the developer picked the wrong order (and no one noticed the error, so it went out to customers that way). Don't let this happen to you!

POSITIONING IN TABBED DIALOG BOXES   Usability experts have noticed that users are often unclear about when changes to settings in a tabbed dialog box take effect (Robinson 1996, 1). For example:

- Do the changes take effect when you move from tab to tab, when you click OK, the next time you start the program, when you click Apply, or when you close the tabbed dialog box?

- If you take some action on a particular page, such as adding a group of users to a network, are the new users saved when you click the Add button or are they saved when you click OK?

Use a consistent method for saving changes to the settings in all tabbed dialog boxs in a product. Avoid doing an auto-save in one tab dialog (changes in one tab are saved when you click on another tab) and manual save (clicking on the OK button) in others.

Also, researchers find that users are most satisfied with explicit information about effects. For example, adding an explicit Apply Settings button means that users no longer have to guess that clicking OK or switching tabs applies their changes. Although the Apply button might add an extra interaction, it eliminates unnecessary cognition. The idea, as ever, is to let users think about *their* tasks, not yours.

Saving the page versus the dialog box   Another source of confusion is what OK, Cancel, or Apply actually affect—the entire dialog box or just the current page? Make effects obvious by positioning your pushbuttons inside or outside the page as needed:

---

6. According to a *New Scientist* note (van Someren 1995), the reason for the difference is historical: "Mechanical adding machines, based on rotating wheels, always have the 0 button adjacent to the 1 button. By convention, most old adding machines had the numbers increasing in value from the bottom and this may be a hangover from when the machines had levers on the wheels rather than buttons. When the numbers were put on to a pad arranged as a three by three grid with one left over, the order of the numbers, as far as possible, kept the same [order]. On a rotary telephone dial, the 0 comes adjacent to the 9 because a 0 in the telephone number is signalled by 10 pulses on the line. When telephones acquired push buttons in a grid, the ordering of the buttons was carried over from the old telephone dial."

- Place pushbuttons that affect all the pages outside the margins of the tab page (Figure 140).

- Place pushbuttons that affect only the page inside the page margins (Wilson 1997a).

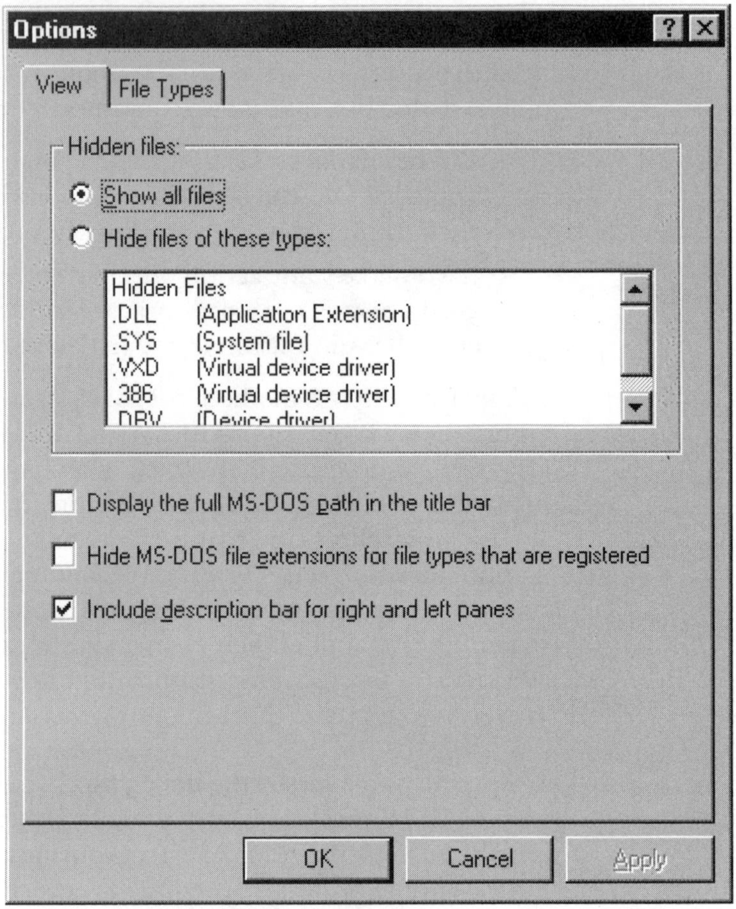

Figure 140

The pushbuttons are placed outside the tabs to indicate that they affect the entire dialog box.

Options

View | File Types

Hidden files:

○ Show all files

○ Hide files of these types:

```
Hidden Files
.DLL      (Application Extension)
.SYS      (System file)
.VXD      (Virtual device driver)
.386      (Virtual device driver)
.DRV      (Device driver)
```

☐ Display the full MS-DOS path in the title bar

☐ Hide MS-DOS file extensions for file types that are registered

☑ Include description bar for right and left panes

OK | Cancel | Apply

INDICATING UNAVAILABILITY To indicate that a pushbutton is unavailable, the platform guidelines say to gray out the label and make sure that the button is unresponsive to user input *except* for a help request. Help should always be available.

However, note that usability expert Jared Spool says that users hate grayed-out buttons and menu items because they never know how to ungray them. He also offers a solution—anticipate and solve the problem for the user. Don't leave it to the user to figure out what he or she is supposed to do.

> In some recent testing, we found that users often tried to click on buttons before they selected the objects those buttons were supposed to help with. We found that by changing the greyed out button to an error message, our users succeeded more often.

> But in most cases, we could go a step further. We could eliminate an error message by replacing it with a dialog box. Here's an example:

> Suppose you have a collection of data elements and a Print Description button. Normally, the button would be grayed out until one or more elements were selected. In our first change, we never grayed out the button. Instead, upon pressing the button with nothing selected, the user would get a message explaining that they need to select something first.

> However, in our second change, we displayed a list box filled with the relevant data elements and a prompt to choose the ones they wanted to print. This way, whether they select the elements first or not, the function still works.

> We've found this strategy to work frequently. (It ends the old object-action vs. action-object debate.) Users tell us the software seems more intuitive. (Spool 1997)

BE CONSISTENT   Consistency is, unfortunately, not as easy to come by as one might hope. It can mean:

- Using common buttons the same way everyone else does.
- Matching the user's idea about how GUIs, in general, work.
- Matching the user's conceptual model of the business task.
- Using the same button for the same function and different buttons for different functions across all parts of the application.

The difficulty is that these definitions can cancel each other out. Following are discussions of each definition.

FOLLOW INDUSTRY STANDARDS   Table 17 shows the industry consensus on a few of the most common buttons. See the *Bellcore Design Guide for Multiplatform Graphical User Interfaces* (1994, 5-138–5-141) for additional buttons.

TABLE 17	Button	Usage	Wrong Usage
Industry Consensus on Common Buttons	Apply	Make changes but leave the window or dialog box open. The Apply button lets a user see the effect of a choice and undo it or add to it if desired.	Do not also close the dialog box. Use OK instead. Do not use as a synonym for Save. Apply is associated with software settings, while Save is associated with the more serious matter of saving actual work.
	Cancel	Cancel any unapplied user settings and close the dialog box. In message boxes with Yes, No, Cancel responses, Cancel should stop the current activity and return to the immediate past state of the software.	Do not use: • To close dialog boxes in which the user made no changes or could not have made changes (for example, a view-only dialog box). Use Close instead. • As a synonym for Quit (or Quit as a synonym for Cancel), since Quit or Exit mean "Leave the application." • To cancel multiple levels of dialog boxes. The user may forget the changes she made in lower levels and cancel them all, mistakenly believing that she is canceling only her most recent changes. Do usability testing to find a better way to apply and cancel hidden settings.
	Close	Close a dialog box when the user: • Has applied changes with an Apply button and now wants to leave the dialog box. • Has made no changes. • Can't make changes (the dialog box is view-only)..	Do not use to cancel unapplied changes. Use Cancel instead.
	OK	Confirm a user's setting and close the dialog box.	Do not use for: • Operations that accept the user settings but don't close the dialog box. Use Apply instead. • Operations that cancel user settings. OK must apply the changes.

Just to prove that developers often ignore or don't know that there is a consensus, Figure 141, Figure 142, and Figure 143 show some examples of button mistakes.

Figure 141

This Apply button in Microsoft Word for Windows 6.0 applies the changes but also closes the window.

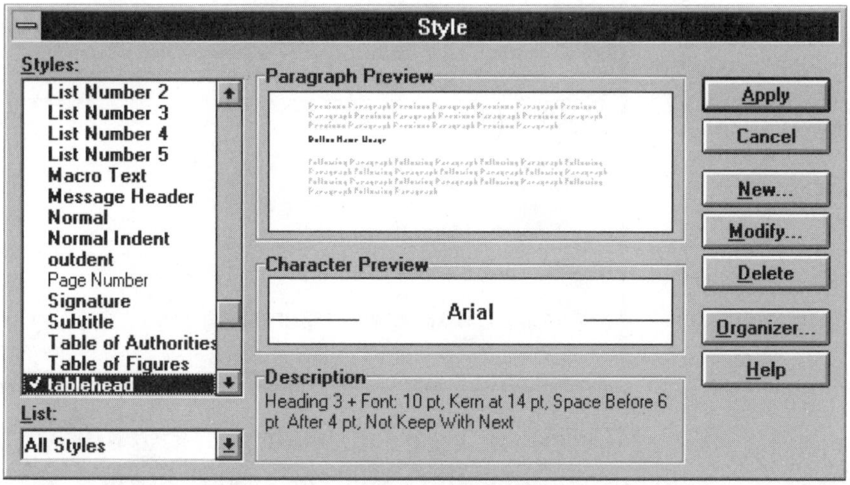

Style

Styles:
- List Number 2
- List Number 3
- List Number 4
- List Number 5
- Macro Text
- Message Header
- Normal
- Normal Indent
- outdent
- Page Number
- Signature
- Subtitle
- Table of Authorities
- Table of Figures
- ✓ tablehead

List:
All Styles

Paragraph Preview

Character Preview

Arial

Description
Heading 3 + Font: 10 pt, Kern at 14 pt, Space Before 6 pt After 4 pt, Not Keep With Next

Apply | Cancel | New... | Modify... | Delete | Organizer... | Help

Figure 142

This OK button in Netscape 2.0 saves changes to the preferences in memory, but not on disk. In most applications, settings are saved automatically, without even confirmation messages. Netscape, however, required that users explicitly save their preferences on a drop-down menu.

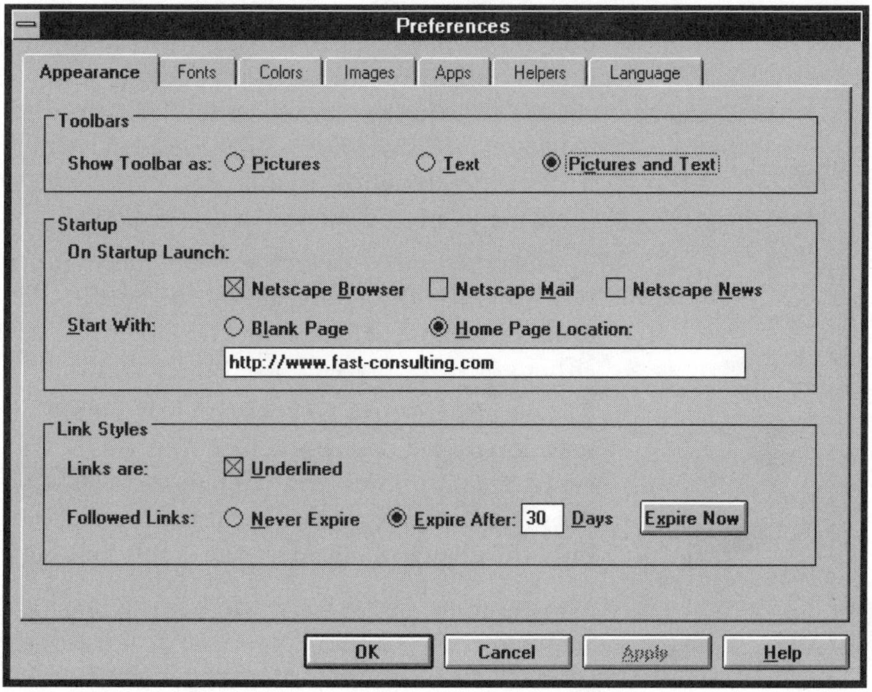

Preferences

Appearance | Fonts | Colors | Images | Apps | Helpers | Language

Toolbars
Show Toolbar as: ○ Pictures   ○ Text   ⦿ Pictures and Text

Startup
On Startup Launch:
☒ Netscape Browser ☐ Netscape Mail ☐ Netscape News
Start With: ○ Blank Page ⦿ Home Page Location:
http://www.fast-consulting.com

Link Styles
Links are: ☒ Underlined
Followed Links: ○ Never Expire ⦿ Expire After: 30 Days [Expire Now]

OK | Cancel | Apply | Help

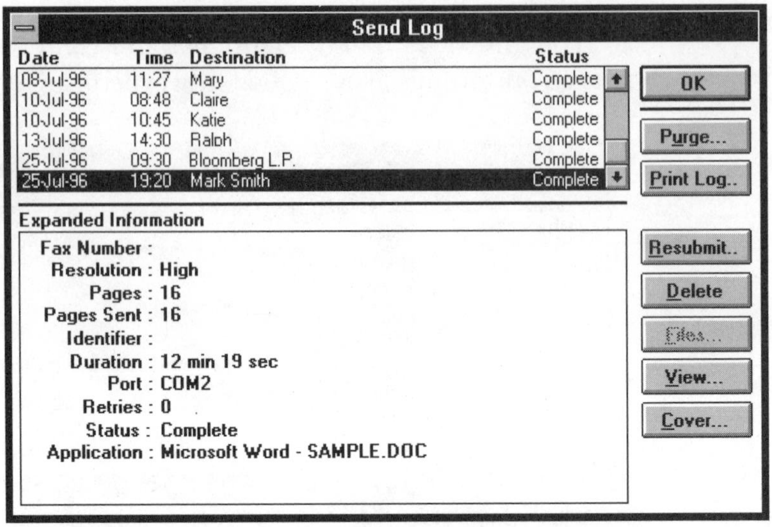

Figure 143

This OK button from WinFax LITE 3.0 doesn't save anything (there is nothing to save). It simply closes the window. The frightening Purge button appears where the relatively harmless Close or Cancel normally appears.

Date	Time	Destination	Status
08-Jul-96	11:27	Mary	Complete
10-Jul-96	08:48	Claire	Complete
10-Jul-96	10:45	Katie	Complete
13-Jul-96	14:30	Ralph	Complete
25-Jul-96	09:30	Bloomberg L.P.	Complete
25-Jul-96	19:20	Mark Smith	Complete

Send Log

OK — Purge... — Print Log..

Expanded Information

Fax Number :
Resolution : High
Pages : 16
Pages Sent : 16
Identifier :
Duration : 12 min 19 sec
Port : COM2
Retries : 0
Status : Complete
Application : Microsoft Word - SAMPLE.DOC

Resubmit.. — Delete — Files... — View... — Cover...

MATCH THE USER'S IDEA ABOUT HOW GUIS WORK These scenarios demonstrate three kinds of mismatches between developers' and users' ideas about how GUIs work:

The user doesn't see it. The user opens a properties dialog box with three standard buttons—Apply, Cancel, and Help. She makes a change and applies it with Apply. The Cancel button's label changes to Close. She doesn't notice that the label has changed, but even if she had, she doesn't know that Cancel means that she can now reverse the setting only by redoing the selection and pressing Apply again.

The user doesn't know which button to pick. A print-parameters dialog box contains OK, Apply, and Close buttons. The user makes a selection, then pauses. He doesn't know that OK is Apply+Close and that either OK or Apply will save his selection.

The user doesn't know what Cancel will cancel. The user opens a font-selection dialog box containing Apply, OK, and Cancel. She selects a typeface and presses Apply. Then she selects italic. She pauses. She doesn't want italic after all, but will Cancel cancel both changes or only the change made after the Apply but before the Cancel?

The developers who write the underlying code know what is going to happen when the users press one of these buttons. However, the users don't. They also aren't interested in the rules, even the ones just promulgated here. They just want to do their jobs and not think about the software.

To avoid any confusion, usability experts suggest that you be very explicit. Instead of OK, use "[action] & Close"—for example, "Set & Close."

Table 18 presents some other pushbuttons that users don't know how to use, plus summaries of suggestions from usability experts.

MATCH THE USER'S CONCEPTUAL MODEL Some pushbutton labels will be obvious. Others will depend on detailed audience analysis and usability testing. For example, on one of the usability news lists, a writer commented that using the standard Commit and Close might be misunderstood by the stated audience, currency traders:

> I have sympathy for the consistency appeal but would also suggest that the best practice is to use meaningful terms, especially where the user community is fairly narrow. For your users, the action following completion of the form may be to commit the contract (and hence their company) to a legally binding securities trade, the consequences of which run into large amounts of money. In this situation, I suspect the case for the more common application of consistency standards demanding Close or Cancel might be outweighed by
>
> a) the need to preserve high awareness of the consequences of selecting the buttons
>
> b) the specific task-related meaning associated with the terms (e.g., Close might mean closing a position—exercising the option—and Cancel might mean issuing a cancelling instruction to the exchange).
>
> You should probably stick to what you have used or perhaps even go further and say "Commit trade," etc. (Choudhury 1996)

USE THE SAME BUTTONS FOR THE SAME FUNCTIONS The meta-rule: Use the same labels for the same function across all parts of your application and different buttons for different functions. However, what if you have two functions that are similar but not exactly alike? Should you differentiate the two options or lump them together under the same label?

To answer these questions, you need to look at the task. For example, an application had a "Go" option on one window and a "Run" option on another. In application terms, "Go" meant "go to the mainframe and re-

TABLE 18

Not-Yet-Standard
Pushbuttons

Button	Usage	Design Notes
Reset, Defaults	There are two possible definitions: 1 Cancel any changes to the dialog box that have not been applied in this session and restore the settings to their last saved state. 2 Cancel all changes since the software was installed and return to the factory settings. Do careful usability testing to find out which is more appropriate for your users and your application.	Depending on which definition you choose, make sure that you use Reset the same way throughout your application.
Undo, Redo	Use to reverse changes to data (deletions, drag and drops, etc.). Whenever possible, make multiple levels of undo (and redo) available. "The biggest problem I've seen with undo is that users don't always notice problems right away, or if they do, they may attempt to correct the problem themselves before trying undo. With a single level of undo, they're out of luck" (Snyder 1996). Undo is valuable because it lets users explore safely. Safe exploration leads to higher levels of user satisfaction as well as expertise.	Undo may not be necessary for changes to operational modes. For example, changing from normal font to italic font probably doesn't require an undo. On the other hand, users may have trouble guessing which activities can be undone (what the rules are). Letting them undo any type of change is much easier to understand.

Table 18 (cont.)	Button	Usage	Design Notes
Not-Yet-Standard Pushbuttons	VCR Navigation Buttons		

◀◀ ■ ▶ ‖ ▶▶ ▲ ◀ ▶‖

Use to:

- Move through video or audio segments.
- Move from scene to scene through multimedia and CD-ROM applications.

Do not use for:

- Book-oriented applications. Use a page-turning model instead.
- Scrolling through lists and files. Use scroll bars or slide bars instead.

Note: Unless your customers are videophiles or audiophiles, restrict your use of VCR-style buttons to the most common ones— stop (■), play (▶), fast forward (▶▶) and rewind (◀◀).

---

trieve the record I asked you for." "Run" meant "run this calculation." However, as far as the users were concerned, "go" and "run" meant the same thing—"wait for some information to come back from somewhere over the network." Having two different labels for the same operation (in the users' minds) was confusing.

On the other hand, sometimes the difference is important, as Janet Borggren (1995) explained in an online thread about "save" vs. "commit":

> The type of saving must be related to the type of work being performed. If you get this right, it appears so natural that you don't have to think about it.

> For example, you may not have noticed that Windows supports both implicit and explicit saves. Word and Excel make you save explicitly, which gives you the power to decide when you have a draft worth saving. It's great to be able to say, 'This is a workable schedule, I'll save it now and then continue to work on it to see if I can make it better. If not, I'll go back to my first draft.'

However, File Manager doesn't make you click Save after you move a file—the action takes place immediately. This is perfect because my logical unit of work corresponds to one action (moving a file), not a series of actions (creating a schedule, which involves many actions). Think how much you would hate it if you had a Commit button in File Manager *or* automatic saving in Word.

To summarize, when two processes have a significant *business* difference, you may need different labels. If two processes have a *technical* difference but only a small business difference, consider using the same label.

Usability Tests

Use "matching" tests: Create two columns, one with labels, the other with descriptions of actions, and ask users to match the labels to the descriptions. Change the labels until most users match most of the test items correctly (define "most" during your test plan).

On prototypes, ask the users to do or find an item and see whether they pick the right button. For unsuccessful choices, ask them what label they would use. Change the labels between tests until most users pick the right button.

See Also

Radio Buttons, Check Boxes.

Radio Button

A button used to turn mutually exclusive settings on and off. Users can set only one radio button at a time. Radio buttons are usually round (in Windows) or diamond-shaped (in Motif).

Good For

■ Selecting only one setting from two to six possible settings (Figure 144).

Figure 144

Radio buttons.

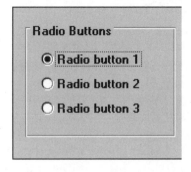

■ Letting users toggle between two states when the states are not opposites or easily inferred from one another (Figure 145).

⊙ Male   ○ Female

Figure 145

A radio-button toggle.

Not Good For

■ More than six or seven settings at a time. Use a single-selection list or a drop-down list box instead.
■ Starting programs or opening dialog boxes. Use pushbuttons instead.
■ Switching between two views of the same data. Use tabbed windows or dialog boxes instead.

Design Guidelines

GROUPING AND ARRANGING RADIO BUTTONS Radio buttons naturally come in groups (except for toggles, described in "Creating a toggle" below). Box or frame each group of related buttons and give each group a descriptive label (Figure 145).

Organize the group by frequency or task order, logically or alphanumerically. See "How to organize lists" in List Box, Multiple-Selection, for additional ideas.

HOW MANY RADIO BUTTONS ARE TOO MANY? When you get more than six settings, switch to a single-selection list. Otherwise, the buttons start taking up too much room on the window or dialog box.

PICK A DEFAULT BUTTON One radio button must always be in selected mode, even when the user first opens the application. As the window's developer, you must pick a default button. Also, since one button must always be on, users cannot choose "none of the above" unless you provide one.

CREATING A TOGGLE Both check boxes and radio buttons can function as toggles. Here, for example, is a typical check box toggle:

☐ Show summary

This is fine for a yes/no, on/off choice. However, what about a toggle like this?

☐ Full duplex

What is the opposite of full duplex? To the uninitiated, probably empty duplex. For modem experts, however, the right answer is half duplex. One solution is to change the label depending on the setting, but that becomes confusing for two reasons (Microsoft 1995a, 138):

■ Changing labels makes the interface seem inconsistent, which is a usability failure.

■ Until the user clicks the button a few times, he or she may not realize that clicking sets the *other* state, not the state shown on the label:

☐ Half duplex   ← First state

☒ Full duplex   ← Second state

You can't solve the problem with two check boxes, since then the user can set both states at the same time or none at all. Rather, the solution is to use two radio buttons:

⊙ Half duplex

○ Full duplex

ARRANGING RADIO BUTTONS You can arrange radio buttons horizontally (in rows) or vertically (in columns). Vertical is better since it's easier to scan—just make sure that you align the buttons.

If you have to use a horizontal arrangement, leave enough space between buttons so that users are not confused about which label goes with which button (Wilson 1997a).

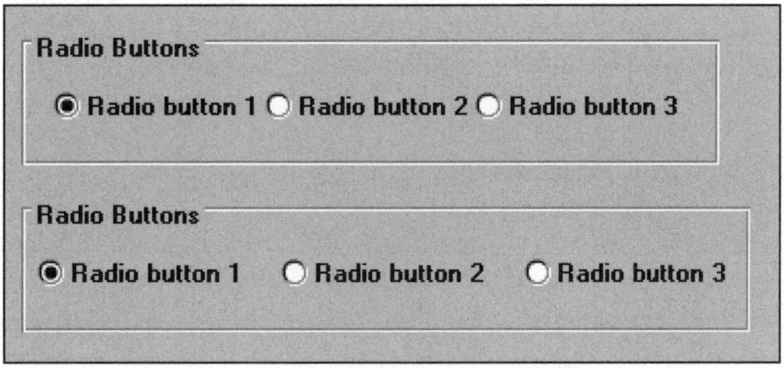

Figure 146

Too close and not too close.

Usability Tests

To find out what the default button should be and whether you need a button meaning "none," first check your specifications and taskflow documentation. Then test the choices with a low-fidelity or high-fidelity prototype. Listen for statements like, "How do I turn off all these buttons?" If you hear, "How do I get the default back?" ask which button should be the default.

See Also

Check Box; Drop-Down List Box; List, Single-Selection.

Scroll Bar

A narrow rectangular area consisting of a scroll area, a scroll box, and arrows or anchors at either end that is used to represent the user's relative position in a document, file, or list. Scroll bars can be vertical or horizontal.

Good For

- Viewing information that is beyond the edge of the scrollable object (list, window, or dialog box).
- With a split bar, letting users see two parts of the same file at the same (Figure 147).

Figure 147

Scroll bars and a split bar.

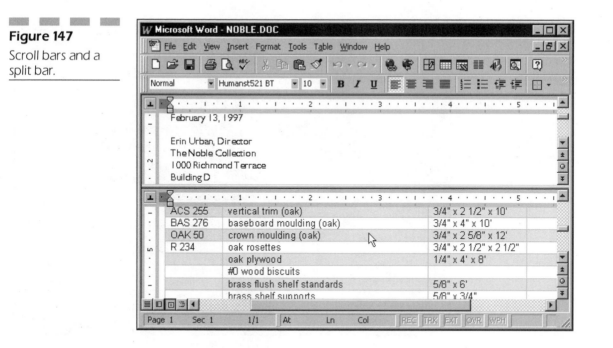

Not Good For

■ Applications that require tiling two or three windows vertically on the screen (Figure 148). The scroll bars take up too much room. Use slide bars instead.

■ Setting values—don't confuse a scroll bar with a slider. See Slider for details.

Figure 148

Too much screen
furniture.

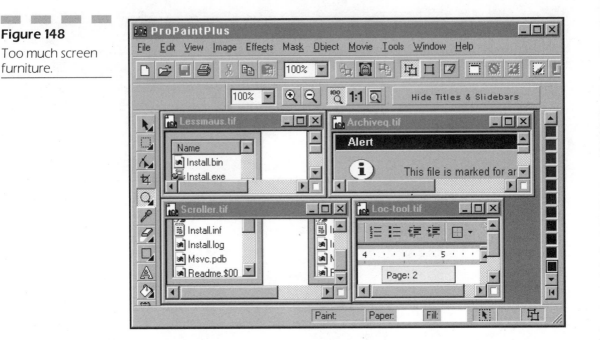

Design Guidelines

GRAY OR TAKE AWAY?   Scroll bars can be set up to:

- Disappear if the scrollable object isn't wide or long enough to scroll.
- Always appear but be grayed out if the object is not scrollable.
- Always appear (without graying or any other indicator).

In general, users think of disappearing and reappearing screen components as unreliable. However, since scroll bars are more like furniture than equipment, they probably aren't even noticed until they're needed. Suggestion: Pick one method (the easiest, say) and stick with it throughout the interface.

LENGTH OF THE LIST   Applications have indicated the length of and the user's location on the list (or other scrollable object) in at least two ways (Figure 149):

1. The scroll box sits at or moves to a spot on the bar proportional to the length of the list or document and the user's location in the list or document.

2. The scroll box itself is proportional in size to the length of the list or document. By its size, it indicates the proportion of information currently visible.

Figure 149

Two ways to indicate the length of a scrolled list: the scroll box's position on the scroll bar or the size of the scroll box.

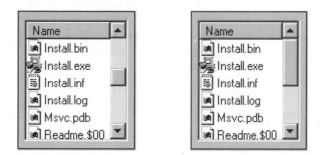

Your platform guidelines or your development environment may pick the method for you. Usability testing will tell you which method makes the most sense to your users.

However, no scroll bar or other component can indicate how long the list is when the application itself doesn't know (when a list is first loading, for example). Rather than trying to change the scroll bar or invent a new widget, just let users know that there may be a delay in showing the size of the list. (Use a status message that doesn't require a user response.) If you can let the user do his work while the rest of the list loads, you will probably have solved the only important problem—being forced to wait.

WIDTH OF ITEMS   When you create a scrolling list of items, you may find that some of the text is too wide to fit. Important parts of long path names or long file names (in Apple systems and now in Windows 95) may thereby be cut off. You can solve the problem in these ways:

■   Make the list wider. If the widths of the lists may vary by customer site—for example, customers with client/server systems have long path names, those with stand-alone systems have short path names—consider making the lists resizable.

- Eliminate text in the middle of the item and insert ellipses (...) there to preserve the beginning and end of the item names.
- Add a horizontal scroll bar to the bottom of the list.

SPLIT BARS The split bar is a nearly invisible feature—as well it should be since most users won't need it (Figure 150 and Figure 151). However, for those who do, splitting a window into panes lets users have multiple views of a single object. (This is a different type of task from having more than one window open at the same time, although the operation is basically the same.)

Figure 150

The user clicks the split bar and drags...

Figure 151

The newly split window.

Some situations in which multiple views are helpful are:

■ Being able to work on a blown-up section of a graphic in one pane and see the effect on the normally sized graphic in another pane.

■ Looking at footnotes in one pane and text in another.

■ Copying information from one part of a document to another.

■ Comparing two parts of the same object.

BETTER LOCATION INFORMATION Some applications, including Microsoft Word 97, now show additional location information. When users click on the scroll box (but not the arrow keys), a tooltip with the heading of the current location appears (Figure 152). In long files or documents, this is very helpful.

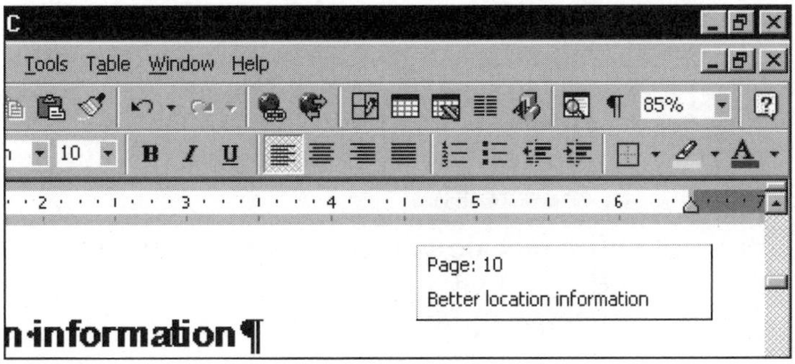

Figure 152

A location tooltip.

DIFFICULTIES WITH SCROLLING Novice windows users may have difficulty understanding how windows work. The chosen development idiom is that the window moves around over data that is fixed in position (the "telescope approach"). This means that the data in a window moves opposite to the direction indicated by the arrow button or the scroll box.

However, users often assume that the arrows will move the data in the same direction as the directional arrow or scroll box—in other words, users think that the data moves under the window, not the window over the data. Why this happens, no one knows. Perhaps it is because users conclude that the data must be moving because the window stays still; or since scroll bars are close to the data, the arrows must be acting on the data, not the window (Galitz 1997, 407).

Another difficulty, even for experienced users, is the amount of mouse movement needed to use scroll bars, since the arrow keys are at opposite ends of the scroll bar (Cooper 1995, 199). Why not put them together? For example, see Figure 153.

Figure 153

A scroll bar that requires less mousing.

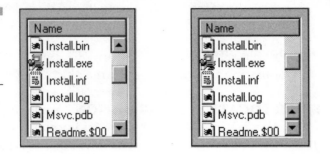

Usability Tests

Here are some tests for inexperienced window users:

- If your user profile indicates that the users are inexperienced with windows, see if the test participants recognize the function of the scroll bar.

- With talk-aloud protocols, find out what conceptual models users bring to looking beyond the edge of the screen. See "Difficulties with scrolling" above.

- If splitting a window into panes is an important part of the application, make sure that users recognize the split bar. Also make sure they know how to unsplit a split window (this is usually a menu option).

Share the results with your training and documentation departments.

CHECK ITEM WIDTHS   During the high-fidelity testing phase, ask the test participants for typical item names. If the list may contain path names, find the longest possible path name as well. Then make sure either that the list box is wide enough to accommodate the longest name or that you've included a horizontal scroll bar or ellipses in the center of the names.

CHECK WHETHER USERS NEED SLIDE BARS INSTEAD
When users are moving from very dense terminal-based or character-based systems to GUIs, make sure that you don't unintentionally nar-

row their views of the information. During tests of high-fidelity proto-types or beta versions, listen for complaints that there isn't enough information on the screen or that the scroll bars and other furniture are blocking the users' view of the data. You may need to replace the scroll bars with slide bars or let users toggle off all screen furniture (see Slide Bar for more information). Use experienced users as test partici-pants; new users may not realize that information is missing.

See Also

Slide Bar.

Slide Bar

A very narrow version of a scroll bar.

Good For

■ Situations in which space is tight, either because the window is very dense or because the main window has to hold many sub-windows or panels (Figure 154).

Figure 154

A window with slide bars instead of scroll bars. They appear at the bottom of the headlines panel and on the right edges of the rightmost panels.

Not Good For

- Occasional or one-time-use applications. Slide bars are too subtle for transient applications.

- Any user population without the fine motor skills needed to manipulate the small scroll box and arrow buttons.

Design Guidelines

When users are moving from very dense terminal-based or character-based systems to GUIs, all the GUI apparatus may unintentionally narrow their views of the information, especially if there are many panes or secondary windows on the main window. (News and financial data applications often tile a dozen windows of various sizes and shapes on the screen at once.)

Consider eliminating even the slide bars: Let users toggle all screen ornamentation on and off. While they set up their windows, they can have the scroll bars and window titles on. Once they're done setting up, they can turn everything off. For more scrolling guidelines and information, see Scroll Bar.

Usability Tests

On a high-fidelity prototype, make sure that the user population has the manual dexterity to click on and drag the small slider. If they can't, try making the hot spot larger than the slider. The slider itself can be made larger if it doesn't obscure live information.

See Also

Scroll Bar.

Slider

A scale or scrolling bar that lets users select a value from a continual range of values. An indicator shows the current setting.

Good For

- Incrementing or decrementing continuous values. Sliders can be read-only or read-write (Figure 155).

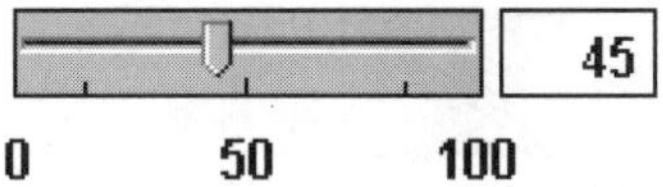

Figure 155
A slider with an entry area.

- Selecting one value or point from an infinite number of values or points.

Not Good For

- Precise entries (unless the slider component also includes an entry area for exact values, as shown in Figure 156). Use a list box or combo box instead.
- Situations in which the range is not continuous.
- Fewer than 10 choices. Use a spin box instead.

Design Guidelines

A well-designed, well-thought-out slider can be an excellent way to map real-life functionality to a software interface. For example, an online thermostat is much more intuitive if you let users raise or lower the temperature by dragging and dropping rather than typing. Just make sure that the values on your slider increase or decrease in some well-known, predictable, and easily understood way.

Show the result of a shift numerically—percentages, size, etc.—or visually. For example, if your application has a color wheel on which users can change colors, show how the color palette has changed.

Let users type an entry or adjust the setting by typing. This offers them the best of two worlds—a slider for the big changes, an entry area for fine-tuning (Figure 155).

SLIDERS ARE NOT SCROLL BARS Don't confuse a scroll bar with a slider. See Figure 156.

Figure 156

A scroll bar vs. a slider.

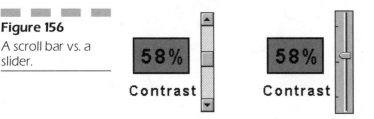

LABELING SLIDERS Make sure that the sliders' labels give the units of measurement. Galitz also offers these guidelines (1997, 399–400):

- Mark the low, intermediate, and high ends of the scale.
- Provide interval markings in consistent increments.
- Let the user change the units of measurement.

READ-ONLY VS. READ-WRITE If the user can change the value shown on the slider, provide a slider box and arrow buttons (like scroll bars). If the user cannot change the slider, do not provide the slider box or arrow buttons. Instead, fill the bar in some visually distinctive way to indicate the value.

Fill vertical sliders from bottom to top. Fill horizontal sliders from left to right. If you intend to internationalize your software, keep in mind that, in some Asian languages, left may indicate higher values and right may indicate lower values. Check with your local representatives.

Usability Tests

Brainstorm to find potential sliders. Look for opportunities to replace entry areas with sliders during low-fidelity prototyping.

However, keep in mind that sliders, although easy to understand, take up more room onscreen and are less precise than simpler entry areas. If you are creating an application with which users will spend a lot of time, make sure that you test the ideas on experienced users *before* you start coding. (If your application comes and goes, on the other hand, use as many sliders as you can. They are helpful because the mapping between the real-world operation and the GUI is usually direct.)

Make sure that users can select an exact value easily. Don't pack the slider so tight that it is hard to stop the indicator on an exact value. Adding an entry area will let users make fine adjustments.

See Also

Spin Box.

Spin Box

A one-line entry area with up and down arrows at one end. Users can either click the arrow buttons or type a choice.

Good For

- For applications with limited screen space, setting predictable, customary, or consecutive values (numbers, days of the week, and so on) with the mouse (Figure 157).

Figure 157

A standard spin box.

Year: [2010 ▲▼]

Not Good For

- In a non-editable spin box, more than 10 increments. Having too many increments forces users to click for long periods of time. Use a combo box or a slider instead.

- Situations in which users need to compare the choices and therefore need to see them.

- Users with limited patience or manual dexterity (for example, laptop users or children). The arrows are small targets and therefore hard to hit.

Design Guidelines

Always add an entry area. Let users enter their own numbers as well as select them with the spin buttons.

MAXIMUM NUMBER OF CHOICES   Weinschenk and Yao recommend keeping the list to under 10 choices (1995, 18). Although this makes sense for non-editable spin boxes, an editable spin box naturally accommodates more choices. The spinner becomes a secondary input device.

LABELING SPIN-BOX INCREMENT BUTTONS   One   problem with spin boxes is that users sometimes can't tell whether the up arrow increments or decrements the values. For example, it may not be obvious which direction the year will move in Figure 157. Clicking the up arrow might change the year from 2010 to 2011 or from 2010 to 2009. Using a plus and a minus rather than the standard arrows might be a better design (Figure 158).

Figure 158

Better labeling for a spin box.

If the range is limited, put that information in the label. For example, if the range of priority levels is between 1 and 10, write the label as "Priority (1–10)."

Usability Tests

Test for appropriate increments and increment sizes.

Watch for difficulties manipulating the arrow buttons. They are small targets and easy to overshoot.

Test that your chosen order actually makes sense to users. "Customary" is not always the same, especially internationally.

See Also

Drop-Down List.

Status Bar

An area at the bottom, or occasionally the top, of a main window. The status bar contains, at a minimum, page or window identification. It may also contain progress messages and screen component definitions.

Good For

- Giving feedback on modes (CAPS, NUM, etc.) and location (page number, window identification). See Figure 159.

Figure 159

A status bar from CompuServe 3.0.1.

- Offering system or application messages that do not require user response.

- Showing descriptions of components when the user holds the mouse pointer over each one. Note: When the development environment allows, What's This? help and extended tooltips are better tools for object identification.

Not Good For

■ Object help that is better handled with tooltips.

■ Important or critical messages that require a response. Users may not notice status-bar messages. Use a message box instead.

Design Guidelines

Responding to the question, "Have you done any testing (or know of any) that indicates whether users actually read [status-bar] messages?" Jared Spool, usability expert, said (1996):

> Our research is very clear on this. Users almost never see bottom-line messages. The larger the screen, the more likely they will miss any important messages.
>
> This has to do with the focus of the user's attention. When the users are exploring menu items at the top of the screen, they don't notice changes to the bottom of the screen.
>
> Lotus (amongst others) tried putting the messages in the top window banner, but that only had a negligible effect.

Spool goes on to say that tooltips were more effective. When Excel 4.0 *without* tooltips was replaced with Excel 5.0 with *tooltips*, icon usage jumped significantly.

STATUS MESSAGES, DEFINED   Status messages are a running commentary on an application's activity. For example, as a program loads, the status message might be "Loading database . . . ." As the program searches, the message might be "Searching for matches . . . ." Once the program has results, the message might be "Found: 22 records."

Status messages are used to indicate either progress toward a goal or the accomplishment of that goal. Progress messages are important when response times may be slow or changeable, while acknowledgment messages are important when a process is not visible to the user (it's running in background, say) or when a process takes so long that the user may have turned away from her computer before it has finished.

Once users know what to expect for particular tasks, *variability* in response times can also create anxiety and dissatisfaction. Variability can occur in either direction: A response that is suddenly too fast causes as much anxiety as one that is too slow (Galitz 1994, 432). The anxiety comes from uncertainty—"Did the process I asked for work?" or "Why is this taking so long? Did I break something?"

As well as providing feedback, therefore, status messages help mitigate the effects of too-long or too-short response times. Users tolerate delays when they know how long the process will take and that the process is, indeed, still continuing. They will tolerate too-fast responses if an acknowledgment message shows that their request was actually acted upon.

HOW TO WRITE STATUS MESSAGES   The messages have to be short because the available space is so small. Feel free to use sentence fragments and implied subjects, objects, or predicates. In progress messages, the action (predicate) is usually more important than the subject (see Figure 160). In acknowledgment messages, the object—the result—is usually the most important (see Figure 161).

Figure 160

The action, "Retrieving," comes first in a progress message.

Retrieving records …

Figure 161

The result often comes first in an acknowledgment message.

23 records found.

If you are going to internationalize the interface, keep in mind that text will expand by at least 30 percent, maybe as much as 200 percent. (See Table 12 on page 111, "Expansion Rates Between English and Other Languages" in Label.) Keep the status-bar messages in resource files to make translation easier.

PUNCTUATION   Use colons to indicate "as follows." For example:

Connected: 23 minutes.

To indicate time passing, use an ellipsis (three periods) at the end of the word or phrase:

Searching . . .

If the process continues for more than a few seconds, continue to add dots.

WHO SHOULD WRITE STATUS MESSAGES   Even though creating status-bar descriptions and messages are development tasks (they are attached to the buttons, menu options, or processes that call them), ask your technical writers to write or edit them. Technical writers will make sure that the messages are grammatically correct, spelled correctly, and consistent from one part of the application to another.

No matter who writes the messages, remember to proofread them. There are often misspellings, missing spaces between words, strange capitalization, and a lack of—or too much—punctuation.

Usability Tests

When testing prototypes (low- or high-fidelity), note points at which the test participants seem to be looking for more information. Ask them what they can't find.

In high-fidelity prototypes or beta versions, see if the participants ask questions that can be answered by status information that they are not noticing.

See Also

Message Box; Progress Indicator; Tooltip.

Table   225

Table

Data organized into rows and columns. In software development, "table" is used in two senses: a report or textual representation of some information; and a view of a database.

Good For

- Showing analysis results in report or table form (Figure 162).

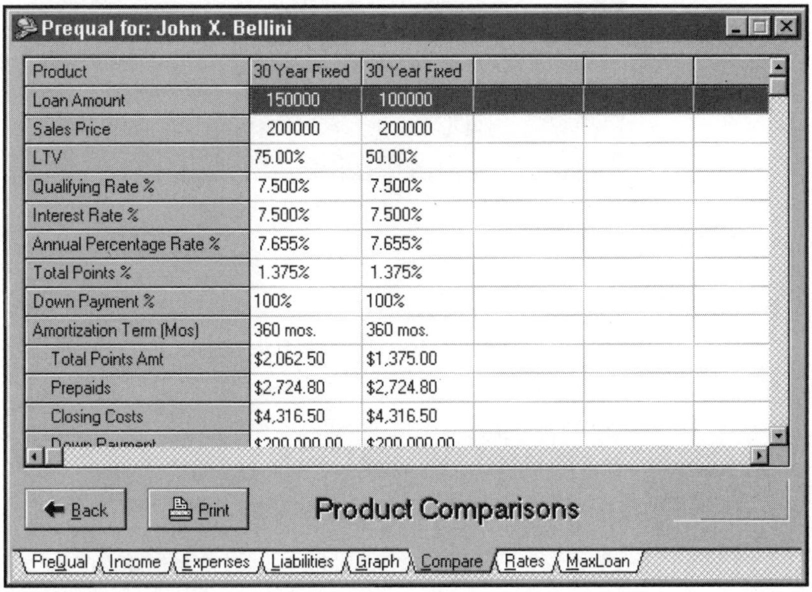

Figure 162

A report from the Laser Pro Mortgage application (CFI ProServices, Inc., Portland, OR).

Product	30 Year Fixed	30 Year Fixed			
Loan Amount	150000	100000			
Sales Price	200000	200000			
LTV	75.00%	50.00%			
Qualifying Rate %	7.500%	7.500%			
Interest Rate %	7.500%	7.500%			
Annual Percentage Rate %	7.655%	7.655%			
Total Points %	1.375%	1.375%			
Down Payment %	100%	100%			
Amortization Term (Mos)	360 mos.	360 mos.			
Total Points Amt	$2,062.50	$1,375.00			
Prepaids	$2,724.80	$2,724.80			
Closing Costs	$4,316.50	$4,316.50			
Down Payment	$200,000.00	$200,000.00			

Prequal for: John X. Bellini

Back | Print | **Product Comparisons**

PreQual / Income / Expenses / Liabilities / Graph / Compare / Rates / MaxLoan

■ Showing the results of a database query (Figure 163).

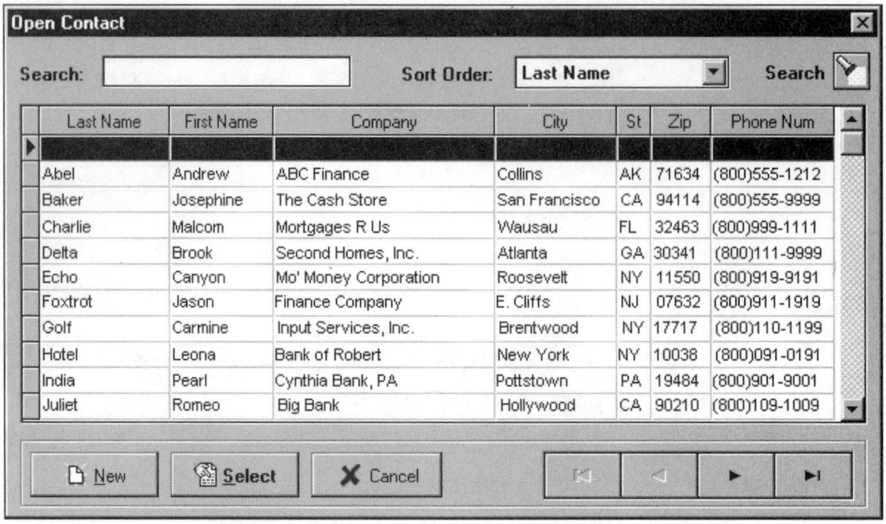

Figure 163

A database view
from Laser Pro
Mortgage (CFI
ProServices, Inc.,
Portland, OR).

Not Good For

Showing overviews. Use graphs instead.

Design Guidelines

PARTS OF A TABLE The topmost row on a table contains the table's title (see "Table titles" below). The left margin on a table is called the "stub." The stub heading should be the type of item to be compared: "Bonds," "Towns," or "Diseases," for example. The names of the items being compared—"ATT 6.0 97," "Waterbury," or "Endometriosis"—are listed in this column. All other columns contain the comparisons (Figure 164).

Figure 164

Parts of a table.

Title			
Stub head	Head	Head	Head
Item name	Data	Data	Data
Item name	Data	Data	Data
Item name	Data	Data	Data

Table   227

Rules (horizontal and vertical lines) can help readers keep their places in the row. Just make sure that the rules aren't overwhelming. Use the narrowest line available to you; use gray lines rather than black lines. For more ideas on reducing visual clutter, see Tufte (1983).

UNITS OF MEASUREMENT   Always show the unit of measurement in the column heading—for example, $, %, "in thousands of ¥," "Celsius or Fahrenheit."

Failure to indicate the unit of measurement causes dissatisfaction. Although experienced users may be able to figure out the unit of measurement from the context, doing so takes time away from studying the data.

Also, if the units are in the headings, you don't have to repeat them for each item, thereby reducing visual clutter.

TABLE TITLES   Make sure that the table title is distinctive—the first few words of their titles should not always be the same. For example, this set of titles uses the same first few words:

Sodium concentrations of the Mississippi River

Sodium concentrations of the Amazon River

By switching the order, you get a more useful set of titles:

Mississippi River sodium concentrations

Amazon River sodium concentrations

A user skimming through a set of tables will be able to pick up the purpose of the table immediately instead of after reading for a few seconds.

For marketing or sales-oriented tables, find a way to let users put a message or point of view in the title—let them emphasize the point of the data. For example, "Company Sales Trend" doesn't say as much as "Company Sales Up in Northwest" or "Sales Down in Southeast." Provide a default title that users can overwrite if they want.

TABLES VS. GRAPHS   Like graphs, tables usually contain "cooked" data or views of a database or spreadsheet. Unlike graphs, tables show details, not overviews. In many applications, graphs and tables are complementary. Whenever possible, let users toggle between tables and graphs.

THE PERFECT TABLE Developers have spent countless hours ago-
nizing over what columns to include, what to call them, how to sort the
data, how to organize the columns, how to let users zoom in on a particular record, and so on.

These are all good questions to ask. However, the problem is that developers often agonize alone, when they could delegate the agony to
the end-users.

In short, make the display easy to change instead of trying to make
the perfect table. Let users reorganize tables on the fly by clicking the
column heads. For example, as shown in Figure 165, clicking Sender
sorts the list of messages by e-mail addresses; clicking Subject sorts it by
subject line; and clicking Date sorts it by date.

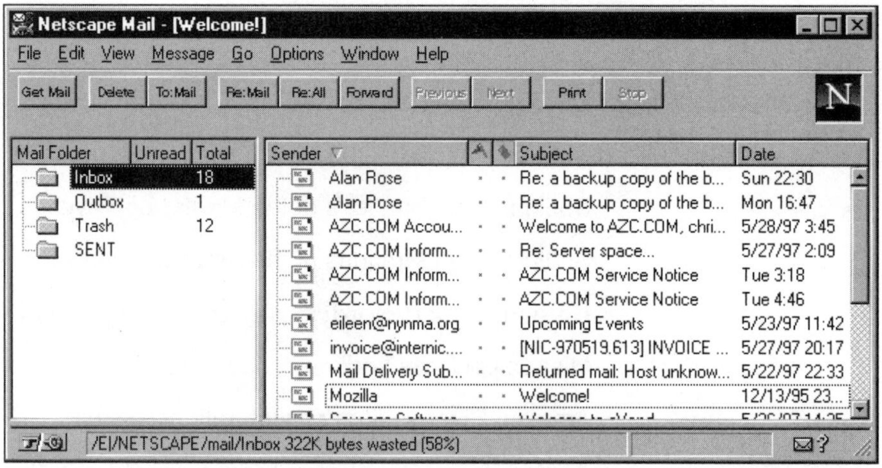

Figure 165

Sorting a table by
clicking the Sender
column head
(Netscape 3).

In Figure 165, the messages are reorganized according to which column was clicked last. This may not be as useful as the two-level sort
shown in Figure 166. In this application, clicking the column head toggles the messages between reverse or standard order, depending on
which column the user clicks and how often. Clicking Date once, for
example, would reorganize the messages in standard chronological order; clicking it again reorganizes the messages in reverse chronological
order.

Table 229

Figure 166

A different approach to sorting—toggling by size (CompuServe 3.0.1).

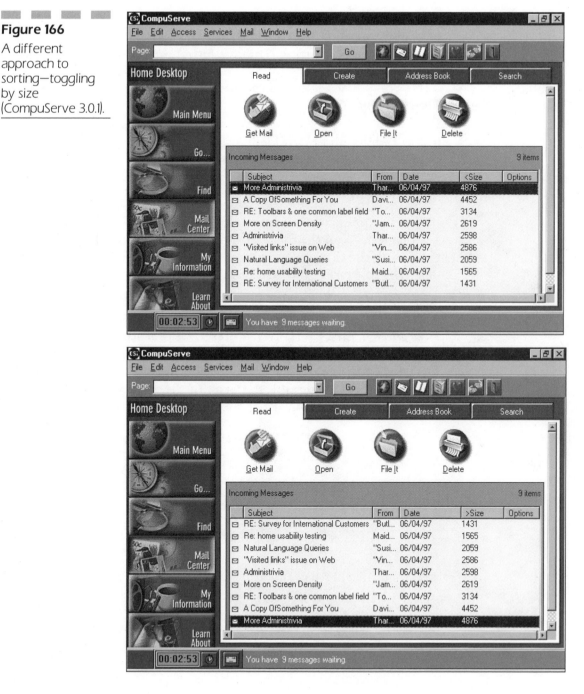

For more complex sort orders (by name within date, for example), you might want to offer a sort dialog box. Do usability testing to find out which style of sorting is more appropriate for your application.

Usability Tests

In low-fidelity and high-fidelity prototypes, note areas in which users seem to be looking for more information—these areas may be good places for tables. Use a talk-aloud protocol.

Also test for these items:

- *Obviousness.* Are the goals of the table apparent? Is the title too generic—can the users recognize the use or contents of the table from the title?

- *Heuristics.* Do experts agree that you've formatted the data correctly? Check with people with expertise in statistics and mathematics.

- *Mechanical.* Users often prefer to see preformatted tables as their first experience with a table program. Later, if they need to, they can fine-tune the display. Have you made it easy for the user to get an interesting table the first time he or she uses the application (perhaps with a wizard, if the display or data are complex)?

See Also

Graph.

Toolbar

A collection of command, action, or function buttons. Toolbars generally appear at the tops or edges of application windows. They may be moveable; if they become moveable, they are called palettes.

Good For

■ Accessing often-used (Save, Cut) or repeatedly used (bullets, numbering) functions with the mouse.

Figure 167

A customized Word for Windows 6 toolbar.

■ Finding important functions easily. Because toolbars make options visible, they also remind users to do important actions—Save, for example.

Not Good For

■ Operations that are done more efficiently using the keyboard.

■ Operations that require many parameters, that have no defaults, or that don't lend themselves to shortcuts. For example, a Fax shortcut button should simply send the document to the fax modem using the current defaults; it shouldn't bring up a fax dialog box.

Design Guidelines

GLOBAL VS. LOCAL FUNCTIONS ON TOOLBARS   Toolbar functions should be global—in other words, they should be usable for an entire window or across several windows. Options that are used in only one section of a window or in a dialog box should appear in the section or dialog box, not on the toolbar.

TRULY GLOBAL TOOLBARS   Some environments accommodate "front panels" (Marcus 1995, 37) or "control panels" on the desktop. When the same functions are available for all windows in an application (or even all applications in the system), it might make more sense to have a toolbar that floats on the desktop rather than repeating the same toolbar on each individual window.

Figure 168

A prototype control panel for a financial analysis system.

The danger is that the floating toolbar may get hidden. However, in the Windows 95 environment, you can create a taskbar that is anchored to an edge of the screen and thereby never gets lost. On Sun or other (usually UNIX) workstations with large amounts of screen real estate, there may enough room for any number of floating control panels.

LOCATION, LOCATION, LOCATION   Palettes generally float, while toolbars are tied to the frame window, usually at an edge of a main window or just below the menubar.

The location of toolbars and palettes takes something from the idea of a workshop—the tension between having a clear space to work and having all the tools you need at hand has to be resolved (Collins 1995, 224). In a physical workshop, you put up wall racks to store the tools you need some of the time and put drawers in the work table for the tools you need all the time. Really well-designed work tables have pockets for tools and hardware around the edges. Toolbars and palettes are like those pockets. Menus are like the wall racks, and dialog boxes are like the drawers.

Figure 169

Status-bar "page view" buttons (at the left) in Word for Windows 6.

TOP VS. SIDE LOCATIONS   Galitz suggests putting toolbars containing the application's primary functions along the top of the window. Toolbars for subtasks can go along the sides of the window (1997, 337).

Some environments let you add toolbar buttons to the status bar or to the scroll bar at the bottom of the window. Windows 95 lets you create "application desktop taskbars" (or "access bars") that act like the Windows 95 desktop task bar. See "Application Desktop Toolbars" in chapter 10 (Microsoft 1995, 271–272).

CHANGING TOOLBARS INTO PALETTES   Microsoft Office 97 and other environments let users drag toolbars away from the window borders, turning them into floating palettes (Figure 170). If it would help users to have certain functions at their mouse-tips, then include this functionality in your application. However, make sure that your training and documentation departments know about it. Users may not notice this feature on their own.

Figure 170

Toolbars into palettes.

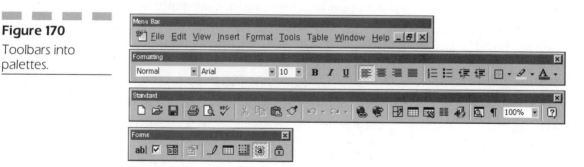

CHANGING POSITIONS   Wherever you put a toolbar, make sure that it can be repositioned. Weinschenk and Yao have these suggestions (1995, 84–85):

- Let users move toolbars (or palettes) to more convenient places.
- Let users customize the toolbar with the options they use most often. Let them remove buttons they don't use.
- Let users toggle the toolbars on and off. Turning toolbars off makes more room on the screen for the "live" information.

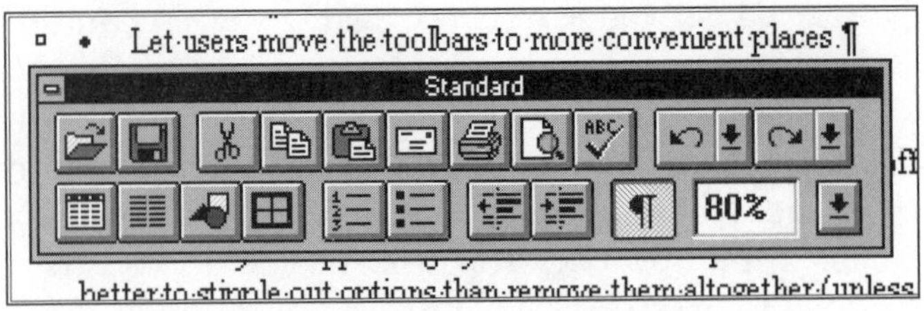

Figure 171

Word for Windows toolbar, dragged into the body of the document window.

OTHER GUIDELINES

- It is better to stipple out temporarily unavailable options than to remove them altogether (unless the options are removed based on user IDs and need-to-know rules). If some buttons are always available and others are sometimes unavailable, consider grouping the two sets separately—at either ends of the toolbar, for example.

- Although you may show different sets of options on different windows, it is better, if possible, to keep the options in the same relative positions from toolbar to toolbar.

- Use the same buttons for the same functions on all toolbars in the application. Don't use a piggybank on one window and a diskette on another for Save.

- Make sure that users can access the same functions from menus and via keyboard shortcuts (except for functions that are truly tied to the mouse, such as free-hand drawing).

ORGANIZING BUTTONS   Galitz offers these guidelines (1997, 336–338):

- Order the toolbar buttons logically—for example, by frequency of use, sequence of use, or importance.

- For buttons ordered left to right, put the most frequent actions to the left. For buttons ordered top to bottom, put the most frequent actions at the top.

- Keep related buttons grouped together. However, to avoid activating potentially destructive buttons by mistake, separate them from frequently selected buttons. (Mouse slips are fairly common.)

BUTTON, BUTTON, WHAT KIND OF BUTTON?   Since toolbars are many functions crammed together, the labels usually end up being small iconic buttons. (See Iconic Label for information on designing and testing the pictures.)

Most are pushbuttons, but some are check boxes (on word processors, for example, the bold, italic, and underline buttons are check boxes) and some are radio buttons (left, right, center alignments).

Usability Tests

Ask test participants to organize the buttons by most used to least used. Also, separately, ask them to identify the function from the label and vice versa. The information you are looking for is:

- Whether users understand the meanings of the pictures immediately (ease of learning).
- Whether they remember the meanings readily, once learned (memorability).
- Whether users can discriminate between similar pictograms or similar ideas.
- How long it takes them to become proficient and whether they graduate to doing complex or sophisticated tasks (Horton 1994, 302).

Ease of learning is especially important when you're developing for casual or inexperienced users. Test using a paper and pencil matching test.

Memorability is most important when you're writing for experienced users. If your user group will use the product daily, you can use "nonsense" pictures (a yellow triangle, a green square, etc.), provided that the icons are visually distinct from one another.

Some pictures may be hard to recognize no matter what you do to improve them. The solution is not to beat your collective heads against the wall, trying to find the best image. Rather, add tooltips. Many researchers have repeatedly found that images combined with text works better than images alone or words alone.

See Also

Iconic Label; Tooltip.

Tooltip

A small pop-up that appears when the user holds the pointer over a button or other screen object for a short period of time. It contains a short "what's this" or "how to use this" description of the object.

Good For

- Finding out what a screen component does, especially when it has no text label (Figure 172).

Figure 172

A tooltip from Word for Windows.

Not Good For

- More than a phrase. Use online help for detailed information.

Design Guidelines

Tooltip help is a property of buttons and other controls. Check the documentation that comes with your development package (or the property box itself) for implementation information.

TIMING Tooltips appear when the user holds the mouse over the button for a certain length of time. Tips are then triggered automatically over each additional button until the user clicks on an object.

User Interface Engineering (UIE) reports that Microsoft sets its delay at 700 milliseconds—when they set the delay at 500 milliseconds, users complained that they popped up too much; at 1,000 milliseconds, users never discovered how to bring them up. However, UIE found another problem during their own tests: Users cruise the toolbar looking for tooltips, but the tips never show up because the mouse hasn't stopped. This problem is compounded, UIE says, by a common user response— trying to make the tips show up by wiggling the cursor over the button. The wiggling, of course, resets the timing so that the tips are never triggered (User Interface Engineering 1996, 7).

HOW TO WRITE THE TEXT   UIE reports that tooltips can be too cryptic (see Figure 173 for a verbose tooltip). In a comparison between Window Access and Lotus Approach tooltips, the researchers found that users preferred Approach's short phrases to Access's terse, two-word labels.

Figure 173

A good, verbose tooltip for Upload from HotDog Pro.

Microsoft's tooltips are designed to match menu labels—for example, "Print Preview" is used both on the button and the menu label. Lotus's tooltips, on the other hand, are designed to help users find the function they need—for example, the tooltip for the Browse button was "Go to Browse to review or modify data."

However, UIE points out that the users ignored the "Go to Browse" part of the message and saw only "modify data," the desired function. For that reason, they suggest concentrating on the function rather than the name (User Interface Engineering 1996, 1).

INTERNATIONALIZATION   If your software may be internationalized, put the text in a separate resource file and a pointer to the text in the component itself. For information on expansion rates between English and most other languages, see Label.

Usability Tests

Test that users describe the control's function the same way that you do. In early phases, use a paper and pencil matching test. In low-fidelity or high-fidelity prototypes, use a talk-aloud protocol and listen for questions about button names and functions.

See Also

Online Help, Context-Sensitive; Status Bar.

Window

The application's container. The main window provides a framework for the application's functions, commands, and data. It also provides a top-level context for secondary windows and dialog boxes.

Good For

- Making the application's conceptual model concrete (Figure 174).
- Offering closure by giving the user a standard starting point and, in some cases, a standard ending point (Figure 175). This is the "home window" idea both on the Web and in standard GUI applications.

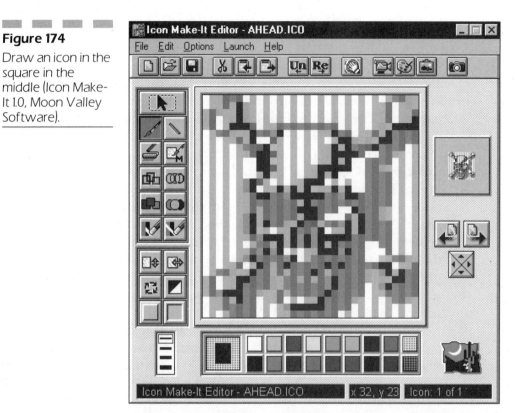

Figure 174

Draw an icon in the square in the middle (Icon Make-It 1.0, Moon Valley Software).

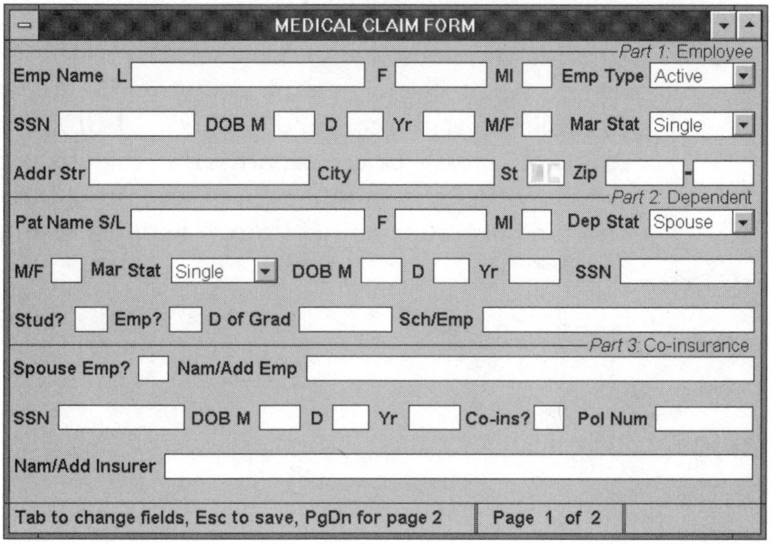

Figure 175

A standard starting point for a data-entry application.

Design Guidelines

Developers, usability experts, users, and designers debate endlessly about how much to put on a window. Some early guidelines suggested keeping screen densities to under 25 percent—in other words, only 25 percent of the window should actually contain fields or displayed information (Galitz 1994, 83). NASA researchers found that densely packed screens (70 percent full) took an average of 5 seconds to scan, while sparsely filled screens (30 percent full) took only 3.4 seconds. By improving the labeling, clustering related information, using indentation and underlining, aligning numbers, and eliminating unnecessary characters, the researchers reduced task time by 31 percent and errors by 28 percent for inexperienced users. Experienced users did not improve their task times, but they did become more accurate. A study of telephone operators found that maintaining a 25 percent density and suppressing redundant family names reduced search times by 0.8 seconds per search (Schneiderman 1992, 318–319).

However, expert users (stock brokers, air traffic controllers, and so on) prefer denser displays because more information per screen means fewer computer-related operations. Since these users are familiar with the data, they can find what they need even on a screen with 80 or 90 percent densities.

The solution to this impasse may be the model shown in Figure 176. This model is based on Cooper's analysis of applications into daemonic, parasitic, transient, and sovereign (1995, 151–170), Galitz's analysis of the three types of sovereign windows (1997, 153–163), and Spool's separation of applications into core and ring (1996a, 1–3). The bars are hypothetical, supported mostly by experience rather than by research data. However, as a hypothesis, it should be testable both clinically (through experience) and experimentally (through usability testing).

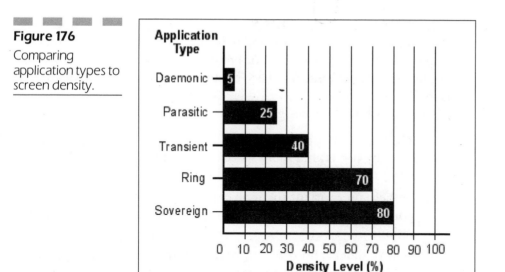

Figure 176

Comparing
application types to
screen density.

Following are definitions of the key terms.

DAEMONIC APPLICATIONS   Applications that do not normally
interact with the user are, in Cooper's model, "daemonic" programs.
They serve quietly and invisibly in the background without much need
for human intervention. Typical daemonic programs are printer driv-
ers and network traffic analyzers. They typically have, or should have,
minimal interfaces—a small window with a few settings. In the UNIX
world (from where the term comes), many daemons have no graphical
interface at all, just a set of command-line flags for changing settings.

PARASITIC APPLICATIONS   Parasitic applications are continuously present but perform only supporting roles. For example, a parasite
may monitor the amount of system resources available, put a clock in
every program's caption bar, or show how much memory is free. They
are physically small and are superimposed on other applications.

A process-reporting parasite has to be both simple and bold. Since it
rides on top of other applications, it must respect their preeminence
and move out of the way if necessary.

TRANSIENT APPLICATIONS A transient application does only one simple function. It comes when needed, does its job, then leaves, letting the user continue with his or her normal activity. Typical transient applications are graphic scanners, document faxers, and e-mail applications.

Cooper offers these design guidelines:

- The transient application should respect the sovereign applications by not taking more space on screen than absolutely necessary.

- To help users orient themselves quickly, its icons and other components can be larger and brighter than those of sovereign applications.

- Skinny sliders and tiny drag-and-drop widgets are out of place here—keep demands on the user's fine motor skills to a minimum.

- Build instructions into the surface—since the user may see the program once a month, she will probably forget what the icons represent and what the steps for using it are.

- Keep a transient application to one window—don't force a user onto a subwindow or dialog box to manage a main function of the program.

RING APPLICATIONS Ring applications are designed to help users do activities in areas with which they are not very familiar. In Spool's model of "core" and "ring" applications, a core application is one that enhances the user's core competencies (the same as a sovereign application in Cooper's model). For example, an engine-analysis system enhances a car mechanic's core competencies. A ring application, on the other hand, helps with tasks outside the mechanic's core competencies. For example, a car-parts locator program makes it easier for the mechanic to do his or her job, but doesn't add to the core competencies.

A core application should be as dense as necessary (see "Sovereign Applications" below), since their users will be spending a lot of time with it and will want to have as much information available as possible. But since users use ring applications only occasionally, they need all the help they can get—not just white space and careful grouping but built-in templates and wizards to get them over the learning hump quickly.

SOVEREIGN APPLICATIONS   Cooper describes a sovereign application as "the only one on the screen, monopolizing the user's attention for long periods of time... Sovereign applications travel in royal splendor, surrounded by their numerous courtiers. They offer a panoply of related functions and features, and users tend to keep them up and running continuously." (1995, 152). Good examples of sovereign applications are word processors and spreadsheets. Many vertical applications are also sovereign applications, as they often stay on the screen for long periods of time—hours, usually—and interaction can be very complex and involved.

One of the most important aspects of a sovereign application is that the users are experienced. Although each user will spend some time learning the application, it will be only a short period of time compared to the amount of time she will eventually spend using the product. Therefore, sovereign applications should be designed for experienced users, not for first-time or occasional users. "Sacrificing speed and power in favor or clumsier but easier-to-learn idioms is out of place here," says Cooper. "Of course, if you can offer easier idioms without compromising the interaction for experienced users, that is always best" (1995, 153). He warns, however, that if a competitor comes up with the same functionality but an easier interface, the competitor will take the market share. Look at WordStar vs. WordPerfect and Microsoft Word in the 1980s or, more recently, Ventura vs. Framemaker.

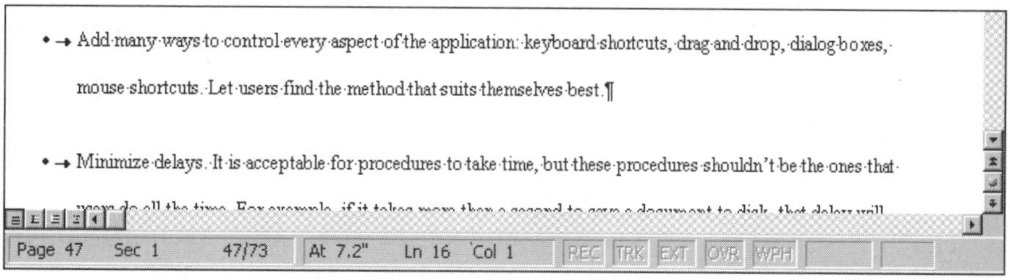

Figure 177

Microsoft Word 7, a sovereign application with extra information and tools tucked into the bottom margins.

Other aspects of a sovereign approach are:

■ Because the user's interaction with the sovereign program dominates his or her sessions with the computer, you should feel free to take as much video real estate as possible.

■ Expect that the users will run the application maximized. Maximize the window by default—although the application must be resizable and minimizable, it should be optimized for maximum size. Unless the user instructs otherwise, documents or views inside second-level windows should also be maximized.

■ Because the user will be staring at the window for hours at a time, mute the application's colors and textures. Bright colors and patterns might be fun the first time the user sees them, but they will start to look unreasonably garish after a few weeks. (Users will complain about the "Mickey Mouse" or "Fisher-Price" colors.)

■ In the same way, screen components don't have to be as big and obvious as they would in transient or parasitic applications. Users will become familiar with the locations of palettes, menus, toolbars, and other items simply because they see them day in and day out.

■ Enrich the interface with extra information (Figure 178). For example, you can add miniature graphs, LEDs, tool icons, and hints to the status bar, to the edges of the scroll bars, and to all the other "dusty corners of the program's visible extents" (Cooper 1995, 154).

■ Add many ways to control every aspect of the application: keyboard shortcuts, drag and drop, dialog boxes, mouse shortcuts, direct manipulation. Let users find the method that suits themselves best.

■ Minimize delays. It is acceptable for procedures to take time, but these procedures shouldn't be the ones that users do all the time. For example, if it takes more than a second to save a document to disk, that delay will quickly come to be viewed as unreasonable. On the other hand, the user won't be irritated if it takes a few seconds to change the format of an entire document—the user can see that it should take time *and* he won't be doing it very often.

THREE TYPES OF SOVEREIGN WINDOWS The sovereign window idea is a GUI design breakthrough, but it doesn't quite go far enough. This is where Galitz's three types of main windows comes in. The three types are form-based data-entry, conversational (also called "interactive"), and inquiry ("result" and "read-only").

In a form-based data-entry window, the user types data from a paper form (for example, a medical insurance form) into the computer. The typist generally looks at the paper form rather than the monitor and, in fact, uses the field labels only to find his or her place again after an interruption.

In a conversational window, the user interacts with the software face to face (so to speak). Activities that fall into this category range from CAD/CAM, games, and automatic teller machines, in which the user interacts only with the software, to airline reservation and telemarketing systems, in which the user interacts with a customer and the software at the same time.

With inquiry windows, the user searches for and retrieves specific information. Applications in this category range from telephone operators' databases to CompuServe libraries to CD-ROM encyclopedias.

The different functions require different window layouts:

- The most important design factor for form-based windows is matching the window to the form, line for line. Visual design is nearly irrelevant. See Figure 175.

- Conversational windows require careful visual organization and should include complete, unabbreviated labels and onscreen instructions. Status and informational messages, prompts, and context-sensitive help are useful here.

- Sophisticated visual design is important on inquiry windows, both because users need to see the desired information immediately and because inquiry applications tend to be market-oriented.

Each type of layout is described below.

FORM-BASED DATA-ENTRY WINDOWS The most important design problem for form-based windows is fitting all the fields in the relatively limited space of the window. The next most important is organizing the fields.

Fitting the data horizontally Figure 176 is a screen developed from the paper form shown in Figure 178.

PART 1: EMPLOYEE INFORMATION			
EMPLOYEE NAME (LAST, FIRST, MIDDLE INITIAL) PLEASE PRINT		• ACTIVE • LONG-TERM DISABILITY	• RETIRED • COBRA
YOUR SOCIAL SECURITY NO.	DATE OF BIRTH MM DD YY	• MALE • FEMALE	MARITAL STATUS • SINGLE • MARRIED • WIDOWED • DIVORCED
HOME ADDRESS - STREET	CITY	STATE	ZIP CODE

PART 2: COMPLETE ONLY IF CLAIM IS FOR A DEPENDANT			
PATIENT'S NAME (LAST, FIRST, MI) IF A DEPENDANT			DEPENDANT STATUS • SPOUSE • OTHER • CHILD
• MALE • FEMALE	MARITAL STATUS • SINGLE • MARRIED • WIDOWED • DIVORCED	DATE OF BIRTH MM DD YY	DEPENDANT'S SOCIAL SECURITY NO.
For a child 19 years or older, is child a full-time student? YES NO	IS THE CHILD EMPLOYED? YES NO	DATE OF GRADUATION:	NAME AND ADDRESS OF SCHOOL/EMPLOYER

PART 3: CO-INSURANCE INFORMATION			
Was your spouse employed at the time of treatment? YES NO		IF YES, NAME AND ADDRESS OF EMPLOYER	
SOCIAL SECURITY NO.	DATE OF BIRTH MM DD YY	CO-INSURANCE? YES NO	POLICY NUMBER
NAME AND ADDRESS OF CO-INSURER			

Since the source is a paper document, the most effective window is an exact image of the document. When the source and target match line for line, the typist can simply type from the form, filling in the entire screen without glancing at it or, at most, looking at it to check for typographical errors and to correct errors detected by software edits (Galitz 1989, 121).

However, a paper form can have a dozen fields on a single line. To fit the fields horizontally, shorten the labels by using a smaller typeface or by abbreviating. If done correctly, abbreviating the labels won't change the usability of this type of window.

Studies of abbreviation methods have found that truncating words is the best method for creating abbreviations. However, since you often end up with the same abbreviation for more than one word, you need back-up methods:

- Contracting words to the first and last letters, deleting vowels, and phonic puns—FX for effects, XQT for execute—are good backup methods (Schneiderman 1992, 163). However, puns rarely translate—don't use them if you intend to internationalize your application.

- Using the abbreviations found in commercial abbreviation dictionaries may help users who move often between jobs in the same industry.

- Creating ad hoc abbreviations doesn't work well because people have different ideas about the "natural" abbreviation for any one word—"meeting" might be "mtg" or "meet," for example (Galitz 1989, 115).

When you use abbreviated labels, teach users the full word or words first, then its abbreviation. Novices who used full command names before being taught two-letter abbreviations made fewer errors than those who were taught only the abbreviations or who made up their own abbreviations (Schneiderman 1992, 162).

It is necessary, but not sufficient, to list all of the abbreviations in lists or combo boxes—also let users know what your abbreviations stand for. Put the definitions online in the help system or hand out commercial abbreviation dictionaries or your own quick-reference guides.

Fitting the data vertically   Abbreviating labels solves the horizontal problem, but not the vertical problem. A paper form can have 60 or more lines or an 8 window has about 20 lines. To display the entire form, you must use scrolling, paging, or tabs.

- *Scrolling.*   Apple suggests that, when a user is at the edge of the window, the application should automatically scroll one line of text for word-processing applications, one field for databases or spreadsheets, and one object (if possible) for graphics programs (Apple 1992, 167).

For form-based windows, however, you might want to scroll by full screens. In other words, when the user fills all of the fields on the first window, pressing [Tab] or [Enter] on the last field moves him to the next page. (Depending on the application, you might want to save the entries automatically between window changes. Multimate and Radio Shack's Scripsit word-processing programs used to save the users' work whenever they changed pages, which was a lifesaver in the days of unreliable hardware.)

Paging. You can let the user page up and down. Although expert users do well with either paging or scrolling, novices prefer paging since it is familiar and less disorienting (Galitz 1989, 75–76).

Paging or scrolling by full screens work best if you divide the set of screens into logical sections. For example, an insurance claim form might be divided into its standard sections—insured name and address; claim information; information on dependants; doctor's information; and so on.

Provide location cues. Here are some recommendations:

— When an application has more than one page or screen per form, show a page or screen number in the status bar. Use the "Page n of n" format to give users a sense of where they stand in the record.

— Put the screen number on the paper form—use an inconspicuous spot in or near the margins.

— If you've broken the form into logical sections, put a subtitle in the status bar. The subtitle should match the title of the same section on the paper form.

Make sure that users can move backward as well as forward through the windows. This is especially important for applications in which corrections to already-saved data are difficult and time-consuming—for example, when saved data are sent by modem to a mainframe in batch and cannot be retrieved, only overwritten. When users can't go back to correct an error, they will often abort the job, losing pages of work, to start over. Consider letting users save data locally, prior to submitting the records, at page breaks or other checkpoints. Temporary saves allow them to look for answers to questions, protect their work against power outages, and take breaks without having to finish and submit an entire form.

■ *Tabbed windows.* A relatively new option is the tabbed window or view. Tabbed windows have the advantage of making all pages (or at least their labels) visible and readily accessible. Just make sure that you add keyboard shortcuts to the tabs so that typists can move between pages using the keyboard.

Organizing the data Paper forms grow in disorganized ways—a legal requirement changes or marketing needs more information so another question gets added to the end of the current form. After a few years, page 2 or 3 of the form is a hash of unrelated information.

Although data-entry clerks don't, strictly speaking, need to understand the information on the forms, they have no way to correct or even recognize errors if they don't understand them. Since repairing errors is far more expensive than doing it right in the first place, ensuring that the forms make sense is more cost-effective than training, job aids, or online help.

For an understandable system, organize the form before you try to program the window against it. The primary organization styles are:

■ *Sequence.* Arrange information in its natural order. An address, for example, is usually written as street, city, state or province, and postal code. If your system has a built-in ZIP code lookup, you might have the users enter the ZIP code first, so that the system can automatically fill in the city and state. (Make sure that they can override the system when necessary, however—commercial postal-code databases contain errors.)

■ *Frequency.* Put the most needed information at the top. For example, since everyone who fills out a medical claim form enters his or her name, address, employer, and insurance ID number, this information appears at the top.

■ *Function.* Group items according to their functions. On federal tax forms, for example, all income appears in one section, all exemptions in another section, and what you owe (or are owed) in the last section.

CONVERSATIONAL WINDOWS Conversational windows include everything from Nintendo games to desktop-publishing systems to financial applications (Figure 179). What makes them "conversational" is that users look at and interact with the window itself—they are not tied to a source document.

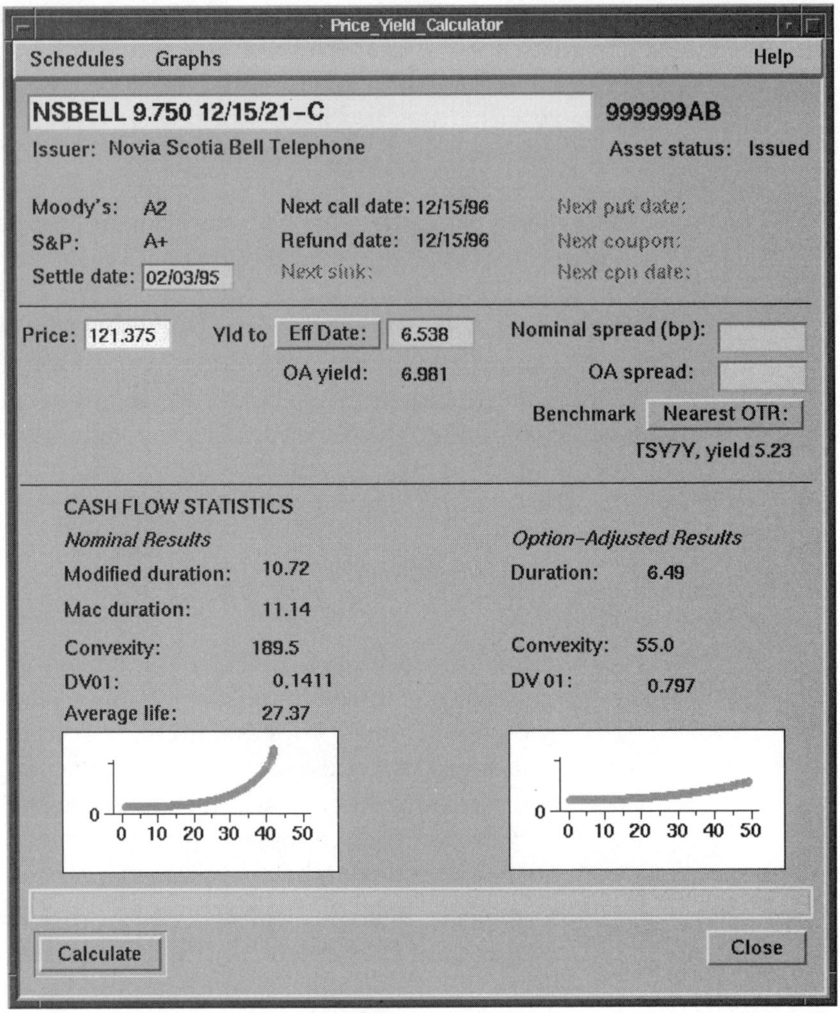

Figure 179

Typical
conversational
window.

Since the user's attention is on the window, more information is better than less. Field labels should be long and detailed; adding onscreen help and cue cards (provided that users can turn them off) is recommended.

Conversational windows can become crowded, however, and highly complex. Without careful design, they can become confusing. Galitz has a simple test for whether a conversational window is designed correctly: "Can all screen elements (field labels, data, title, headings, types of controls, etc.) be identified without reading the words that make them up?" (1994, 58). For help designing windows that pass this test, see Label.

In general:

- Provide need-to-know information at the top of the window or on the primary window. If the user is looking for price relative to yield, then show her price and yield at the top of the window. Information about the company issuing the stock, the number of shares outstanding, the broker recommending the stock, and so on, can go at the bottom of the window or in secondary windows.

- Put nice-to-know information in secondary windows. For instance, a lab analyst needs to know whether a test result was positive or negative—therefore, this information goes on the primary window at the top left. However, he might also like to know the statistical likelihood of a false positive using this batch of reagent, this level of humidity, and so on. This information can go in a separate window, tabbed view, or dialog box.

INQUIRY WINDOWS At a minimum, inquiry windows let users search for and look at information. However, the idea of "inquiry" goes far beyond answering simple questions or checking a view of a database. Inquiry can also mean answering a child's question about dinosaurs or sending an adult on a chase from "wild goose" to "Chinese cuisine" to "influenza epidemics."

- Careful organization, easily scannable text and instructions, and the right amount of information per window are just as important on inquiry windows as they are on conversational windows. However, designing a sophisticated inquiry window—for the World Wide Web, for example, or for a multimedia presentation—is more like designing a magazine page than a software window—shape, color, and typography are paramount.

- To create an easily understood window, remember consistency, placement, and proportion. The following sections are oriented around a multimedia or Web inquiry window, but the ideas are applicable to less complex applications as well.

Consistency Maintaining consistency is simple—define one or two standard layouts for the entire application and fit all text and graphics into those layouts. Magazine designers use the "grid system" to define pages and simplify layout, and this system works just as well for window design.

The first step in defining a grid system is selecting margins and, within the margins, a number of columns (Hurlburt 1978, 47–64). See Figure 180.

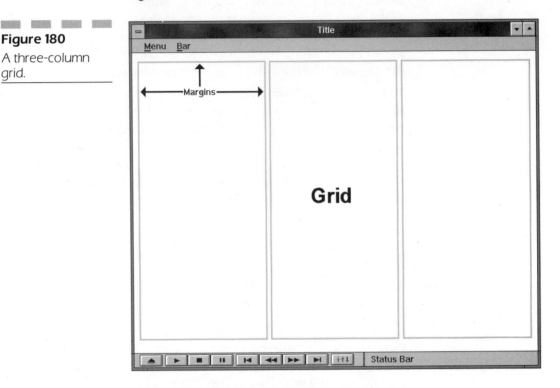

Figure 180

A three-column grid.

The columns can contain either text or pictures. Chunks of text and pictures can remain within the confines of the columns or break out across multiple columns, as shown in Figure 181.

Since all window elements remain within the grid, the windows look consistent as the user moves from one to the next. Since the elements are not rigidly restricted to one column, however, you can accommodate a variety of picture shapes and sizes. Note: The grids in Figure 181 and Figure 182 are visible as gray boxes around the columns. However, the grid in the finished product can be visible or invisible.

Figure 181

Picture, text. (Photo • 1997 by John D. Watson, Brooklyn, NY.)

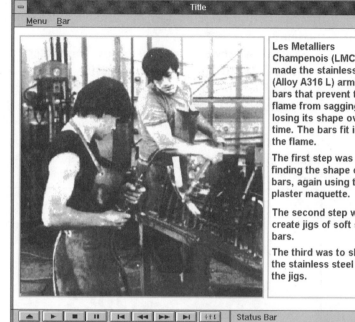

Les Metalliers Champenois (LMC) also made the stainless steel (Alloy A316 L) armature bars that prevent the flame from sagging and losing its shape over time. The bars fit inside the flame.

The first step was finding the shape of the bars, again using the plaster maquette.

The second step was to create jigs of soft steel bars.

The third was to shape the stainless steel on the jigs.

Figure 182

Picture, text, video.

Les Metalliers Champenois (LMC) also made the stainless steel (Alloy A316 L) armature bars that prevent the flame from sagging and losing its shape over time. The bars fit inside the flame.

The first step was finding the shape of the bars, again using the plaster maquette.

The second step was to create jigs of soft steel bars.

The third was to shape the stainless steel on the jigs.

Much of the actual shaping of the steel was done with a simple acetyline torch. The torch was faster and much easier to use than the furnace, since the workers could use it right where they were working.

Placement Can the user find what he's looking for immediately? Or, in a marketing presentation, does he see what you want him to see immediately?

You can satisfy either criterion by knowing two facts: People look at pictures first, and (in Western societies, at least) their eyes move from the upper left-hand corner to the lower right-hand corner. Therefore, put your most important piece of information at the top left. In a marketing presentation or multimedia application, put your pictures or headlines at the top left, the text to the right. If you can, try to have something in the picture point to the text, as shown in Figure 183.

Figure 183

Point towards the text.

Proportion For graphic elements such as photographs and illustrations, certain proportions are more pleasing than others. The "golden rectangle," whose proportions are 1 to 1.618, has intrigued Western artists, designers, and philosophers since antiquity. If you draw a line through the golden rectangle to create a square, the remaining area is another golden rectangle—a most interesting property. Another popular rectangle, especially in Japan, is the double square (Marcus 1992, 7–8).

Typography requires a good sense of proportion as well. Luckily, there is a simple rule of thumb for the correct relationship between line length and type size for optimum readability:

A line of text should be about one and a half alphabets long
(39 characters, in other words).

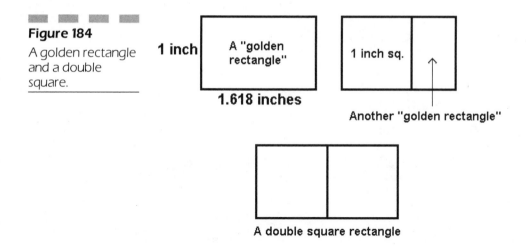

Figure 184

A golden rectangle and a double square.

Most type books say 40 to 60 characters per line is fine, depending on how wide or narrow the letters in the typeface are (Romano 1984, 86–87). Forty to sixty characters is about five to eight words (an average word is eight characters long). The easiest way to find the right size is to create a "ruler" in your chosen face by typing 1 to 0 four times:

12345678901234567890123456789012345678901234567890

Change the type size of the ruler until it fits the desired line length.

SECONDARY WINDOWS   In Windows 95, secondary windows are defined as nearly anything that isn't a main window—property windows, property inspectors, pop-up windows, and dialog boxes are all called "secondary windows." However, historically, as well as on other platforms, secondary windows are defined as supplemental windows.

Secondary windows are derived from the main window and typically appear on top of or inside the frame of the main window. They are resizable, movable, and scrollable. Although structurally they resemble a primary window, using the same controls in their title bars, they use the main window's menu bar.

They are used to do supplemental tasks, such as:

- Holding additional documents, spreadsheets, or other items without opening additional copies of the application.
- Holding second-level tasks—page 2 of a data-entry form, for example.

■ With the help of modes, moving users through a task in a highly structured way. See Dialog Box, Standard, for more on modes.

■ Showing secondary information. Secondary windows are useful when the main window is filled by top-level information, but users require backup information. The backup information can appear in secondary windows, especially tabbed secondary windows (see Figure 185).

Figure 185

A multi-document interface using tabs (HotDog Pro version 2.057, Sausage Software).

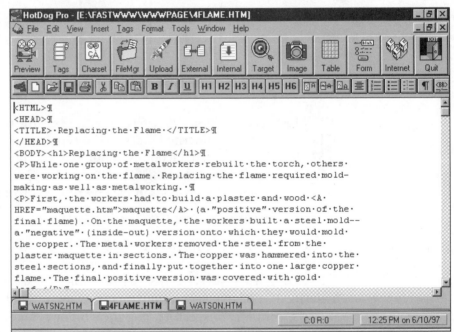

MDI and other multiples   In Windows 3.0, Microsoft defined the "multiple document interface" (MDI) type of window. An MDI window holds any number of documents, in contrast to the "single document interface" (SDI) that can display only one document at a time. In an SDI system, users who wished to cut and paste (for example) between two documents would have to open two copies of the application. In MDI, users simply open both documents inside one application, thereby simplifying the interaction and using fewer system resources. Once the multiple documents were opened, users could tile or cascade the set or flip between them using a keyboard shortcut. Word for Windows is a typical MDI application.

In Windows 95, however, Microsoft argues against MDI and for three other paradigms:

■ Workspace, which is a window that holds a set of objects. It is based on the idea of a desktop or table. Like MDI, it is used to present multiple views of the same object or views of multiple objects.

■ Workbook, which is a set of views or child windows organized into a tabbed notebook. Every page of the notebook is maximized, making side-by-side comparisons difficult. However, the interface is simple and easy to understand—there are no child windows to manage. Figure 186 is a good example of the workbook approach.

■ Project, which is a container holding or actually managing a set of objects. The objects do not have to stay inside the main window frame and can be minimized and restored separately from the main window. Because they are separate, they must have their own menubars and other elements. Visual Basic is a good example of a project-style application (Figure 186).

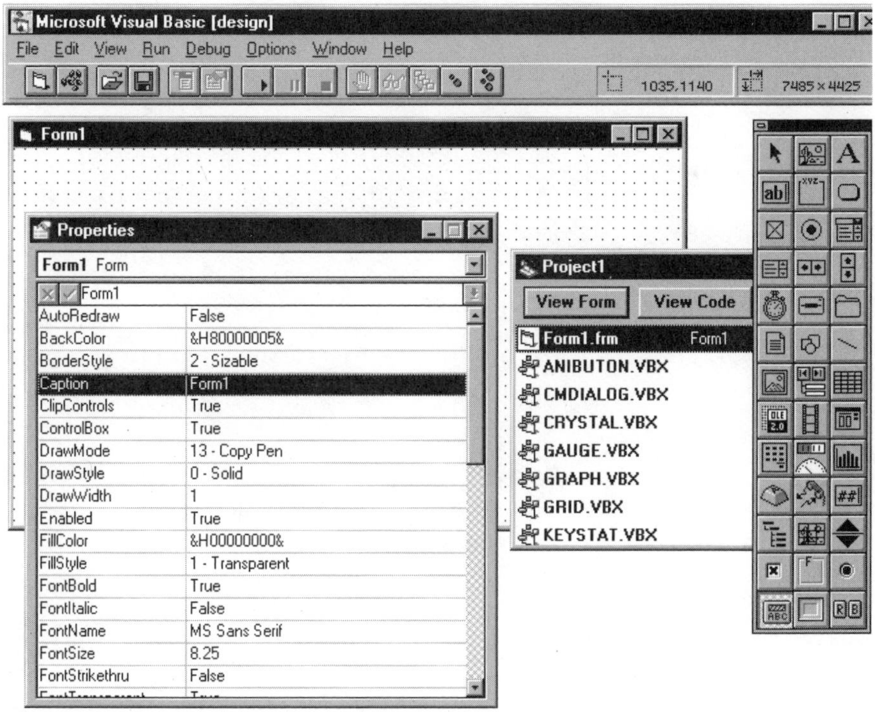

Figure 186

Visual Basic as a project-style application: the windows are not restricted to a frame.

For more information about these paradigms, see Microsoft (1995, 220–235) and Galitz (1997, 226–232).

Usability Tests

Finding the "home" or main window is the function of conceptual modeling and low-fidelity prototyping. See Appendix A, "Creating a Good GUI," for more information.

See Also

Dialog Box, Tabbed; Dialog Box, Standard; Label; Pushbutton.

Wizard

A set of dialog boxes that automates a task by asking users questions, usually one question per dialog box.

Good For

- Automating infrequent tasks that users do not need to learn—installing a software package, for example (Figure 187).
- Helping new or casual users do complex or sophisticated tasks (Figure 188).
- By giving new users a successful first experience with the application, encouraging them to graduate to the regular interface.

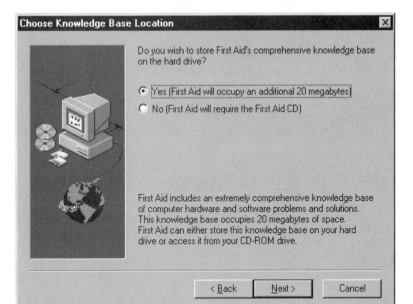

Figure 187

A panel from an
installation wizard.

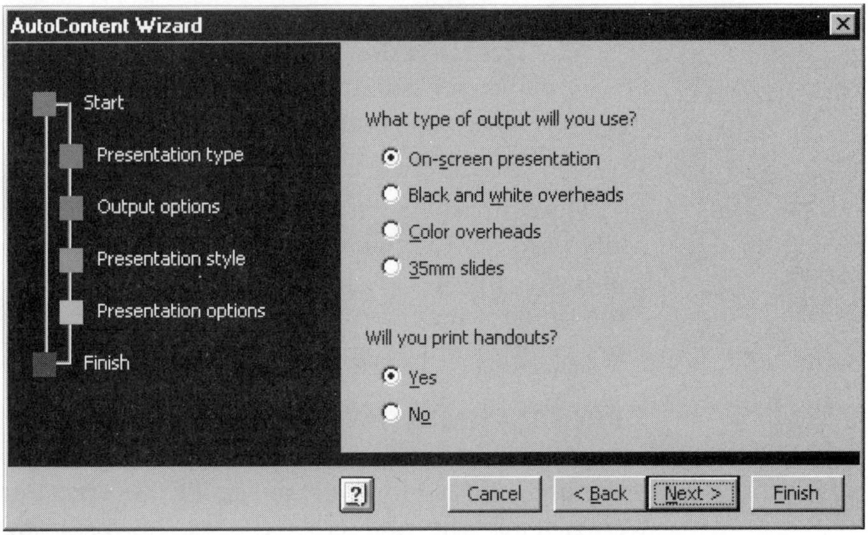

Figure 188

A panel from
AutoContent
Wizard, Microsoft
PowerPoint.

Not Good For

■ Tasks that are used so frequently that users would be expected to learn them. Experienced users may find wizards to be too slow and not adaptable enough.

■ Teaching users how to do a task. Use printed training guides, online tutorials, or online procedural help instead.

Design Guidelines

For one-time tasks and for getting first-time users up and running quickly, wizards are excellent tools. However, they have two shortcomings: Rigidity and a slow pace.

■ Wizards are rigid because the outcomes must be programmed in advance and the templates restricted to a certain likely group. For example, the Microsoft Word 7 "Letter" wizard restricts the user to seven page designs and three letter styles.

■ Wizards are slow simply because they restrict the user to one choice per panel. In a standard interface's dialog boxes, on the other hand, users can usually make many choices at once (Boggan, Farkas, and Welinske 1996, 92).

The primary design guideline, therefore, is to make sure that you really need one. As the Microsoft guidelines put it, "Do not rely on wizards as a solution for ineffective designs; if the user relies on a wizard too much it may be an indication of an overly complicated interface, not good wizard design" (Microsoft 1995, 359).

PROGRAMMING WIZARDS Microsoft says that you can, if you want, define wizards as a series of secondary windows through which the user moves. However, since all these extra windows can lead to increased modality and screen clutter, they recommend using a single secondary window instead, replacing the contents as needed (1995, 359).

WIZARD SCREEN COMPONENTS Typical screen components in wizards appear on Table 19. Panels also generally include graphics. See "Graphic feedback for wizards" below.

TABLE 19	< Back button	Lets users return to an earlier panel and change values if necessary. Remove or disable the button on the first panel.
Wizard Screen Components	Next > button	Lets users confirm the choices on the current panel and move to the next panel. Remove or disable the button on the last panel.
	Browse button	Lets users find a particular file, path, application, or piece of hardware.
	Cancel button	Discards all user-supplied settings, terminates the process, and closes the wizard. Note: For complex tasks, you might want to offer a save option, letting users save their choices up to the point at which they canceled.
	Finish button	Completes the task. May apply user-supplied or default settings from all panels. However, check your task analysis before putting Finish on all panels. It might not be advisable or possible to let users generate a result based only on the defaults. Put Finish to the right of the Next > button.
	Help button	Offers background information and advice.
	Radio buttons	Let users select one option from the available options.
	Text entry area	Lets users enter text that will appear in the end product (a title, for example) or type a value that the wizard needs.
	Title	Identifies the wizard's purpose.

GRAPHIC FEEDBACK IN WIZARDS   Provide feedback by including a graphic on the left side of the window (see Figure 187 and Figure 188). On the opening window, this graphic establishes a reference point. It can be either/or:

- A conceptual rendering (for hardware set-ups, for example, show pictures of the hardware that will be set up).
- A snapshot of the area of the application that will be affected.
- A preview of the result (Microsoft 1995, 360).

On the subsequent panels, change the graphic to show the results of the user's choices. For example, if you are designing a newsletter wizard and the user can set one, two, or three columns, change the graphic to show the result for each choice. So that the user can see the end product emerging step by step, each subsequent graphic should reflect all previous choices. For example, if the user picks a two-column format in panel 3, make sure that panel 4 and all following panels show the newsletter in two-column format.

If the graphic is not interactive, make sure that it looks that way. If you illustrate part of the interface, for example, make it larger or smaller than its actual size or render it more flatly (Microsoft 1995, 362).

WRITING THE WIZARD TEXT   Following are some writing guidelines:

- Use simple, jargon-free language.
- Present options to users as questions: "What style would you like for your newsletter?" or "How many columns would you like?"
- Provide short conceptual tips so that users can understand the implications of each option. "What's This?" help tied to the various radio buttons could be an appropriate way to deliver this type of information.
- Wherever possible, suggest the actions that the user might take after finishing the task. Encourage the user to customize the result using the application's usual interface. Point to the most likely next task in the user's workflow. Provide jumps to useful help topics or tutorials (Boggan, Farkas, and Welinske 1996, 95).

DESIGNING THE FLOW   In designing the correct flow through the wizard, you need to look for the most likely or obvious route through the task. Once you find it, stick with it and make sure that the user knows what it is.

FIND THE OBVIOUS ROUTE   Obviousness is important for inexperienced users. Think about giving driving directions to your house: If your friend Sally has never been in your town before, you try to keep her on the main or best-marked streets. If your friend John lives the next town over, on the other hand, you might tell him about the shortcuts or have him go by the scenic spots (the local golf course, the local swimming pool, etc.). Sally is the inexperienced user; John is the experienced user. Their needs are different and must be met differently.

STICK WITH IT   Stick with the obvious route by making sure that the users can actually answer the questions the wizard asks them. This is especially a problem with installation wizards. For example, many installation wizards ask for the brand name of the system's modem. But how many people know anything about their system's modem, especially if it's internal? One solution is to provide best-guess defaults—for example, "Hayes compatible" should work for most personal computers. (It might not work for such sophisticated systems as Sun workstations and Cray supercomputers, but these machines are tended by system administrators who know everything about them and do all installations by hand anyway.)

ADD A ROADMAP   Once you have your flow, let the users know what it is—provide a roadmap. Just putting "step 1 of 5" in the title bar isn't enough, says Carolyn Snyder. Several types of problems occur when an application doesn't have a good roadmap:

> *User looks in the wrong place*—In Step 4 of the Microsoft Excel Chart Wizard, one user became frustrated when he couldn't figure out how to enter the chart title (which the Chart Wizard lets you do in Step 5). He eventually gave up and clicked Finish, never realizing that the Chart Wizard had the functionality he wanted.

> *User knows the destination but can't determine the route*—We saw this in our desktop scanner study, where users didn't know if they were supposed to scan from the scanning software, the image editing application, their word processor, or what?

> *User's don't know where they are*—When a user completes the Microsoft Access Form Wizard, Access puts the user into Design mode. But users didn't realize Access had switched context on them, and they looked in the menus for commands that had been there just a minute ago, when they were still in Browse mode. We found similar problems in PowerBuilder 3.0, which also changes its menus depending on the state of the application. Most of the time, new users couldn't describe what mode they were in, what they could do there, what mode they needed to be in or how to get there (Snyder 1996, 8).

Roadmaps can be:

- As simple as listing the steps on the first panel (Figure 189).
- Putting the steps on tabs and checking off each tab as the user finishes the panel.
- On operations with many steps (such as doing a federal tax form), putting the steps on a list that reappears at the beginning of each section. The finished steps are marked on the list.

Figure 189

Roadmap from
Microsoft
PowerPoint
AutoContent
Wizard.

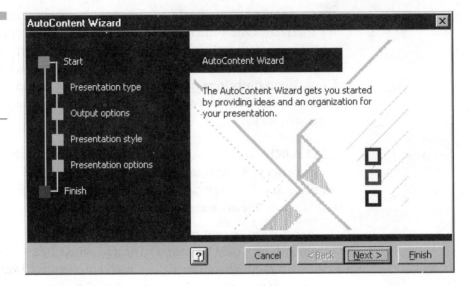

Usability Tests

TEST FOR TIME SAVINGS   Wizard development is often the *result* of usability tests—users cannot figure out how to do a complex task, so wizards are brought in as a solution. When you test the wizards themselves, make sure that you:

■ Compare times to *complete* tasks and times to *learn* tasks with and without the wizard.

■ Test how quickly experienced users become frustrated with the pace of the wizard and the restricted set of choices.

The solution to experienced users' frustration is not to add more functionality to the wizard. Rather, the solution is to state on each panel or on the last panel how the user can change these settings using the standard interface.

TEST WHETHER YOU NEED HELP BUTTONS   Usability and technical communication experts disagree as to whether wizards should have help buttons—why offer help on help? Also, since you ask only one question per panel, there should be plenty of room on the panel for long labels and instructions. However, sometimes background information can be helpful. Do usability tests of the wizard with and without help buttons.

See Also

Online Help, Context-Sensitive; Online Help, Procedural.

APPENDIX A

HOW TO DESIGN A GOOD GUI

The problem with computers is that you can turn the same basic box into almost anything—jet cockpits, cash machines, jukeboxes, typewriters, general ledgers, elevator control panels.... This problem, however, is also what makes the software industry so fascinating for many of us— "How do I flatten this three-dimensional thing onto this two-dimensional surface, but still make it look and act the same?"

This appendix contains an outline of a GUI-design process (rather than step-by-step instructions). You will fill in the details yourself as you develop your own system, keeping in mind that designing the GUI can be incorporated into your regular software design process. Note, however, that creating an interface is very different from creating the underlying code. An interface requires visual thinking and enough imagination to guess what this application might look like to end-users ("calculator" or "phone"), whereas the underlying programs require logic and a process model ("database" or "spreadsheet").

Aside from the difficulty of shifting between left-brain and right-brain thinking, the design method described here, called the "fourteen-step drill-down method," is pretty simple. First, you do the standard preparation work—you pick a brainstorming/design team, list the users' tasks, and come up with some likely conceptual models. Then you narrow the models down to one (using low-fidelity prototyping) and, from the model, you pick the home or main window. Once you have the home window, you can create the fields, dialog boxes, the menus, icons, and buttons you need to control the application, and finally the messages and other text users need to keep on track. At each point, you test your guesses with various usability tests and evaluations (see Appendix B, "Usability Tests," for details). If you do one step a week, you can have a workable interface in 14 weeks.

Here is a summary of the steps:

1. Pick a team.
2. Do a task analysis and create user profiles.

3. Find a good conceptual model (the user's mental model) by brainstorming, then test the most likely candidates with low-fidelity prototypes.

4. Define the home or main window (where the user starts and ends).

5. Define the application's structure—the menus.

6. Create the user's path with dialog boxes and secondary windows.

7. Create the fields and entry areas.

8. Brainstorm a look for the icons and the iconic buttons.

9. Create the shortcuts: mouse shortcuts using toolbars and palettes, expert user shortcuts using pop-up menus and other options.

10. Name all the pushbuttons.

11. Create the radio buttons, check boxes, and lists.

12. Define all data displays—tables, graphs, spreadsheets, and so on.

13. Write the error, alert, and status messages, plus online help.

14. Look at what you've done and prepare for the next release.

1. Pick a Team

In a 1988 book, "The Sources of Innovation," the M.I.T. researcher Eric Von Hipple found that 77 percent of the innovations in equipment used to make semiconductors and printed circuit boards and 67 percent of the breakthroughs reported in four major types of scientific instruments came from customers. With software, these trends are even more dramatic. (Gladwell 1997, 47)

The drill-down method is not something you can do alone in your own cubicle. It requires a team of right-thinking people. Table A.1 lists the team members, their importance to the team, and notes on the roles, including who can substitute for whom if necessary.

Try to have only one of each type of team member, since large groups tend to be unwieldy. For practical help on developing both teams and software, see Gause and Weinberg (1989).

TABLE A.1	Role	Importance	Notes
Team Members	Artist/designer	Can find the correct visual style and create sensible graphics	If you don't have an artist on staff, ask the design firm you used for your logo and letterhead if you can borrow one of their employees.
			Also ask around in the office: One or more of your receptionists, developers, technical writers, or project managers might have a design background or know how to draw. (Do you have any ex-architects on staff, for example? Architects know drafting and design.)
	Developer	Knows what's possible; good stand-in for expert users	It's hard to find a substitute for a developer, but an analyst or manager with a development background might do.
	End-user	Has the business acumen; knows the job	Using actual clients is key, and interested clients will be happy to join your team. (To put it another way, if you can't get anyone for the team or for user testing, why would you expect anyone to want to buy the application?)
			For early iterations, an account representative or customer service representative can act as a reasonable stand-in.

Table A.1 *(cont.)*

Team Members

Role	Importance	Notes
Facilitator	Keeps the design sessions on track	The facilitator may have one of the other roles (developer, technical writer, etc.). Look for someone who understands brainstorming and team building, and who can be an enthusiastic sponsor of the process.
		Human-factors experts are trained to facilitate. If the human-factors expert declines the role, a project manager might be a good substitute.
Human factors/ cognitive psychologist	Knows how minds work, how people do things	If you don't have an in-house human-factors expert, you can easily hire someone. Ask him or her to teach you how to design and test usable applications. See Appendix B, "Usability Resources," for help finding a human-factors expert.
		The expert can also train the person who will be the in-house facilitator.
Marketing director	Knows what will sell the software—what the point of it is	Use sales and account representatives as substitutes if necessary.
Quality assurance expert	Knows what will make an application easy to support and maintain	A customer-service representative might be able to fill this role if necessary.

	Role	Importance	Notes
Table A.1 *(cont.)* Team Members	Recorder	Keeps track of all decisions, interesting sidetracks, and unresolved issues	The recorder can have one of the other roles or the recording role can change at each session. Don't make the job onerous: The recorder records only the decisions and unresolved questions, not every discussion. Until the team gets the hang of it, the facilitator might want to review the list at the end of each meeting, not the beginning of the next, to make sure that nothing was lost.
	Technical writer	Knows how to analyze functionality from a user's point of view; good stand-in for novice users	Most professional technical writers can design competent interfaces on their own, without any specific training, simply from having to "fix" so many interfaces in the documentation. There is no good substitute for a technical writer except, perhaps, a specifications writer.
	Trainer	Knows what angers or confuses users first-hand; may notice that users are changing the ways they use the application	Trainers are valuable because they are on the front lines and see new users' first encounters with the application. Account representatives, customer-service representatives, and technical writers can be reasonable substitutes if necessary.

2. Do Task and User Analysis

Before you start designing, it helps to figure out who's going to use the system to do what. However, it is not necessary to go overboard at the beginning. If you use the "waterfall method," all aspects of the application are specified in advance and heaven help you if you deviate. But most shops do not and cannot use such a highly structured format. Instead, they iterate—as you will do, too, if you follow this method. (For more information on development styles, see DeGrace and Stahl, 1990.)

The reason to do task and user analysis is not to fulfill some obsessive organizational need for order, but to replace opinions (which foster arguments) with data. You can start your brainstorming with opinion, however, provided that you get *each* team member's opinion and note the differences. Where there are differences, the facilitator assigns team members to resolve the differences (with interviews or research) and report back at the next meeting.

Writing down the results is also very important. Like any other type of documentation, it lets you return to earlier decisions if you need to ("Why *ever* did we do that?") and lets you give clear, consistent information to management, marketing, customers, and other interested parties.

Popular methods for doing task analysis are use cases (Constantine 1995) and task scenarios (Lewis and Reiman 1993). For user analysis, see Rubin (1994) and Dumas and Redish (1994). For a good overview of the analysis process, plus an interface-activity notation system, see Hix and Hartson (1993).

Guidelines for a Good Workflow

Once you have a good idea of the workflow, check it against the following set of guidelines (Zetie 1996, 124).

1. Do not automate bad workflow—re-engineer the process first, then automate it. (Hint: Check the data-entry forms, where appropriate, for bad workflow.)

2. Make hidden dependencies visible. Indicate constraints clearly.

3. Give the users as much freedom as they can use, not as much as you can give them technologically.

4. Eliminate unnecessary restrictions; throw away unhelpful freedoms.

5. Support incomplete work and work in progress.

6. Different types of users may need different types of workflow; there is no single right answer, even for a single application.

7. Don't let the user start down a path that may not be closable.

8. Match points of closure to the user's needs, not the system's, whenever possible.

9. Confirm successful closure to the user.

3. Find the Conceptual Model

Once your team has written down as much as you can find out about your application's tasks and users, you are ready to brainstorm conceptual models: "The conceptual model or metaphor of a software user interface is the means by which it communicates the software's underlying operations and functionality to a user.... For example, the desktop metaphor, the primary conceptual model in used for the development of commercial software for the last several years, has enabled a host of less sophisticated users to enter the computing arena—a group who otherwise might never have mastered the much less friendly DOS model of computing" (Rubin 1996, 130).

Some models will be apparent or preordained—a new foreign-exchange data desktop had better look like its predecessors. However, whenever you computerize a task for the first time or move from one platform (mainframe, say) to another (Sun OS), you don't necessarily have a good idea of what the application should look like. Ergo, the need for a conceptual-model brainstorming session.

To find *the* right conceptual model, you need to come up with at least a dozen possibilities. Why? Because conceptual models have these peculiar characteristics:

- They are always formed. No one is going to come to your application with *no* expectations.

- Once formed, conceptual models are sticky—they're hard to break, like habits.

■ They have a primary effect on usability. If the application's conceptual model closely coincides with the user's mental model, then the application will be easier to use and learn. If not, the user will have difficulty learning the application and, once learned, getting beyond the novice level.

To find the models, the team should plan to spend a few hours brainstorming together. The facilitator must make sure that everyone understands that no idea is wrong or silly, and keep pushing the group to come up with ideas. The obvious models show up early in the session; the oddball models, which tend to be richer and more provocative, usually appear only after the team is ready to give up. For more on finding conceptual models, see Rubin (1996, 133–134).

Once you have a dozen or so ideas, eliminate and consolidate until you have two or three possibilities. Pick them based on:

■ How well they can be extended—for example, a "fireplace" model for a creative-writing application is fine for the contemplative aspects of creativity but not for brainstorming activities).

■ Whether they will be readily understood by the target audience—for example, a toaster icon to indicate "new bank account" will amuse older employees who remember when banks offered irons and toasters to draw new customers, but will bewilder younger employees.

■ You are now ready for low-fidelity prototyping and testing.

Low-Fidelity Prototyping

To find out which of the three models has the most resonance with users, create low-fidelity ("lo-fi") prototypes for each one. Don't do full-scale interfaces, however: Just pick the most important functions—the home window (see "Define the home window" below), two or three menu items, and one or two dialog boxes.

By testing the lo-fi prototype on potential software users, you can find out if you've gotten the *concept* right. Once the concept is right, you can move on to the next set of steps.

The design tool-kit consists of colored paper, acetate sheets, glue sticks, sticky notes, and markers. The lo-fi team generally consists of three people: recorder, facilitator, and computer. The recorder watches the test participants and takes notes, while the facilitator acts as the test participant's advocate and contact. The third member, who works the hardest, plays the computer: He or she moves the pieces of paper representing different user-interface screens, dialog boxes, messages, and so forth around in response to the test participant's actions. For example, if the participant points to a button that calls up a color palette, the "computer" has to find and display the palette. If the computer stays in character, the test participants tend to forget that they're *not* watching a real computer.

For more information on lo-fi prototyping, see Rettig (1994), Snyder (1997b), Rauch, Gillihan, and Leone (1997), and Fowler (1996).

4. Define the Home Window

Most of the information you need to formalize the design of the main window appears in "Window" in the main section of this book. In general, you have to decide whether the application is daemonic, parasitic, transient, ring, or sovereign, and if sovereign, whether it's a form-based window, a conversation window, or an inquiry window. (You may have defined the type while developing the lo-fi prototype. In that case, you're simply making your choice conscious and unambiguous in this step.) Once you've decided on the type, you can follow that type's guidelines.

Keep in mind, however, that the main window should, first of all, embody the conceptual model (if the conceptual model is "telephone," the main window should look or act like a telephone), and secondly, act as the "home" window. The home window is the window on which users start doing real work; they may end their task on the same window as well. Like Internet home windows, a good application home window provides users with the first rungs on the ladder—it makes it easy for the users to start. For example, the "Document1" blank page in Microsoft Word for Windows provides an obvious starting point—a writer can simply start typing on the screen. (A ladder with a few missing rungs would be a word processor that offered just a gray background with no insertion point.)

Having an obvious ending point is useful as well, since it provides closure. For a good discussion of this aspect of interface design, see Zetie (1996, 93–101).

5. Define Menus

Here is one way to define menus using the team:

1. Hand out a stack of index cards.

2. Ask half the members of the team to write out names of menu items (rather than the menu names themselves, although some cards will probably end up being menu names anyway). They should have copies of the task analysis to work from. (Also see Menu, Drop-Down and Menubar in this book.)

3. Once the first half has written all the names, ask the other half of the team to organize the cards into logical groups and give the groups names.

4. Pin or paste the cards on the wall and let everyone on the team (and outsiders as well) inspect the menus. Make any final adjustments.

When everyone is satisfied that the team has defined the menu structure, create a menu map (Figure A.1).

A menu map essentially opens up all the menus and makes all options and submenus visible at the same time. The map, if you publish it in your documentation and training materials (recommended), is an invaluable quick-reference guide to the structure of the application. Developers like them too, because they can post them in their cubicles as a reminder of where they are and what they're doing.

Creating the menu map isn't the last step, however. Before you actually code menus, test them on customers using one of the low-impact tests described in Appendix B.

Figure 1

A sample menu map.

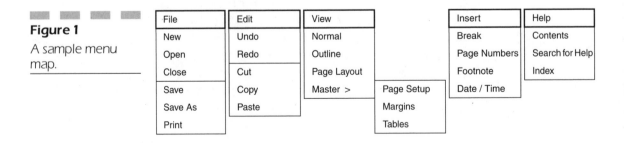

6. Create Dialog Boxes

Dialog boxes and secondary windows hold extra tools, keep the application running smoothly, and direct users through the workflow. To give team members a sense of the trail-blazing aspect of secondary windows, use this warm-up exercise:

> Develop, as a group, driving instructions between [a local landmark] and this building. The person who needs the instructions is driving a car with out-of-state plates. With each individual step, include feedback (for example, signs that the driver will see along the route) and error correction (for example, how to get back to the right exit if the driver overshoots it).
>
> When you've finished, do the same problem again, but this time write your instructions for a friend who knows the area and wants the most efficient way to get from the [local landmark] to this building. Include feedback and error correction.

The facilitator should pick a location close enough that the team can do the exercise in 10 minutes or less per problem (the second problem will be quicker because most of the feedback and error correction will have been done already). The team should work together, with one person recording the steps on the white board or blackboard and the rest offering directions and corrections. (By the way, you usually get two forms of directions out of the exercise—numbered steps and a map.)

At the end, the team can talk about what they discovered by doing the process and how it relates to defining paths through the application. (Hint: The driver with out-of-state plates is the new user; the local driver is the expert user.) Take no more than five minutes or so.

The final step (of course) is to create the main path through the application starting from the home window and including feedback and error correction. Also do the expert path. Make sure that the recorder records all details—the feedback and error correction information will become part of the online help and the error messages file.

If your application includes wizards, design them using the same technique but stick to the main path only. Or use your customers' expertise—ask one or two expert customers how they would do a particular task and create the wizard the same way. If the task already exists in a different application or an earlier version of your application, record these users' actions (on video tape if possible) and copy them with the wizard. Be careful to test the results on new users, however. Expert users might skip steps that new users need to follow if they are to understand how the application works.

7. Create Fields

Creating fields and entry areas should be nearly automatic at this point. Just make sure that you organize fields into logical groups, and organize the groups to match the workflow you identified earlier. Do quick lo-fi tests with customers to check that the workflow is correct and that the labels make sense.

For help creating entry areas, see Field, Entry, and Field, Protected. For information on creating labels, see Label and Iconic Label. You can find help on organizing windows and dialog boxes in Label as well.

For help defining required fields, see Field, Required.

8. Brainstorm Icons

Applications use desktop icons to start the program and iconic labels to run operations from palettes and toolbars. "Iconary," based on the game Pictionary, is a good team method for brainstorming icons. Here are the instructions:

1. List all required icons on index cards, one icon name per card. The required icons should have been identified during the task and user analysis, but others may have surfaced since then—check your lo-fi prototypes and other notes. Shuffle the cards and lay them face down on the table.

2. Create two teams and have each team pick a starting artist and a recorder. Make sure everyone has paper and a pen or pencil.

3. Let the artist on Team #1 pick a card. He or she has five seconds to look at it and come up with an idea. At the end of five seconds, the artist must start drawing. The other team members try to guess the concept within 60 seconds.

- If they can't, that card is put back on the bottom of the stack for another attempt. The sketch is given to the recorder who labels it with the icon's name and sets it aside.

- If they can, the sketch is given to the recorder who writes down the icon's name, as well as what seemed to work and what didn't.

4. If Team #1 got the concept within 60 seconds, the same team picks another artist and recorder and starts over from step 3. If Team #1 didn't get the concept, then Team #2 takes over.

Keep going until all the icons have been sketched, the time has run out, or the participants are exhausted. The team with the biggest pile of good icons wins.

If this application is very important to the corporation, ask a professional designer to do the final versions from the team's sketches and notes. Remember that your icons, especially the desktop icon, should remind customers of your corporate logo. For the final designs, try to use the same colors, shapes, and fonts as appear in your corporate identity materials. For more help designing icons, see Icon, Desktop, and Iconic Label in the main part of the book.

For case studies on the design of Sun's Web-site icons, see Nielsen and Sano (1997) and Nielsen (1997d).

9. Create Shortcuts

You defined many of your mouse shortcuts when you defined iconic labels for your toolbars and palettes (see Palette and Toolbar for more information). However, you might also want to brainstorm for ideas in these areas:

- Define keyboard-oriented shortcuts, especially if many of your users are touch typists (see Keyboard Shortcuts: Accelerators and Mnemonics for the most common types of keyboard shortcuts).

- Add pop-up menus to put context-sensitive tools at expert users' fingertips.

- Look into adaptive technologies—whether or not your users will need adaptive technologies, you might be able to use them in other ways. For example, technologies designed for blind or partially sighted customers can be very helpful in dark environments; technologies designed for deaf customers can be helpful in very noisy environments (like financial markets).

■ If your customers often use specialized pointing devices or other equipment, look for ways to write shortcuts for that equipment.

10. Name the Pushbuttons

The three keys to naming pushbuttons well are:

1. Be specific. Instead of labeling a button "Cancel," add what the user is canceling—for example, "Cancel Save."

2. Use the customer's terms. If the customers are not system administrators, write "Save on network drive" instead of something like "Push to network." (If they *are* system administrators, use the more specific label.)

3. Use industry standards whenever possible—Apply to save changes on a dialog box without closing the dialog box, for example.

For details, see Pushbutton in the main section of this book.

11. Create Radio Buttons, Check Boxes, Lists

Follow the guidelines for creating radio buttons, check boxes, and lists in the main section of the book. Watch especially for situations in which lists (multiple-select or single-select) might be more useful than buttons and vice versa. Also look for opportunities to replace free-form data-entry fields with combo boxes. Test these components using high-fidelity prototypes, or during alpha and beta releases. Using the customers' own data may bring out problems you wouldn't see any other way (for example, names that are too wide for the list box you designed).

12. Define Data Displays

Data displays include tables, graphs, spreadsheets, and other displays. Tables can contain "raw" information generated from SQL, Oracle, and other databases, or "cooked" data using a table generator.

Brainstorm for opportunities to transform data from one form into another—for example, if your application contains a spreadsheet, add an option to display the data in graph form as well. If you display a graph, make it possible to see the underlying numbers.

Guidelines for designing graphs and tables appear in the main section of this book.

13. Write Messages and Help

Follow the guidelines for creating messages and online help in the main section of the book. Be on the alert for internationalization problems: Make sure that the developers put all messages in resource files. They should not embed them in the code (this is a good idea for all labels and text).

A good team exercise is to take your current list of messages, or the messages from an earlier release, and rewrite them in goal-action format. For example, say that this was the current message:

Do you want to create FILEDIR? It does not exist.

You should reverse the action and problem so that the problem comes first:

The directory FILEDIR does not exist. Do you want to create it?

The first few times you use the 14-step drill-down method, it may be a good idea to work as a group and out loud, doing the revisions together on a white board or blackboard. For subsequent design sessions, it may be more effective to split the messages up among the team members, then let them edit each other's revisions.

Make sure that you include online help in your user tests. The technical communication department can either write up some test items for the main usability tests or set up their own tests of the help and the manuals. For more on testing documentation for usability, see Coe (1996) and Hackos (1994).

14. Set Up for the Next Release

Software always changes. Users pick up new skills and expectations, the hardware becomes faster and more accommodating, and the social context changes (laws change, new financial products come on the market, and so on), which forces changes in the workflow.

Plan to respond to opportunities, not just to bugs and problems. The usability tests may already have indicated that users have new and unexpected uses for your product—make sure that these possibilities are recorded. Look through the customer-service reports for requested changes and bug reports that don't seem to make sense—you may be looking at future enhancements or at least at a different conceptual model.

A month or so after the application is released, hold a wrap-up session for the team. Find out which parts of the design process worked and which didn't. Talk about the possibilities for the next release; brainstorm a few ideas as well. Then put every memo, lo-fi prototype, index card, and what-have-you into a box or loose-leaf binders and store it in the facilitator's office (or in the office of whoever wants to "own" the record). Remember: This archive might not seem very important at first, but like all handmade objects, it will become more valuable over time.

APPENDIX B

USABILITY TESTS

Probably the best reason to test for usability is to eliminate those interminable arguments about the right way to do something. Your design team can go around in circles for years without finding the right solution to an interface problem. Worse, you can stumble onto a right answer without knowing it—and, if you can't recognize it, you are just as likely to design it out of the application as leave it in. With human-factors input and testing, however, you can replace opinion with data. Real data tends to make arguments evaporate and meeting schedules shrink.

Another good reason is the cost-benefit ratio. For one usability study, Nielsen cites a ratio of $10,500 in costs to $500,000 in expected benefits (1997c, 3). With that kind of return, why isn't everyone doing usability?

"One important reason," Nielsen says, "is the perceived cost of using these techniques.... It should be no surprise that practitioners view usability methods as expensive considering, for example, that a paper in... *Communications of the ACM* estimated that the 'costs required to add human factors elements to the development of software' was $128,330," a sum that is several times the total budget for usability in most smaller companies (Nielsen 1997b, 7—14; Bias and Mayhew, 1994). However, discount usability methods, in which traditional usability methods are simplified and numbers of test participants are reduced, bring cost-benefit ratios down to manageable levels. *Any* usability testing is better than none, Nielsen argues, since any usability testing has a positive cost-benefit ratio.

When To Do Usability Testing

Although usability is often seen as a separate discipline managed by a priesthood of human-factors experts, many of the techniques are similar to ones already used in software development firms. For example, a cognitive walkthrough is the same idea as table-topping or storyboarding, but with a concentration on the interface; an interface heuristics evaluation is the same idea as a technical review or inspection; prototyping the interface is the same concept as prototyping the functionality (for information on standard walkthroughs, inspections, and prototyping, see Freedman and Weinberg, 1990; DeGrace and Stahl, 1990). In other words, software houses should be able to incorporate usability tests and inspections into their regular design and development lifecycles without too much trouble. Human-factors expertise is readily available—usability specialists and firms are happy to demonstrate and teach usability techniques. See "Resources" below for details.

Note: Before you test, make sure that you know what you want to test by developing a test plan. For step-by-step instructions, see Rubin (1994) and Dumas and Redish (1994).

Contents of this Appendix

This appendix describes some common usability tests. Some tests are simple, others are more complicated.

- For quick answers to terminology questions, simple tests like the matching test, card-sorting test, and paper and pencil test are fine.

- For new interface designs, low-fidelity prototyping helps you identify the right conceptual model (what's in the user's head)—see Appendix A for more information.

- For projects on which you're betting your entire business, use heuristic evaluations, cognitive-walkthroughs, and full-blown usability tests.

Following Nielsen's recommendations for discount or "guerrilla" usability, the tests list the minimum numbers of iterations, test participants, and expert reviewers. For more information on this approach, see Nielsen (1997b).

Low-Impact Tests

"Low-impact" doesn't mean low impact on the user interface but rather on resources and budget. Use low-impact tests to check the intelligibility of pieces of your application. For the application as a whole, use the high-impact tests.

Matching Test

Most people learn to do matching tests in kindergarten—you match two terms or a picture and a term by drawing a line from one column to the other.

If the test participants make many mistakes with icons, ask them what they *think* the icon represents. It might be cost-effective to have your graphic artist on-site during test sessions. He or she can watch the tests, ask questions at the end of each test, and revise the buttons between sessions until you have a set of workable icons.

Note that recognizability makes icons easy to learn and therefore most appropriate in transient applications (applications used only occasionally). Recognizability is helpful but not as necessary in sovereign applications. See Windows for more information about the types of applications.

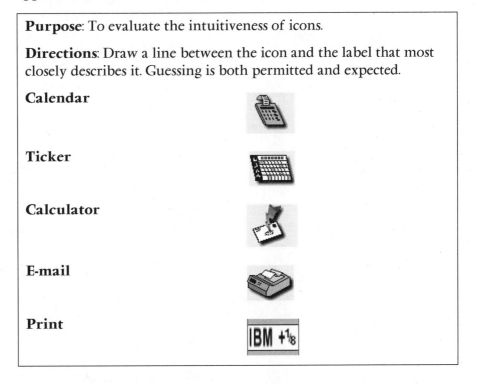

Purpose: To evaluate the intuitiveness of icons.

Directions: Draw a line between the icon and the label that most closely describes it. Guessing is both permitted and expected.

Calendar

Ticker

Calculator

E-mail

Print

PAPER AND PENCIL TEST   Use this test for any kind of structural question—Web-site structure, menus, table of contents, and so on. It can also be adapted for indexes and synonym lists.

The following sample paper and pencil test is designed to test whether users can easily figure out which menu name on a word processor's menu bar contains the tasks they're looking for. For example, would the user who wants to save changes to a template look on the File menu or on the Format menu?

If test participants have trouble with your choices, ask them what they would call the task and where they would put the option. Feel free to revise names between test sessions until most participants get most of them right (define "most"—75 percent? 90 percent?—before you start the test).

Purpose: To evaluate the intuitiveness and ease of understanding an application's internal structure.

Directions: Names of menus appear above the questions. For the tasks listed in the questions, please write the name of the menu on which you think you might find the option for that task. Guessing is both permitted and expected.

File   Edit   Print   Format   Attach   Book   Help

1. Create labels by doing a mail merge.   _____

2. Include a video clip in the document.   _____

3. Create a new chapter in a book.   _____

4. Create a new book.   _____

5. Create a chapter template.   _____

6. Copy a paragraph of text.   _____

CARD SORTING   Card sorting is another method for testing an application's structure. To prepare, the design team creates a set of index cards with the name of one menu item or Internet page on each card. The test participants are then asked to:

- Sort the cards into piles according to similarity or relationship. Note: If a card doesn't fit into any category, ask them to put the card in an "Other" or "Miscellaneous" group.

- After they have collected the piles, ask them to group the piles into larger groups. Note: Some participants will create ad hoc larger groups first, then break them into smaller groups, if you tell them the goal up front.. If you want a bottom-up analysis rather than a top-down analysis, do not mention all three steps at the beginning of the session.

- After they have created the larger groups, ask them to name each group.

Collect rationales for the participants' choices using a "think-aloud protocol"—the participants are asked to say why they're making various choices and what may be puzzling them—or by interviewing them at the end of the session. You can also collect the information on post-test questionnaires, described below in "Questionnaires."

The more participants you have, the more accurate your results will be. Why? Because at least one participant will create completely idiosyncratic piles. In a small sample of three or four participants, the outlier will skew the data; in a larger sample, the idiosyncratic results will fade into the background as noise.

Note that the index-card method is also a good way to start defining a Web site or application windows and dialog boxes. As you brainstorm the site, put each possible page or window name on a card. When you think you've identified each page or window, lay the cards out on the table and create a flow-chart or tree structure. You can shuffle the cards around easily until you think you've identified the right structure.

QUESTIONNAIRES   Software houses often send out questionnaires with beta releases and with the final release's documentation. Some Web sites also include short surveys (Nielsen 1997f, 1—2). These questionnaires are not as useful as they might be because most users don't complete or return them and because they are not usually designed to collect satisfaction and usability levels. However, any data are better than no data—try to get access to the results. You might also try to write or rewrite the questionnaires using some of the techniques described below.

STATISTICALLY FRIENDLY QUESTIONNAIRES Professional usability studies use questionnaires—Likert scales, semantic differentials, fill-in, and others—that are designed to be analyzed statistically. Questionnaires will give you information on preferences, opinions, and suggestions for improvement. Don't use them for performance-related questions (for example, "How did you print a form?") because performance is better measured with observation. For best results, use questionnaires while the audience is still thinking about the application—for example, at the end of formal usability tests or at the end of training sessions.

Hint: When writing a questionnaire, use the problem statements from the test plan as your starting point. For example, if you want to find out if the icons make sense to users, some of the questions should ask how understandable the icons are.

Following are brief descriptions of three type of usability questions. For additional formats, see Rubin (1994, 199—210).

LIKERT SCALES On Likert scales, participants register their agreement or disagreement with a statement. For example:

	Strongly disagree				Strongly agree	
The site has exactly the information I need.	☐	☐	☐	☐	☐	☐

Hint: To force participants to decide whether they like or don't like a feature, use even numbers of boxes. If you use an odd number, participants tend to use the middle box as for "don't know, don't want to think about it."

SEMANTIC DIFFERENTIALS In semantic differentials, participants are asked to register the degree to which they agree with one or another of two adjectives. They can be used to gather usability as well as aesthetic preferences. Both ends of the scale read from 1 to 3, with 0 being the no-preference choice.

This software is:

Simple	3	2	1	0	1	2	3	Complex
Reliable	3	2	1	0	1	2	3	Unreliable

FILL-IN QUESTIONS   The point of a fill-in questionnaire is to let participants expand on their ideas and feelings about the application. The key to a tester-friendly fill-in questionnaire is to limit the answers and thereby make the participants prioritize their answers. You can do this by using small fill-in areas and by limiting responses to three or four points. For example:

I found these aspects of the Web site particularly informative. (Please list from 0 to 3 aspects).

_____

_____

_____

ANALYSIS OF PRODUCT REVIEWS   One often-overlooked source of usability information is published product reviews of your own and your competitors' products. Competitive analyses are especially useful when you are designing a new product or a significantly different version of an existing product. Use them to set usability goals and to convince upper management of the importance of usability in your product.

Hint: Why rely on second-hand accounts? Test your competitors' products for usability in the same way as you test your own. By testing competitive products, you can develop a deeper understanding of what you should or should not include in your own product (Hackos 1994, 447).

INFORMATION RACE   This test can be used to develop or check timings for individual tasks and documentation searches. It requires expert users. Trainees on their last day of training may make good candidates.

To run an information race, give two or more test participants a set of questions and tell them that they are racing one another to find the answers (Wilson 1997b, 2). Whoever gets the right answer first receives a prize (or should—look for leftover company T-shirts, coffee cups, and other freebies to give away as prizes).

INTERNAL DEBRIEFINGS Certain members of your staff have regular contact with your customers—for example, customer service representatives, account representatives, quality-assurance testers, installers, trainers, and sales representatives and executives. Use them as resources. For example:

- Meet with your customer service representatives once a month to review any usability problems that seem to be coming up. If setting up usability meetings is unrealistic, sit in on regularly scheduled customer-service meetings and listen for usability issues.
- Check bug reports for usability problems. You might recognize some reports as actually indicating usability problems, not bugs or "requested features."
- Accompany account representatives to customer sites. Watch the customers interact with the software and make notes of any difficulties.
- Sit in on training classes and watch trainees interact with the software. If you notice that some trainees have trouble with a particular task, ask about the problem during the breaks.

High-Impact Tests

High-impact tests cost more in money and time, but the impacts on usability far outstrip the costs, provided, of course, that the tests are done well. Following are descriptions of some of the most popular tests. For human-factors experts who can do the testing as well as train your staff to do it themselves, see "Usability resources" below.

COGNITIVE WALKTHROUGH A cognitive walkthrough is an inspection rather than a testing method. It requires a team of experts who understand the type of application and the users as well as usability criteria (Nielsen and Mack 1994, 105—140).

To conduct a cognitive walkthrough, the team tries to anticipate the user's actions and thoughts while trying to do a particular task. The walkthrough starts with a clear statement of the user's objective in performing a task. Then the team moves through the task as the user would, looking for confusing steps, missing information, likely sources of error, and any other issues that they might uncover. Note: Scenarios or use cases defined during your analysis phase can be used as inputs to the action here.

Cognitive walkthroughs can supplement or, in a pinch, even substitute for user-based testing. If the team can accurately mimic the actions and mental models of the actual users, the results will be much the same as those uncovered during user testing. As a supplement to user-based testing, it is especially useful in uncovering consistency, terminology, and task sequencing problems. A cognitive walkthrough can also be used very early in development, before a working simulation or prototype is available. The evaluators can easily work from hardcopies of window designs (or a low-fi prototype).

The team should include at least one person with human-factors experience (this category may include technical communicators, many of whom have picked up human-factors expertise formally or informally in the course of their work). But also consider inviting account representatives, trainers, quality-assurance testers, and customer-service representatives to do the cognitive walkthroughs. Since they work so closely with your customers, they are good stand-ins for actual users.

A variation of the cognitive walkthrough is the pluralistic usability walkthrough. The difference is that the evaluators include three specific types of participants: actual users, product developers, and usability experts. The product developers act as "living publications"—any time a participant has a question that he or she would normally look in the documentation for, he or she can ask the "living publication." The developers also have the advantage of immediate feedback on their designs and ideas (Nielsen and Mack 1994, 67).

HEURISTIC EVALUATION A heuristic evaluation is another inspection method. In this type of evaluation, a small team of evaluators checks the interface and judges its compliance with recognized usability principles (the "heuristics").

A heuristic evaluation can help you decide how well an application conforms to accepted usability criteria and may help you uncover problems earlier in the development process. It may also be less expensive than formal usability testing. However, don't short-change formal usability testing—evaluators are likely to overlook usability problems if the system is highly domain-dependent and they have little domain experience (Nielsen 1997a, 1—2). Heuristic evaluations may also miss mismatches with actual users' conceptual models. Experienced users put applications to unexpected uses; heuristic evaluations cannot anticipate this type of activity.

To do an evaluation, each evaluator inspects the interface alone to ensure unbiased and independent results. The evaluators go through the evaluation twice, first to get a feel for the flow and the general scope of the system, then to focus on specific interface elements. Only after all evaluations are done are the evaluators allowed to communicate and have their findings aggregated. The results can either be written up by each evaluator or the evaluators can describe the problems to an observer as they go through the interface. Using an observer reduces the workload for the evaluators, although it adds overhead to the sessions. However, the observer can answer evaluators' domain questions or get them back on track if the prototype blows up (Nielsen 1997c, 1–2).

Heuristic evaluations work best when they are conducted by three to five evaluators. Heuristic evaluation is hard for a single individual to do because one person never notices all the usability problems in the interface. More evaluators will find more problems since, luckily, different people find different usability problems (in the same way that different editors find different grammatical errors and different quality-assurance analysts find different types of bugs). The more evaluators you add, the more problems they will find. However, as Nielsen points out, the cost-benefit ratio begins to drop after you reach eight evaluators—additional evaluators don't find exponentially greater numbers of errors (1997c, 4–6).

Table B.1 is a shortened version of Nielsen's ten usability heuristics, which seem to have become a standard for heuristic evaluations (Nielsen, 1997e). Note: Add weighting factors appropriate to your application—not every guideline is equally important in every situation. For details, see Nielsen (1997d, 1).

FORMAL USABILITY TESTING　Formal testing (what most people think of when they think of usability testing) is used to evaluate the ease of use and intuitiveness of your application. The application can be still in the design phase, in prototype, or in beta. You can also test finished applications (you might test the last release, for example, to act as a baseline for the next) or your competition's applications.

To do formal testing, you need three to five test participants (Nielsen 1997b, 4—5), a facilitator, observers, and when testing paper prototypes, someone to play the computer. You test the participants one at a time

TABLE B.1 Nielsen's Ten Usability Heuristics	Visibility of system status	The system should keep users informed about what is going on with appropriate and timely feedback.
	Match between the system and the real world	The system should use the user's language rather than system-oriented terminology. Follow real-world conventions and make information appear in a natural and logical order.
	User control and freedom	Users often choose functions by mistake and need clearly marked "emergency exits." Support undo and redo.
	Consistency and standards	Users should not have to wonder whether different words, situations, or actions mean the same thing. Follow platform guidelines.
	Error prevention	A careful design that prevents a problem from occurring is better than good error messages.
	Recognition rather than recall	Make objects, actions, and options visible. The user should not have to remember information from one part of the dialog to another. Instructions should be visible or easy to retrieve whenever appropriate.
	Flexibility and efficiency of use	Accelerators, which are not seen by novice users, may often speed up the interaction for the expert user. Let users tailor frequent actions.
	Aesthetic and minimalist design	Dialogs should not contain information that is irrelevant or rarely needed. Every extra piece of information in a dialog box competes with the relevant pieces of information and diminishes their visibility.
	Help users recognize, diagnose, and recover from errors	Error messages should be expressed in plain language, precisely indicate the problem, and constructively suggest a solution.
	Help and documentation	Even though it is better if the system can be used without documentation, it may be necessary to provide help and documentation. Any such information should be easy to search, focused on the user's task, list concrete steps to be carried out, and not be too large.

by giving each participant a task to do using the software. Each individual test takes three to four hours, including the debriefing at the end for a total of three to five days of testing (formal tests also require time to develop the scenarios and test plans, plus write up the results). Observers can also analyze their notes at the end of each session or at the end of all sessions. However, it is best to at least sort the notes as close to the test as possible, before you forget the details.

ROLES   The roles in a usability test are facilitator, user, and observer. If you are testing a low-fidelity prototype (no actual software yet), a fourth person must act as the computer. During the test, only the facilitator can speak to the test participant. The observers watch and take notes, and the computer reacts to participant requests.

Facilitator   The facilitator gives instructions and a task scenario to the test participant ("user"), encourages the participant to say out loud what he or she is thinking, and keeps the test on schedule.

The facilitator must assist the participants without directing them. Since the point of the usability test is to find confusions and misunderstandings, the facilitator cannot answer direct questions such as, "How do I do this?" Instead, the facilitator must say something like, "How do you think it's done?" or "Try it and see what happens." However, he or she may offer hints following predefined rules—for example, "If the participant cannot do the subtask after four tries or 10 minutes, the facilitator can offer a hint. After six tries or 15 minutes, the facilitator can say, 'Let's assume that the task was done' and go on to the next step."

The facilitator also debriefs the participants after the session using a questionnaire or a structured interview. The observers may also join in at this point. Use the debriefing to find points of confusion—theirs *and* yours; to bounce ideas off the participant; to find out how well the application meets their expectations.

The most difficult task for the facilitator is maintaining focus. Most people cannot, without training, concentrate on a task or another human being for four hours straight. Rubin suggests seven methods for growing into the facilitation job (1994, 76—78):

■   Learn the basic principles of human factors and ergonomics. Go to conferences and classes, read books and magazines. See "Usability Resources" below for the organizations that sponsor publications and conferences.

- Learn from watching others. See what works and what doesn't firsthand. Ask why the facilitator uses particular techniques, what she thinks of other techniques, and so on.

- Watch yourself on tape. Review your session with the intent of improving your skills. Note which things you did well and which you need to work on.

- Work with a mentor. Help an experienced facilitator do a test and have him or her do the same for you. Ask for criticism and advice.

- Practice facilitating. One of the advantages of practice is that you learn that everyone makes mistakes; one ruined session does not invalidate the entire test.

- Learn to meditate by sitting down in a quiet spot once a day and watching your breath. As thoughts come up, you acknowledge them and let them go. The result, Rubin says, is that your thoughts become more transparent, which in turn frees you to perceive many things more clearly and directly.

- Practice "bare attention" by setting aside brief periods of time during the day to intentionally heighten your awareness of everything you do and your surroundings.

Test participant   The test participant, who should be drawn from your user community, does the tasks using the application or prototype and, by his or her actions, shows where there are difficulties. The facilitator asks the participant to think out loud during the session.

The "thinking aloud" protocol makes it easier for the observers to understand confusions and to spot mismatches between the users' and the developers' conceptual models. Note that some experts have had good results testing two children, a parent and child, or two co-workers together—it makes thinking aloud about the software more natural. However, you have to watch out for power disparities. One participant may overwhelm the other.

Usability testing can be hard on the participants. The facilitator and everyone associated with the test must make it clear that you are testing the software, *not* the participant. Nevertheless, participants can be frustrated to tears. Before engaging participants in a test, check your protocols against the Human Factors and Ergonomic Society Code of Ethics (Rubin 1994, 313—314).

Observers   The observer (or observers) takes notes on index cards or Post-It notes, one observation per card. The observers document the performance, reactions and comments of the participant, which includes noting where he or she hesitates, shows confusion, and makes incorrect choices. If a participant suggests a solution, the observer can jot it down as well, but finding solutions is not the observer's main purpose. There can be as many observers as will fit in the room, provided that they stay out of the participant's direct line of sight and remain silent throughout the test (not as easy as one might think). In fact, the facilitator must be prepared to remove observers from the room if they cannot follow the rules.

The difficulties for the observers are to remember to make notes, rather than get caught up in the drama of watching the user struggling through the application, and to keep quiet. It is a natural human tendency to offer advice or sympathy, but neither is helpful during a test.

Computer   When you are testing a low-fidelity prototype, the computer play-acts the actions and responses of an actual computer program. The computer is responsible for arranging, finding and displaying the various elements of the user interface in response to the user's actions. He or she must know the application's logic so thoroughly that he or she creates the illusion that the prototype is actual software. For example, if the user attempts to pull down a list box on the prototype, the computer must display it. If the user double-clicks on an icon, then the computer displays the results of picking that icon. If an interface object is not yet implemented, then the computer either says out loud, "Not yet implemented" or displays an error-message card with that text.

RESULTS   At the end of the three to five days of testing, the lead observer and the facilitator must analyze the data and develop recommendations. As Lewis and Rieman say, "The point of the test is to get information that can guide the design. To do this, you will want to make a list of all difficulties users encountered. Include references back to the original data so you can look at the specifics if questions arise. Also try to judge why each difficulty occurred, if the data permit a guess about that" (Lewis and Rieman 1993, 5.5.4).

To make the analysis process more manageable, some testers use large Post-It notes and write one problem on each note. When the tests are done, they do affinity diagramming (by sticking the notes on a wall and moving them around until the similar problems are near one another) and quickly categorize and prioritize the problems. Other observers write their notes on screen shots and then organize those. The key is to avoid copying observations from many logbooks or lists to another. Rather, you simply put all the problems from all the observers up on a wall and summarize the results from the single display.

If you had a large group of developers as observers, the report will simply remind them of what they saw. (Human-factors experts say that watching users struggle through his or her design does more to convince a recalcitrant developer than any other activity.) If there were few observers, the report will have to convince as well as describe.

For more information on analyzing results, see Rubin (1994, 257—293), Dumas and Redish (1994, 309—355), and Lewis and Rieman (1993, 5.5.4—5.6.2).

Usability Resources

To find experts or classes in your area, contact these organizations:

The Human Factors and Ergonomics Society, P.O. Box 1369, Santa Monica, CA 90406-1369; voice: (310) 394-1811; fax: (310) 394-2410.

SIGCHI (Special Interest Group, Computer-Human Interaction) of the Association for Computing Machinery (ACM), 1515 Broadway, 17th Floor, New York, NY 10036-5701; voice: (212) 626-0500; fax: (212) 944-1318; e-mail: acmhelp@acm.org.

Usability Professionals' Association, 4020 McEwen, Suite 105, Dallas, TX 75244-5019; voice: (972) 233-9107; fax: (972) 490-4219; e-mail: UPADallas@aol.com; Web site: http://www.UPAssoc.org.

BIBLIOGRAPHY

Apple Computer. 1992. *Guide to Macintosh software localization.* Reading, MA: Addison-Wesley Publishing Company. Also available online at http://devworld.apple.com/dev/techsupport/insidemac/HIGuidelines.

Bailey, R. W. 1996. *Human performance engineering: Designing high quality professional user interfaces for computer products, applications, and systems.* 3rd ed. Upper Saddle River, NJ: Prentice-Hall.

Bellcore. 1994. *Design guide for multiplatform graphical user interfaces.* Piscataway, NJ: Bellcore (orders 1-908-699-5800).

Bias, Randolph G. and Deborah J. Mayhew. 1994. *Cost-justifying usability.* Boston: Academic Press.

Boggan, Scott, David Farkas, Joe Welinske. 1993. *Developing online help for Windows.* Carmel, IN: Sams Publishing.

Boggan, Scott, David Farkas, Joe Welinske. 1996. *Developing online help for Windows 95.* Boston, MA: International Thomson Computer Press.

Borggren, Janet, <Janet_R_Borggren@cstar.ac.com>. 1995. "RE: Using SAVE or COMMIT control buttons." [E-mail.] Accessed October 31, 1995.

Carroll, John M. 1992. *The Nurnberg funnel: Designing minimalist instruction for practical computer skill.* Cambridge, MA: The MIT Press.

Chicago Manual of Style, The. 1993. Chicago: The University of Chicago Press.

Choudhury, Khaled <khaled@msn.com>. 1995. "I have sympathy for the consistency appeal . . . ." [Personal communication].

Coe, Marlana. 1996. *Human factors for technical communicators.* New York: John Wiley & Sons, Inc.

Collins, Dave. 1995. *Designing object-oriented user interfaces.* Redwood City, CA: Benjamin/Cummings Publishing Co.

Constantine, Larry. 1995. Essential modeling: Use cases for user interfaces. *interactions,* April, 34–46.

Cooper, Alan. 1995. *About face: The essentials of user interface design.* Foster City, CA: IDG Books Worldwide, Inc.

DeGrace, Peter and Leslie Hulet Stahl. 1990. *Wicked problems, righteous solutions: A catalogue of modern software engineering paradigms.* Englewood Cliffs, NJ: Prentice-Hall, Inc.

Del Galdo, E. M., Jacob Nielsen, eds. 1996. *International user interfaces.* New York, NY: John Wiley & Sons.

Digital Equipment Corporation. 1995. *Digital Common Desktop Environment: Style guide and certification checklist.* Massachusetts: Digital Equipment Corporation.

Dumas, Joseph S. and Janice C. Redish. 1994. *A practical guide to usability testing.* Norwood, NJ: Ablex Publishing Corp.

Feldberg, Steven. 1997. Personal communication.

Fowler, Susan, Victor Stanwick. 1995. *The GUI style guide.* Chestnut Hill, MA: Academic Press Professional.

Fowler, Susan. 1996. Designing multimedia: Back to the drawing board. *I.D. Magazine,* March/April, 82.

Freedman, Daniel P., Gerald M. Weinberg. 1990. *Handbook of walkthroughs, inspections, and technical reviews: Evaluating programs, projects, and products.* 3rd ed. New York: Dorset House Publishing.

Galitz, Wilbert O. 1989. *Handbook of screen format design.* 3rd ed. Wellesley, MA: QED Information Sciences.

Galitz, Wilbert O. 1993. *User-interface screen design.* Wellesley, MA: QED Information Sciences.

Galitz, Wilbert O. 1994. *It's time to clean your windows: Designing GUIs that work.* New York: John Wiley & Sons.

Galitz, Wilbert O. 1997. *Essential guide to user interface design: An introduction to GUI design principles and techniques.* New York: John Wiley & Sons.

Gardner-Bonneau, Daryle Jean. 1992. "Human factors problems in interactive voice response (IVR): Do we need a guideline/standard?" *Proceedings of the Human Factors Society 36th Annual Meeting.*

Gause, Donald C. and Gerald M. Weinberg. 1989. *Exploring requirements: Quality before design.* New York: Dorset House Publishing.

Gladwell, Malcolm. 1997. Just ask for it: The real key to technological innovation. *New Yorker,* April 7, 1997, 45–49.

Hackos, JoAnn T. 1994. *Managing your documentation projects.* New York: John Wiley & Sons.

Hix, Deborah, and H. Rex Hartson. 1993. *Developing user interfaces: Ensuring usability through product & process.* New York: John Wiley & Sons.

Horton, William. 1994. *The icon book: Visual symbols for computer systems and documentation.* New York: John Wiley & Sons.

Huff, Darrell. 1982. *How to lie with statistics.* 40th ed. New York: W.W. Norton.

Hurlburt, Allen. 1978 *The grid.* New York: Van Nostrand Reinhold Company Inc.

International Business Machines Corp. 1992. *Object-oriented interface design: IBM Common User Access guidelines.* Carmel, IN: Que Corporation.

International Organization for Standardization. Working draft of March 19, 1993. *User interface to telephone-based services: Voice messaging applications,* Pub. No. ISO/IEC JTC1/SC18/WG9 N1219.

Kano, Nadine. 1995. *Developing international software for Windows 95 and Windows NT.* Redmond, WA: Microsoft Press.

Kohl, John R., Rebecca O. Barclay, Thomas E. Pinelli, Michael L. Keene, and John M. Kennedy. 1993. "The impact of language and culture on technical communication in Japan." *Technical Communication,* 1st Quarter.

Leavens, Alex. 1994. *Designing GUI applications for Windows.* New York: M&T Books/Henry Holt and Company, Inc.

Lewis, Clayton, and John Rieman. 1993. *Task-centered user interface design.* <ftp://ftp.cs.colorado.edu/pub/cs/distribs/clewis/HCI-Design-Book/>.

Lunde, Ken. 1993. *Understanding Japanese information processing.* Sebastopol, CA: O'Reilly and Associates, Inc.

Marcus, Aaron, Nick Smilonich, Lynne Thompson. 1995. *The cross-GUI handbook: For multiplatform user interface design.* Reading, MA: Addison-Wesley Publishing Co.

Microsoft Corporation. 1993. *The GUI guide: International terminology for the windows interface.* Redmond, WA: Microsoft Press.

Microsoft Corporation. 1995a. *The Windows interface guidelines for software design.* Redmond, WA: Microsoft Press. Available online at http://www.microsoft.com/win32dev/uiguide.

Microsoft Corporation. 1995b. *Microsoft Windows 95 help authoring kit.* Redmond, WA: Microsoft Press.

Motte, Susan <SUSANMOTTE@aol.com>. 1995. "Re: Visual cues for required fields" [UTEST posting]. Accessed August 23, 1995.

Mullet, Kevin, Darrell Sano. 1995. *Designing visual interfaces: Communication oriented techniques.* Englewood Cliffs, NJ: Prentice-Hall PTR.

National Language Technical Center. 1991. *National language design guide: Designing enabled products,* Vol. 1 (part number SE09-8001-01). IBM Canada Ltd., National Language Technical Center, Dept. 979, 895 Don Mills Rd., North York, ONT, Canada M3C 1W3.

National Language Technical Center. 1992. *National language support reference manual,* Vol. 2 (part number (SE09-8002-02). IBM Canada Ltd., National Language Technical Center, Dept. 979, 895 Don Mills Rd., North York, ONT, Canada M3C 1W3.

Nielsen, Jakob and Robert L. Mack, eds. 1994. *Usability inspection methods.* New York: John Wiley & Sons.

Nielsen, Jakob and Darrell Sano. 1997. *SunWeb: User Interface design for Sun Microsystem's internal web.* <http://www.ncsa.uiuc.edu/SDG/IT94/Proceedings/HCI/nielsen/sunweb.html>. Accessed July 18, 1997.

Nielsen, Jakob. 1997a. *Characteristics of usability problems found by heuristic evaluation.* <http://www.useit.com/papers/heuristic/usability_problems.html>. Accessed June 27, 1997.

Nielsen, Jakob. 1997b. *Guerrilla HCI: Using discount usability engineering to penetrate the intimidation barrier.* <http://www.useit.com/papers/guerrilla_hci.html>. Accessed June 27, 1997.

Nielsen, Jakob. 1997c. *How to conduct a heuristic evaluation.* <http://www.useit.com/papers/heuristic/heuristic_evaluation.html>. Accessed June 27, 1997.

Nielsen, Jakob. 1997d. *Icon usability.* <http://www.sun.com:80/sun-on-net/uidesign/icons.html>. Accessed April 22, 1997.

Nielsen, Jakob. 1997e. *Severity ratings for usability problems.* <http://www.useit.com/papers/heuristic/severityrating.html>. Accessed June 27, 1997.

Nielsen, Jakob. 1997f. *Ten usability heuristics.* <http://www.useit.com/papers/heuristic/heuristic_list.html>. Accessed June 27, 1997.

Nielsen, Jakob. 1997g. *User surveys on the Web.* <http://www.useit.com/papers/surveys.html>. Accessed June 27, 1997.

Norman, Kent L. 1991. *The psychology of menu selection.* Norwood, NJ: Ablex Publishing Corp.

Open Software Foundation. 1993. *OSF/Motif style guide,* rev. 1.2. Englewood Cliffs, NJ: PTR Prentice-Hall.

Rauch, Thyra L., Dana L. Gillihan, and Paul Leone. 1997. Low-fidelity prototyping for technical communicators. *Society for Technical Communication 44th Annual Conference 1997 Proceedings.* Arlington, VA: Society for Technical Communication.

Rettig, Mark. 1994. Prototyping for tiny fingers. *Communications of the ACM,* April, 21–27.

Robinson, Mavis. 1996. Tabbed dialogs: semantic minefields. *Eye for Design,* March/April, 1–7.

Romano, Frank J. 1984. *The TypEncyclopedia: A user's guide to better typography.* New York, NY: R.R. Bowker Company.

Rubin, Jeffrey. 1994. *Handbook of usability testing: How to plan, design, and conduct effective tests.* New York: John Wiley & Sons.

Rubin, Jeffrey. 1996. Conceptual design: cornerstone of usability. *Technical Communication,* 2nd Quarter, 130–138.

Ruby, Laconya <lruby@raleigh.ibm.com>. 1997. "Re: Placement of buttons" [UTEST posting]. Accessed May 29, 1997.

Schneiderman, Ben. 1992. *Designing the user interface,* 2nd ed. Reading, MA: Addison-Wesley Publishing Co.

Schumacher, Jr., Robert M. 1992. "Phone-based interfaces: Research and guidelines," *Proceedings of the Human Factors Society 36th Annual Meeting.*

Smith, Daniel P.B. <dpbsmith@world.std.com>. 1997. "Re: Recalculating fields" [personal e-mail]. Accessed March 20, 1997.

Snyder, Carolyn. 1996. Roadmaps. *Eye for Design,* May/June, 6, 8.

Snyder, Carolyn, <csnyder@uie.co>. 1996. "UNDO, what to expect?" [UTEST posting]. Accessed April 30, 1996.

Snyder, Carolyn, <csnyder@uie.co>. 1997a. "Can you folks help me with this Letter to the Editor?" [Personal e-mail]. Accessed February 5, 1997.

Snyder, Carolyn. 1997b. Using paper prototypes to manage risk. <http://world.std.com/~uieweb/paper.htm>. Accessed April 20, 1997.

Spool, Jared, <jspool@uie.com>. 1995. "Re: Toolbar design issue" [UTEST posting]. Accessed June 19, 1995.

Spool, Jared. 1996a. Is your application a core or a ring? *Eye for Design,* November/December, 1–3.

Spool, Jared, <jspool@uie.com>. 1996b. "Status line messages" UIETIPS [online newsletter]. Accessed June 14, 1996.

Spool, Jared, <jspool@uie.com>. 1997. "Eliminating greying out" UIETIPS [online newsletter]. Accessed May 20, 1997.

Sun Microsystems, Inc. 1990. *Open Look: Graphical user interface application style guidelines.* Reading, MA: Addison-Wesley Publishing Co.

Tufte, Edward R. 1983. *The visual display of quantitative information.* Cheshire, CT: Graphics Press.

Tufte, Edward R. 1990. *Envisioning information.* Cheshire, CT: Graphics Press.

Tufte, Edward R. 1997. *Visual explanations.* Cheshire, CT: Graphics Press.

Tuthill, Bill. 1993. *Solaris international developer's guide.* Englewood Cliffs, NJ: Prentice-Hall.

Uren, Emmanuel, Robert Howard, Tiziana Perinotti. 1993. *Software internationalization and localization: An introduction.* New York, NY: VNR Computer Library.

User Interface Engineering. 1996. Effective "Tool Tips." *Eye for Design,* January/February, 1–8.

Van Someren, Nicko. 1995. "Key problem" (The Last Word section). *New Scientist.* January 28, 1995, vol. 145, no. 1962.

VanDevender, Steve. 1993. *The (much requested) translation manifesto,* <http://insoft-l/doc/guidelines/manifesto>. Accessed April 22, 1993.

Vatovec, Bogo <bogo@hermes.si>. 1997. "Re: Placement of buttons." [Posting.] Accessed May 30, 1997.

Weinschenk, Susan, Pamela Jamar, Sarah C. Yeo. 1997. *GUI design essentials for Windows 95, Windows 3.1, World Wide Web.* New York: John Wiley & Sons, Inc.

Weinschenk, Susan, Sarah C. Yeo. 1995. *Guidelines for enterprise-wide GUI design.* New York: John Wiley & Sons, Inc.

Wilson, Chauncey, <cwilson@ftp.com>. 1997a. "Draft of design guidelines." [Personal e-mail.] Accessed January 27, 1997.

Wilson, Chauncey. 1997b. "Documentation usability techniques" handout at Society for Technical Communication 44th Annual Convention. Available upon request from Wilson at <chaunsee@aol.com>.

Yourdon, Edward. 1992. *Decline & fall of the American programmer.* Englewood Cliffs, NJ: PTR Prentice-Hall, Inc.

Zelazny, Gene. 1991. *Say it with charts: The executive's guide to successful presentations in the 1990s,* 2nd ed. Homewood, IL: Business One Irwin.

Zetie, Carl. 1995. *Practical user interface design: Making GUIs work.* New York: McGraw-Hill, Inc.

INDEX

Symbols

key, telephony 140

A

abbreviations 107, 247
accelerator
    definition 98
    guidelines 101
    on pop-up menus 146
    usability tests 102
access bar. See toolbar
access key. See mnemonic
accessing
    commands and operations quickly or when
        mouse is unavailable 98
    often-used functions with the mouse 231
    properties of selected objects 145
    related mouse operations quickly 175
    secondary tasks 126
ACM (Association for Computing Machinery),
    SIGCHI 297
action button. See pushbutton
adaptive technologies, audio 143
alert message. See information message
always on top option 27, 31
American National Standards Institute
    (ANSI) 160
ANSI (American National Standards
    Institute) 160
application window. See window
Apply button 198
area graph 82
asking for user responses 148
attention panel. See information message
audio menu 139, 140
audio technologies 143
auto exit. See auto skip
auto fill 64

auto object help. See tooltip
auto-completion. See auto fill
automating infrequent tasks 258

B

Back button 262
balloon help. See tooltip
bar graph 81
bell curve. See frequency polygon
belt graph. See area graph
Borggren, Janet 203
Browse button 262
bubble help. See tooltip
butterfly chart. See segmented bar
button. See pushbutton

C

cake graph. See pie chart
Cancel button 154, 198, 262
capitalization
    all uppercase hard to read 110
    headline style 134
    labels 110
    pushbuttons 191
    sentence style 134
card-sorting usability test 286
cascading menu. See menu, drop-down
changing settings 24
chart. See graph
check box
    changing the label 5
    definition 3
    internationalization 7
    labeling 4
    maximum number of 6
    menu items 4
    mixed-value state 6